THE YEW-TREE AT THE HEAD OF THE STRAND

An 'ordinary/extraordinary' woman: my mother in her late twenties.

THE YEW-TREE AT THE HEAD OF THE STRAND

Brian Cosgrove

… I dreamt the past was never past redeeming:
But whether this was false or honest dreaming
I beg death's pardon now. And mourn the dead.
Richard Wilbur, 'The Pardon'

LIVERPOOL UNIVERSITY PRESS

First published in 2001 by
LIVERPOOL UNIVERSITY PRESS
4 Cambridge Street, Liverpool L69 7ZU

British Library Cataloguing-in-Publication Data
A British Library CIP record is available.

ISBN 0-85323-737-9 *hardback*
ISBN 0-85323-747-6 *paperback*

Typeset in Minion with Chianti by
Northern Phototypesetting Co. Ltd, Bolton, Lancs.
Printed and bound in the European Union by
Bell and Bain Ltd, Glasgow

To all those who have worked – publicly or behind the scenes – for peace and reconciliation in Ireland.

Note

The place-name Newry is of ancient origin, and derives from the Irish: *An t-Iúr* meaning 'the yew-tree'. The full Irish place-name, however, is *Iúr Cinn Trá*, the literal translation of which is 'the yew-tree at the head of the strand'.

Contents

Acknowledgments

Under different circumstances, this book would have been dedicated to my parents; but the work as a whole is, I hope, sufficient testimony to the high regard in which I hold them.

I owe a special debt of gratitude to my brother Peter, without whose industry few if any of the illustrative photographs would have been available. It was he who, some decades ago, compiled, dated and arranged in sequence the treasury of family photographs which might otherwise have disappeared, or been dispersed beyond recovery.

A special expression of gratitude also to Jonathan Williams. Like many who have worked with Jonathan, I have reason to appreciate the efforts he has put in, over and above the duties of a literary agent. My thanks for his support and encouragement.

A brief extract from 'Dante and the Lobster' is reproduced with the permission of The Estate of Samuel Beckett and The Calder Educational Trust, and one from *Waiting for Godot* with the permission of The Estate of Samuel Beckett; brief quotations from T. S. Eliot's *The Waste Land*, Seamus Heaney's 'Clearances', and Richard Wilbur's 'The Pardon' with the permission of Faber and Faber Limited; a quotation from John Ciardi's translation of Dante's *Inferno* by permission of Myra Ciardi and W. W. Norton Inc.; a brief excerpt from the short story 'Grace', two from *A Portrait of the Artist as a Young Man* and one from *Ulysses* with the permission of The Estate of James Joyce – © Estate of James Joyce; quotations from Frank O'Connor's *An Only Child* and 'Uprooted' with the permission of Harriet O'Donovan Sheehy; and a short extract from *To the Lighthouse* with the permission of the Society of Authors, acting as the literary representative of the Estate of Virginia Woolf. The lines from

Robert Frost's 'Out, Out –', from *The Poetry of Robert Frost*, edited by Edward Connery Lahem, The Estate of Robert Frost and Jonathan Cape as publisher, are used by permission of The Random House Group Limited. The author and publishers are grateful for the permissions to quote these copyright materials.

CHAPTER ONE

A Public House

Side by side, through the centre of Newry town, parallel and (so it seems) forever divided, run the Clanrye river and the Newry Canal. The river, gift of nature, is native to the landscape; the canal, completed under British overseers in Newry's prosperous mid-eighteenth century, is the fruit of man's ingenuity, and was, in its day, a remarkable feat of industrial engineering. My father's pub, known for most of his lifetime as 'The Buffet Bar', on one side looked out on these two waterways; but, since it occupied a corner site where two thoroughfares meet, the pub had two entrances. One was from The Mall, which ran parallel to the Clanrye river, and became, if you crossed the junction with Margaret Street, the departure point for a number of buses, stops for which ran along its length (hence the pub's later name: 'The Bus Saloon'). The other point of access was from the aforementioned Margaret Street, which runs perpendicularly from The Mall into one of Newry's main shopping precincts, Hill Street.

The Mall entrance provided, above the door in fine black lettering, information regarding 'A. J. Cosgrove, Wine and Spirit Merchant'. The 'A. J.' stood for Arthur Joseph, but to all and sundry he was always known as 'Joe'. According to an obscure family tradition, however, there was a certain irony in the fact that he was called Joe or Joseph at all. The story goes that his mother, Brighid, sent him with a nurse or minder to the christening with instructions that he was to be called Art (the Irish form of Arthur) – she, for reasons unknown, being unable to attend herself. In the absence of his mother, however, he underwent the Shandean fate of being mischristened (though in his case with results neither as comic nor as dramatic as those that befell Sterne's hero, Tristram), and ended up as Joe Art. When and why he decided to reverse Joe Art to make of it Arthur Joseph is not known. Nor is it known who was responsible for adding the 'Joe' in the first place. But that, in any case, was the name that was to stick with him for the rest of his days.

He was small and wiry, with a head slightly larger than the proportions of his body seemed to warrant, a high forehead, shrewd and genial eyes under bushy eyebrows, and a generous laugh. He carried into death a full head of hair (a feat which, it is now all too clear to me, I cannot hope to emulate: genetically I am in that regard my mother's son, for all her brothers rapidly went thin on top).

I rarely knew my father to take a holiday, except once or twice, most notably when, in 1947, he travelled on the *Queen Elizabeth* to the United States to see two sisters who were married there, and some nieces and nephews, all of them living in Boston or elsewhere in Massachusetts. After that unusual extravagance, it was back to the old routine. Year after year, Monday to Saturday, he entered the bar at about 9.50 a.m. (it opened at 10), took two thirty-minute breaks in the course of a long day, for dinner and tea, and was lucky to be out of the bar (after closing-time at 10 p.m.) by 10.15 or even (on a Saturday) 10.45. (Christmas Eve meant an even later release, and of course, after the brief respite of Christmas Day, it was mayhem all over again on Boxing Day.) Most nights he signalled his imminent retreat by calling out in the time-honoured fashion, and in his professional tone of voice, 'Time, gentlemen, please!' It was my earliest introduction to formulaic proceeding. Years later, I was delighted to have the formula recalled for me when I read the similar bar-cry, 'HURRY UP PLEASE ITS TIME', towards the end of the second section of T. S. Eliot's *The Waste Land*.

*

(Three men are standing at the bar counter, two in close proximity and in a kind of loose alliance, while the third stands a little apart, but certainly within earshot. (So I fill out the details in my imagination, for I never witnessed this episode, though I assure you that it did actually happen.) My father stands behind the bar, wearing, as usual, his long white apron, which reaches almost as far as his trouser-bottoms. The two men close together wear derbies, and one has a moustache: the other man has a cap, from under which he casts a somewhat suspicious regard at the world at large.)

First Man (*with derby and moustache: addressing my father*): What's the time there, Joe?

Father: Nearly one. Time for a Christian to go home and have his dinner.

Second Man (*derby but no moustache*): Aye, true bill. I've a nice eel the missus is cooking for me.

First Man: Eels, Pat, is it? *Eels?*

(*Cap Man is now all ears*)

Second Man (*Pat*): Aye eels, Matty. Eels. Great stuff! Couldn't bate it with a big stick! Have you ever tried them?

Cap Man (*jumping in*): Mother of God! You don't eat bloody eels, surely. Yewch!

Pat: Ah, don't knock it, Jimmy, till you try it.

Cap Man (*now identified as Jimmy, his face twisted in disgust*): Jasus, I don't know how anybody could put those slimy yokes in their mouth! Jasus (*he takes another good swill of his Guinness*), do you know what it is? Anybody who would eat eels would eat shite.

(*My father laughs, a good-natured laugh, a laugh of bonhomie – perhaps because he has seen the other man bridle, and wants to keep the situation cool.*)

Jimmy (*warming to his theme*): No, I'm serious. It would not surprise me to see you eat shite.

Father: You wouldn't want to see poor oul' Pat here reduced to that.

Jimmy: Tell you the truth, Joe, I would not. It would make me sick for a week – shite *or* eels, all the same to me.

Matty (*up to now keeping his counsel*): So d'you think then that Pat here *would* eat shite?

Jimmy: Christ, I do not! Sure no human being could eat shite, eh?

Matty: Begod (*and he winks at my father*), you'd be surprised now.

(*A glitter of mischief in my father's eye; a conspiracy is imminent.*)

Pat (*the eel-eater, trying to sense out the conspiracy, and playing for time*):

Well, there's a time for everything. The human animal has all kinds of possibilities.

Jimmy: Animal is right. Only an animal would eat shite – or eels, for that matter.

Matty: What do you think, Joe? I think Pat here could do it.

Pat (*catching the drift from his companion, and getting in on the act*): Eat shite, you mean? Oh, I think so, if it came to it.

Jimmy (*now a little fierce*): Never! You'd never eat shite! That's just pre-posterous, Joe, what?

Father: Well, I don't know…

Pat: Oh I would. I betya I would. Betya anything I would!

Jimmy (*now fully drawn*): And I betya you wouldn't. You would *not*!

Matty: Is this bettin' now we're talking about? Are we talking (*he looks to my father for support, and is tapping the bar counter with an index finger*) serious betting?

Father: Sounds like that to me.

Pat: Well, bet away then. Bet away. I'm betting that I can eat shite. Are you (*to Jimmy*) betting I can't?

Jimmy: Bloody right I am! I bloody well bet you can't!

So, the bet was struck, and, subsequently, in the absence of Jimmy, the plot was hatched by the other three (my father included). I cannot say who the prime mover was, but what they did was this. They sent to the hardware shop around the corner in Hill Street for a brand new cham-ber-pot, filled it with red lemonade (actually brown in colour), and pos-sibly diluted that with water until it bore a more than passable resemblance to urine. The final touch was to drop three or four ginger biscuits (ginger 'snaps', as they were known) into the pale brown liquid, and allow them to grow suitably soggy. At a time prearranged, Jimmy came in to see if his challenge had been taken up; and my father with due ceremony placed the chamber-pot (or 'po') on the bar-counter in front of Pat.

'Would you have an oul' spoon there, Joe?' says Pat.

My father duly obliges. Pat then plunges the spoon into the po, lifts the soggy brown mush to his mouth and begins to eat it off the spoon …

'Jesus Christ!' says Jimmy. 'Here's your effin' money', and exits, almost retching, throwing the ten-shilling note (or whatever the agreed amount was) behind him, eager to get out to the refuge of the street as fast as he possibly can.

*

My father's sense of humour was of the kind best described as 'robust'; and perhaps that was the sort most men of that generation had. (Beckett's father, going back a generation further still, seems also to have had a liking for scatological jokes.) Operative in all this, pretty certainly, was an obscure law of compensation: forbidden by religious scruple or by other pressures in the culture to speak too openly (even in jest) about sex, the male allowed himself a generous measure of freedom in colourful (if mild) invective and 'dirty' talk of a more innocent kind. My father could, for example, call upon a number of vigorous terms for those who irritated him. These ranged from the contemptuous putdown 'sparrowfart' to the more angrily dismissive 'gobshite'; while, in his highest satiric mood, he would damn some unfortunate in the most scathing term of all, 'coul' [cold] trousers', which in one caustic phrase impugned both his capacity for generosity and his virility.

But this recourse to basic language may also have been a way of acknowledging the harsh realities of existence. My father had been through a tough school. Coming from a very poor farm and a large, impoverished family in Clady, County Armagh, he had been apprenticed at the age of fourteen as barman to a Catholic in Portadown who owned a small hotel. I never heard him speak of this first employer with anything but affection, but at the same time, from remarks he let fall, it seems to have been the case that the hours were long and demanding and the rewards small. Hence one of his jokes: about the apprentice barman just new to the job who asks his employer about the 'conditions of employment'. 'Sixpence a week,' is the curt reply, 'and your dung home in a string bag.'

From one point of view, he was a highly sociable man (and fortunate for him that he was, being in the bar trade at a time when the customers expected more chat and personal attention than they generally do now). Part of his sociability was his ability to tell a joke in what was almost exclusively male company, and he told a story well. But there was quite another side to him. If his sense of humour was robust, his mind was sharp and well-informed. Moreover, many of us in the family suspected that he suffered from a degree of frustration – perhaps even intellectual frustration – in the day-in, day-out routine of running a bar in a provincial town. The story was that he had been originally earmarked for a career in the law in America: he was the youngest in his large family, and the plan was that an elder brother, having gone first to the States, would then send him his fare so that he could join him. Once there, he would study law. For some reason, though, this never materialised; so off he went into the bar business, making, it must be said, quite a success of it. Eventually he and another brother (his favourite, Peter) were owners of a public house in Cookstown, County Tyrone. When that brother married, there came the parting of the ways (amicable, it seems), and with his share of the Cookstown enterprise, my father bought what was then a small hotel in Newry, which thereafter did double duty as pub and family residence (there were five children, myself the youngest, so the largish hotel quarters were very welcome).

Yet there remained about him a sense of unfulfilment. It was, perhaps, this frustration that sometimes (though, thankfully, not often) led him to the drink. It is no pleasure to me to recall how he could throw back neat whiskey (the only alcohol he would touch, as far as I know) until he was very far gone. My impression is that there was little sense of gratification in the exercise, and one reason for the choice of neat whiskey was to speed up the process as much as possible. Unlike some of his customers, one of whom in particular could demolish an entire bottle of whiskey on Christmas Eve and then walk out in a state of self-possession, he was unable to 'hold' his drink: but then he did not really want to 'hold' it. I have one painful memory in particular: aged about nine or ten, I saw him one evening carried down to our sitting-room out of the bar where he had been tippling for most of the day. He was literally unable to walk, and, with his arms draped round the shoulders of two of his best customers, decent men both, was borne forward, his feet trailing on the floor, until they managed, with some awkwardness, to deposit him in an armchair.

I looked with a mixture of fascination and distaste at this caricature of a familiar and authoritative figure, his eyes sparkling with irrationality, his mouth a foolish grinning gash, his speech slurred into inarticulacy. When, later, I saw John Mills give his extraordinary Oscar-winning performance as the feeble-minded Michael in David Lean's *Ryan's Daughter*, I suspect that, for me, some of the disturbing resonance in that performance may have derived from that image of my father exposed in all his weakness. Mills in that film part became for me, if only fleetingly, a symbolic embodiment of the failed father, the respected elder collapsed into caricature; and when, in one scene, Mills swings his heavy boot against the wooden underside of a bar-room bench, I identified with an unusual degree of empathy with the young shell-shocked English soldier (played by Christopher Jones) who is severely rattled by the persistent noise and begins to return in his imagination to the horrors of the Front.

It is some mitigation to my pain to remind myself that, to the best of my knowledge, my father was never, when he had drink taken, given to violence, either in deed or word. He would be either foolishly happy, as the drunk man can be, or else, more problematically – this was the case in his closing days – given to demeaning self-pity, as if the pains he had borne throughout his life could find an outlet in that way only. For there had been tough experiences early on, as he fought to make his way in the world; and his own account of how he had started on the whiskey was illuminating. In the business he shared with his brother Peter in Cookstown, he would sometimes have to work long unbroken hours in the less salubrious of the two locales in the pub (known as the 'back bar'), operating under pressure and going without food for lengthy periods. By his own account, he began to drink shots of whiskey just to keep warm and, I suspect, simply to keep going.

These explanations, however, came late on: all that the boy of nine or ten saw was a sadly diminished figure, suddenly revealed as ridiculous, for whom, in more normal contexts, he had both affection and respect. I leave it to those qualified in psychology to estimate the effects of such an experience as this one: but I note in my readings in literature a deep, instinctive interest in the irrational (Joseph Conrad is a favourite), along with a profound distaste for rational optimism. (Thus, I sometimes find it difficult to believe that anyone of even minimal intelligence can repose any substantial faith in 'The Enlightenment', or find in that eighteenth-century movement any serious basis for a compelling account of human affairs.)

And I think, too, that the painful sight of a worthy father, a dedicated and hard-working *paterfamilias*, reduced to a powerless marionette encouraged in me a habit of detachment; I began to withdraw my emotional engagement from a world in which the objects of such emotion were unreliable, and cultivate a separateness which might render me less vulnerable. It is certainly the case that as I grew up I was marked by the other members of the family as 'independent': and in my early reading of Wordsworth's *The Prelude*, my heart leapt up in sympathy when I came upon the poet's confession that in his formative years he

> was taught to feel, perhaps too much,
> The self-sufficing power of solitude.

*

I sometimes think that for most of my early life my father remained a puzzle that I was always trying to interpret. And towards the end of his days I felt a real urgency not only to get to know him better, but to win, in turn, both his attention and respect. I often studied him, particularly in his later years after my mother had died (not long after her sixtieth year), as he sat quietly on the old couch in the bar, at a time of the day when the customers were few, or the bar was, as it might happen to be, empty. He struck me then as a deeply introspective man, very self-absorbed – one who had some major problems to resolve in his own mind. And that effect was heightened when he resorted to a compulsive pastime, which involved repeatedly tossing a coin; as if he were attempting, by some reading of the sequence of heads or tails, to divine a pattern in his life. The coin-tossing was, perhaps, his version of the *sortes*

Virgilianae, an attempt to read the auguries in the gambler's throw of the coin.

For gambling (or, to be more specific, betting on the horses) was after all the mainstay of his existence. The truth is, of course, that, given the nature of the bar culture at that time, it was hard not to get involved with the bookies. Our bar had its own resident bookie's runner, who would place your bets for you in one of the two or three bookies' (or turf accountants') shops a hundred yards away in The Mall (not at all, in spite of the name, the kind of place you would associate with that other famous Mall with the word 'Pall' in front of it). The runner, who was the kind of being known in the US as a 'bar-fly', could hope for suitable reward (a free drink) if the bet was successful (though such is the nature of human life that he had to take the bad days with the good; and it is a well-known fact that a man in sore need of a drink makes a poor philosopher).

It was in the nature of the Newry experience, with its high level of unemployment (it was after all a Nationalist town, and Stormont was never going to do it any favours), that many men spent their days triangulating between the three Bs: bar, bookie's and 'bru' (as the bureau for unemployment was always called). Even allowing for the inescapable influence of this pervasive culture, however, my father's passion for betting on the horses was extreme. It might be said, in fact, that he approached the business of betting on the horses with an almost religious fervour; while with regard to religion proper, his attitude was less than enthusiastic.

I do not for a moment mean to suggest that he was in any sense an agnostic or even a sceptic of the radical type (though there was in his character what I now feel to have been a saving scepticism of a general kind, and a well developed sense of irony). But he held that open displays of devotion or religious fervour were for women mainly: men did not go in for that type of thing. It was all very well for the women to go off to church, beating the pious breast (or 'batin' their croppin'', as he put it); but the duty of men was to remain in the real world, of business, politics, sport and professional duty. So, as I now view it, he may have transferred to horse-racing the enthusiasm which might have been expended on religion. Perhaps, though, that is a confusion in my own mind between two nightly rituals which often followed hard on each other's heels: the family rosary, and the radio tipster's 'three best' for the next day's racing. Certainly, the family rosary was dutifully said, by my father as by everybody else – though my two brothers and myself were often less than fully reverent. (As we each knelt somewhat awkwardly at a chair in the sitting-room, it was not unknown for one of us to pass wind, sometimes audibly, and even if not audibly, still not beyond immediate notice (one of my father's sayings, which intrigued me as much by its rhythm and poetic pretensions as by its appositeness, was: 'The fart that makes the least report is the damnedest fart of all'). All three of us would end up in a fit of stifled gig-gles, which threatened to erupt into disruptive noise when we tried to keep up our articulation of the responses.) But, whether reverently said or not, the rosary (and the 'trimmings' added at the end in the form of special petitions or devotional prayers) had to be out of the way before the 'three best' were announced on the radio. This happened at the end of the Irish Hospitals' Sweepstake programme, one of the announcers being Bart Bastable (who was fairly swiftly mythologised – by myself, I think – as Fart-Best-of-All). What added to the difficulty, of course, was that the programme in question was broadcast from Radio Eireann (the Athlone transmitter); and even though Newry was close to the border with the Republic (or the 'Free State', as it continued to be known), it was still far enough north to make the reception sometimes uncertain (depending, doubtless, on the weather, or other uncontrollable circumstances).

I retain the most vivid picture of my father in his armchair, hunched over that evening's *Belfast Telegraph*, holding his Parker pen to write the priceless information on the top of one of the newspaper's pages, while, as the rest of us went about our business in a hush that must rightly be termed sacred, he struggled to make out the names of the horses against a background of insistent static. Often, I fear, he ran the risk of forfeit-ing any grace merited by his earlier patient involvement in the family rosary by venting his frustration in muttered imprecations (a favourite was 'God's curse!', tersely invoked against those obscure forces which were thwarting him; he might sometimes in addition make very liberal use of the Holy Name).

It is certainly the case that he did not gamble primarily for the base material motive of making money. Indeed, my general impression is that he was never really interested in becoming wealthy; and that attitude, combined with my mother's habitual concern for spiritual rather than material realities, meant that we children, while encouraged to succeed, never felt that success was to be measured in merely financial terms. In one of those moods of self-flattery to which we are all prone, I was delighted to apply to my own background a comment by John Butler Yeats to his gifted son William. A gentleman, the poet's father informed him, 'was a man not wholly occupied in getting on'.

My father, then, was too much of a gambler to accept gambling primarily as a means to financial reward, for the true gambler relishes much more the satisfaction of beating the odds, bucking the system, or even (as I think) finding himself for a brief golden moment the favoured child of an otherwise hostile fate. The material reward of a successful bet functions mainly as the symbolic proof of that casual beatitude so rarely bestowed by an indifferent or even hostile world. Yet on one occasion at least his financial reward was indeed considerable. In 1946 the winner of the November Handicap (Las Vegas, ridden by Harry Wragg) came home at 100/6, to complete for him a complex series of successful bets known as a 'yankee' (six doubles, four trebles and an accumulator involving all four horses selected). His winnings amounted to something like £500 – a mighty sum in 1946.

I have only recently learned that it was this unusual stroke of luck which paid for the one extravagant holiday he ever permitted himself – his trip to America on the *Queen Elizabeth* in 1947.

*

My father's politics were consistently held and clearly defined, but tempered by pragmatism and, above all, tolerance. He was unreservedly Nationalist in his outlook, having lived through the emergence of the modern Irish state, and having played his part (though in a minor and non-active way) on the Nationalist side in that emergence. He once briefly met, on a historic public occasion in Armagh city, the legendary Michael Collins, and contributed to the mythologising of that figure in my eyes, a process later accelerated by my reading of Rex Taylor's *Michael Collins* (my attitude subsequently has been one of greater scepticism). There were, however, some anomalies: for instance, he would make a point of tuning in to the King's message on radio on Christmas Day. So it was that we often shared with all those loyal families in Britain the ritual of listening to the annual broadcast by George VI – even if my father would compensate for this possible betrayal of Nationalist purity by referring disparagingly to 'stuttering George'.

In other matters of a political nature he was not about to risk compromising himself. Thus, he was scathing about the Unionist-dominated Northern Irish parliament at Stormont, and made it clear that his sympathies lay with the Northern Ireland Nationalist Party (this being some time prior to the establishment of the later Nationalist grouping, the SDLP), even though he must have felt the futility of a politics in which a Protestant majority was assured of power (and the Catholic minority equally assured of permanent exclusion) for the foreseeable future. On one dramatic occasion he and a number of other prominent local Catholics resigned from the Board of Newry's Daisy Hill Hospital, because once again a Protestant majority on the Board had ensured that one of their own got the job in question. I like to think, though, that his reaction did not at all arise from a fit of pique at the failure of himself and his fellow-taigs to 'get the taig candidate in'; he was in principle anti-sectarian, as the mixed nature of the clientele in his business readily suggests.

His pub was a deeply ecumenical one, not only in religious but in class terms, long before that word became ready currency: Protestant and Catholic, members of society both high and low, businessmen and wage-earners from both sides of the community consorted happily in the bar-room, with no sense of unease or, for that matter, that forced bonhomie which sometimes in these situations tries to do duty for genuine tolerance. A representative tableau might be the following. In one corner, engaged in conversation (possibly about the prospective winner of the three-thirty), would be a prominent Protestant business-man, a member of the local aristocracy (Lord K—), a retired British army major-general (Northern Irish by birth and, as it happens, a Catholic), and a colonel who was a staunch Unionist. Across the room you would find Jock (unemployed and the father of fourteen children: with two such clues, no prizes for guessing his religious background), Sergeant Daly (a Southern-born ex-member of the Royal Ulster Constabulary, to which he came after a spell in the old Royal Irish Constabulary, the all-Ireland police force which existed prior to Irish independence and the partition of the island), and the egregious and forever thirsty 'Champ', unemployed, except when acting as bookie's runner, often for the select group in the far corner. The thirst and the occupation as runner were intimately connected, since his reward for relaying the bets of others was (especially if they were successful) the utterance of those magical words which made his existence tolerable, 'What'll it be, Champ?' He eventually late in life went 'on the wagon' (he had 'found religion', it was rumoured). For a while we used to joke that he was the *second*-best-dressed man in the neighbourhood, since he was the recipient of my wealthy brother-in-law's 'cast-offs'.

My father could relish a sectarian joke (he enjoyed telling the story of a Catholic on a crowded bus on a Saturday evening in Belfast, turning ostentatiously to the sports pages and reading in the loudest voice, to all who could hear, his own factitious headline, 'Celtic 2, Rangers 0: Pope to Get Very Drunk in Vatican Tonight'). But his pub was very strictly a 'no party songs pub', and he was determined to keep it that way. Equally, he refused to divide up the pub-space into a 'public bar' and a 'select lounge': it was one large open area, accessible to all who had business there (either buying drink or, when television came in, watching the races on TV), and could, as the saying is, 'keep a civil tongue in their head'. It has always since haunted my imagination as the image of the ideal community, individuals freely mingling and exchanging views, adapting in a civilised (if often spirited) way to each other without compromising their own cherished individuality or deeply held beliefs. It was in many ways an advantage to grow up in close proximity to such a social scene, though, introspective and apolitical as I undoubtedly was,

I may have assimilated less from the experience than other members of my family.

Of all the Protestants who were regular customers in my father's pub, it is 'Big Alf' who stands out most in my memory. As the name suggests, he was above average height, with all his other features in proportion; his hands seemed especially capacious. His face, too, was unforgettable: large and coarse and friendly, looking as if it had been carved out of some potato of abnormal size, and one of those faces that quite simply seems to merit the term 'human' more richly than others. In sum, he had the kind of features that would not have been out of place in a canvas by Brueghel. But what was most extraordinary about Alf was the way in which he had transcended sectarian bitterness: for he had every motive to reject Nationalism and any who were even vaguely associated with that creed. In the Troubles of the 1920s, in a particularly barbaric act, his own mother, as well as other members of his family, had been burnt to death by the Republicans in an attack on their small house in one of the townlands outside Newry. Yet Alf was ready to forgive and forget. No wonder, then, that he should be such a permanent fixture in my mind, a figure who grows almost mythic at this distance, still invested, as he was, with something of the Dickensian power of the child's imagination: for he was one of the singular figures who first appeared as part of that exotic collection of human beings I glimpsed through the bar-door in my ear-liest years, at busy Christmas or at other times.

Yet even for Alf there was one day in the year when he could not appear in our pub: that was the Twelfth of July. I have no doubt that this was not personal choice on his part, but a matter rather of what we have come to know as 'peer pressure', or, not to put too fine a point on it, of the politics of the tribe. And he was not the only Protestant customer who felt obliged to submit to this enforced absenteeism: many others would stay away for one or two days or even longer around the Twelfth, in some instances for evident pragmatic reasons, such as that they were socialising, during that period, with other Protestants who were not habitués of our (Catholic) pub or of any similar establishment. Yet, when all allowance had been made (and in my recollection someone like Alf was always a reluctant absentee, and felt almost ashamed to be so), the whole thing was a sad reminder of the ineradicable divide between the two sides, and the limits to the possibilities for true fusion. In that regard, my image of the bar as an ideal community looks sentimental and fatally flawed: there were some realities that it simply could not accommodate.

It was perhaps in order to escape from these narrow horizons that my father fed his political interests elsewhere, which he did by taking the most lively interest in international affairs. He was an avid reader of the newspapers and an obsessive listener to the radio news: natural enough in one who runs a pub, where your customers (before the arrival of television or even more distracting electronic knick-knacks) expect to exchange 'weighty' views on the latest in world news (and if they have 'had a few', then you need to be especially well versed to keep the whole process rational). But my father's interest in world politics was something undertaken as a matter of personal urgency rather than professional obligation: he seemed to relish summoning up the evocative names of Roosevelt, Truman and Eisenhower, of Churchill and 'Joe' Stalin, of Douglas MacArthur and Field-Marshal Montgomery (for the latter he felt a certain contempt, dismissing him as a 'showman'). It is in this perspective, in truth, that his habit of listening to the King's Christmas message should perhaps be viewed: it was another gesture towards the cosmopolitan, a way of keeping his views turned outward. It may even have been the case (though I am by no means certain of this) that he had in some obscure way a sentimental sense of the Commonwealth of nations, extending around the globe in a network of distant affinities.

World affairs, in any case, frequently impinged upon family life. Some of my earliest memories of table-talk at lunch- or tea-time concern the Korean War; born only four years before World War II ended, I have of course no memories of that (though I was utterly fascinated as a child when I came upon some old gas-masks lying around the house, these seeming to me as exotic as screen-props in the cinema, until with repeated familiarity they became rubbersmelly and banal). I found my father's comments deeply disturbing: it appeared that a monstrous weapon called an atomic bomb had been not only invented but used against the Japanese at Hiroshima and Nagasaki, and that this weapon could well be used again. The Korean War was between the Chinese and the Americans: we were, of course, on the side of the Americans (we had lots of cousins in the US, and they sometimes sent us presents, especially during the shortages after World War II). Korea was a comparatively small country, but China was not, and neither was the US, so if push came to shove, then the Americans might have to use the A-Bomb...

'And that,' my father would solemnly intone, 'would be the end.'

There would be a brief pause as the implications of this pronouncement began to sink in. Then one of the older members of the family would seek further clarification.

'The end of...everything, you mean?'

'The end,' my father would repeat with significant emphasis.

The end of the world! Unthinkable – yet here was Father telling us all that it was a very real possibility.

I have not often thought of myself as one profoundly affected by growing up in that peculiar Age of Anxiety known as the 'Cold War': but it is undoubtedly the case that these comments by my father provoked a radical sense of insecurity, entering deep into my imagination with a substantial if not fully formed sense of foreboding. Later, at school, and some time after the Korean War was over, we made jokes about it. While on the one hand we read our *GI Joe* comics, which extolled the bravery and ingenuity of the Yanks against the yellow peril of the Chinks, on the other we enjoyed stories of hordes of fighting Asiatics throwing themselves with fiendish commitment against GI strongholds shouting 'Fug you, marine! Fug Babe Ruth!'

Yet the fear of universal nuclear war was far from dispelled. I was from the age of eight or nine a fervent devotee of (among others) Captain Marvel; and I shall forever remember a special edition of a Captain Marvel comic, peculiar in its size (something less than the usual thirty-two pages) and colour (it did not use the full range, but was limited to browns and greens and oranges). It was an unashamedly propagandist piece, warning against the horrors of nuclear war: in it, Captain Marvel tries in vain to deflect the world-powers from their aggressive ways, and, himself invulnerable, ends up as sole survivor on the planet. The last picture shows him lamenting over a desolate world. It was an image that stayed with me longer than I wished: not that I had nightmares about it, but it left me, as Wordsworth phrases it in a completely different context, with 'a dim and undetermin'd sense' of possibilities I would have preferred to consign to the realm of the unimaginable.

*

I think of my father as a tough man, and treasure in particular one story of his courage in the face of real danger. The event happened before I came to consciousness, and so possesses something of the character of family myth; but it really did take place. It was during World War II, when American soldiers were stationed in County Down at a camp in Ballykinlar. They came up to Newry one night on leave, and proceeded to paint the town red. Very much the worse for drink, they ended up in our bar; my father, assessing their condition correctly, refused to serve them. One of them threatened him with a knife, but he still stood his ground. So the American GI threw the knife at him, and it hurtled past and stuck in the back of the wooden entrance-door. Eventually the Military Police arrived, and the episode ended without anyone much the worse for the experience. But the mark where the knife had stuck in the door remained, and could repeatedly provoke in subsequent years a retelling of the event, which, perhaps embellished as the years went on and the incident receded in time, became a significant episode in the family folklore.

Yet my father had a gentler side, however well he sometimes managed to hide it. He made a point of keeping canaries in the bar, their cages hung aloft the high sunstreaming windows. I think he enjoyed their bursts of song as a reminder of the birds he had heard on the farm in his childhood. He was assiduous in his care for them, replenishing their seed-trays and refilling the water-containers as the need arose. In a word, he cherished them. One morning, though, when he opened up the bar as usual, he was met by an ominous silence. He let up the blinds, and, as the light poured in, quickly realised the reason for the silence. All the canaries (there were, I think, three or four) lay stiff and dead at the bottom of their cages. What affected him as much as anything was that he never did find out what had caused their sudden deaths. He could only surmise that a rat had somehow got close to them, and scared the creatures to death. That day his pub was sombre in its lack of joyous birdsong.

Tough though my father was, however, his harsh and demanding life took its toll. My memory of him is of one who suffered from recurrent ill-health. By the time he died, he had had God knows how many operations for ulcers, and among my recollections is the sight of my father reduced to a strict milk diet, and putting up with it as patiently as he could. I think that, in the course of a hard life, he had the greater part of his stomach cut away by the surgeon's knife. In later years, too, he developed a stiff leg, which meant that he had to limp slowly and perhaps painfully around the bar. Yet even in his late years, and in that physical condition, he exercised his authority. As a young man in my early twenties I saw him one day eject from the bar a man who had become objectionable through drink. The man was a good foot taller than himself; but he took him by the shoulder and forced him out onto the street, in a way that brooked no contradiction. To a number of his customers, as to the barmen he employed, he was always known as 'the Boss'.

At times querulous in his final years, and desolate after the death of my mother, he nevertheless saw out the end of his days with stoic dignity. Nor did he ever lose his sense of humour. I prefer to remember him, not as a semi-invalid, battling on with a grim stoicism, but as one who both told and enjoyed a good joke. One of his better ones concerned the rustic type (my father probably called him a 'Ballyholland man', after one of the more notorious townlands outside Newry), who goes to the doctor with haemorrhoids. The doctor shows him some suppositories.

'Do you know what these are?'

'Oh I do begod,' says the patient, not wishing to reveal his ignorance.

'Well, then,' says the doctor, 'take one of these every night and put it up your back passage. If things don't improve, come back and see me, OK?'

Two weeks later the patient returns.

'Is there any improvement?' asks the doctor.

'Not a bit,' says the patient, obviously angry because he feels he has been conned.

'And did you,' says the doctor, 'follow the instructions I gave?'

'Every night,' says the patient, increasingly filled with righteous indignation, 'I opened the kitchen door and threw one of them things up the back passage. And for all the good it done me, doctor, I might as well have shoved them up my arse!'

*

If the bar on occasion featured a number of multi-coloured canaries, in the house itself it was more usual to find a solitary budgerigar, to whom we strove to teach (often without much success) various phrases (usually decent rather than obscene). The budgie Joey (light blue, with brownish markings on his wings) arrived one afternoon with a highly specified pedigree, produced with a flourish by the man who was selling him (a Mr Clarke, let us call him). Unfortunate man that he was, Mr Clarke suffered from a pronounced stutter; so that, while he was relaying the details, we had to keep our faces straight, and, subsequently, in his absence, repeatedly imitated his halting delivery: 'H-h-his f-f-father was a s-s-s-cinnamon wing and his m-mother was a sk-sk-sk-sky blue.'

It was doubtless because of our mocking repetitions of that sentence that the words stayed in my mind; but in due course I began to feel, at first obscurely, and then more directly, that – however incongruous the analogy and ridiculous the origin of the words – that formula might have something to say to me about my own parentage (or, more correctly, about my attitude towards my parents). For if my father was imperfect (if lovable) – sinnerman/cinnamon – it was difficult for me not to see my mother in ideal terms as 'a thing enskied and sainted'; though thankfully, she was in reality a prosaic being of the earth, and far too human to be perfect.

CHAPTER TWO

Mother

Here was a man who now for the first time found himself looking into the eyes of death – who was passing through one of those rare moments of experience when we feel the truth of a commonplace… When the commonplace 'We must all die' transforms itself suddenly into the acute consciousness 'I must die – and soon', then death grapples us, and his fingers are cruel…

(George Eliot, *Middlemarch*)

The centre of our house was the kitchen, and appropriately enough that was also the house's hearth. For at all times when the weather was chilly or even cool, a fire burned in its grate, warm and red-glowing beneath its thick black cap of slack. To the right of the fireplace a door opened into the much smaller scullery; opposite that door was the deal table at which we had some of our meals (though as we grew older, the preference was for the table in the adjacent dining-room, and that, in any case, was where we ate when there were guests). But what I most remember about the kitchen was that it was in that domestic centre that my mother did her baking: here, with an inexhaustible energy, she sliced apples for tarts or for dumplings, mixed her madeira or 'marble' cakes (magically, three colours and flavours, vanilla, raspberry, chocolate), beat up by hand her sponge-cake mixes and the cream to fill them, rolled and spread the pastry cover for the brown stew pie, chopped up the vegetables for shin soup, prepared the mix for the steamed puddings (orange, coconut), or layered the bread in the pyrex dish which, duly covered with a frothy egg-white top, became the 'queen of puddings'. Coming up to Christmas, activity was more frenetic than ever: there were Christmas cakes to be made, and mince pies, the turkey to be cleaned out and stuffed. The Christmas pudding required a separate ritual: first mixed, then a bottle of stout added, it was left at least a day to mature before we all stirred it and made a wish. Only then was it ladled into a number of bowls, beginning with the largest and on down to the smallest (we always had a series of plum puddings, the last of which was eaten at Easter).

It was not only on occasions like Christmas that my mother made the essential contribution. She presided likewise over the festivities at Hallowe'en. For not only did she ensure that we had our apple strung up in the kitchen (to be bitten into without using your hands) and set up the basin of water so that we could 'dunk' for apples (again using your mouth only), but she provided as centrepiece of the *Winterfest* a large apple dumpling. Along with a number of local children we would do our rounds, dressed up as outlandishly as our resources would permit, and collect whatever gifts and money we could. If, as sometimes happened, a drunk contributed a half-crown where he meant to give a penny, we had no compunction about taking advantage of his error; for this was a night when we were liberated from responsibility, and the continual explosions of fireworks, near and far, confirmed us in our hectic freedom. Then the group of us would return to our house, laden with spoils (not only money, but nuts, apples and sweets), and enjoy our pagan feast in the warm kitchen.

The main attraction was the dumpling, containing, as tradition dictates, a number of symbolic items which, on this ominous night when the dead were supposed to walk, predicted your future. These were wrapped in greaseproof paper, and randomly distributed among the apples. A ring meant marriage, a button a single life, a piece of rag poverty, a coin (usually a silver sixpence) wealth. In theory, it was possible for one person to be the recipient of contradictory symbols (for example, you could conceivably end up with both the ring and the button), but in practice this rarely happened. Neither do I remember any such ritual as that found in Joyce's short story 'Clay', where the spinster, Maria, is blindfolded and asked to reach out and touch one of a number of items placed on a table in front of her. Cruelly, Maria touches the saucer filled with clay, symbolising death.

When I first came across the famous phrase in Thomas Mann's *Tonio Kröger*, 'the bliss of the commonplace', it probably acquired its sense and substance from my experience of our kitchen. Here was all the ordinary sustenance one could ever need: warmth and comfort, food and nurture. What further endeared the place to me was the fact that I often read by the fireplace there (comics mostly); or, most vivid in my recall, I sometimes baked small potatoes in the roasting fire, peeled them out of their blackash skins, and mashed them up with butter and salt, relishing the exotic smoky flavour (perversely, I often then proceeded to eat the charred black skins as well). There was only ever one other hearth that meant as much (or more) to me: that was the big kitchen range in my Uncle Johnny's farmhouse in Lislea, where, in the lazy Sunday silence, the big ticking clock, fixed securely on the upper wall, would 'sing peace into my breast'.

It is odd, then, to remember that it was precisely in the home kitchen, that rich haven of domestic security, that I first deeply and insidiously tasted death. Not that any death occurred there: but rather that I, at the age of eight or nine, thought that a death sentence had been pronounced – that it was all over for me, and that I was destined to be nipped in the bud before I should ever have the chance to bloom. How common, I wonder, is this kind of experience? Perhaps it is more frequent than we like to remember, though in my own case the memory is ineradicable.

It happened this way. I had developed, at that young age, a very heavy cold or 'flu; the doctor (a well known local man, Dr Laverty, let us call him here) was called out, and I was duly examined in the kitchen, probably because that was the warmest room in the house. So I lay back again on the big couch which lined the wall opposite the fire, fascinated in retrospect, as ever, by Doc Laverty's ability to talk, wield the stethoscope, and conduct the examination (including auscultation) without once removing the cigarette from the corner of his mouth. It was a further object of fascination to observe the way the cigarette grew increasingly soggy with saliva and, above all, to wonder if the lengthening end-ash would fall off (onto the floor or his clothes or wherever) before he had time to deal with it (his success rate in that regard was something less than fifty per cent). But I was disposed to make the best of it, and snuggled down, feeling a little miserable because of my condition, but comforted by the proximity of the quietly glowing fire, and thinking that I was bound to be soon on the mend, once the doctor had seen me. As I lay there, however, I became aware of low voices in the dining-room next door. It was my father and the doctor talking together. Nothing, of course, unusual in that, since they often chewed the fat about the horses or the international or national news. But I was intrigued by the fact that they seemed to be keeping their voices conspiratorially low; and, idle and unoccupied as I was, I strained my ears to listen.

'No, no,' said Dr Laverty, in deliberative professional tones, 'it doesn't look well at all.' Then the breathy intake on his cigarette.

'Is he...' began my father, but I could not pick up the rest.

'Matter of days' (Dr Laverty exhaled). 'There's no hope.' His voice was more audible than my father's. 'Ach, we've done what we could for him, but...'

I imagined the concluding gesture, and a slow horror stole across my heart. I could no longer focus on what my father was saying in reply: perhaps it was a commonplace 'That's very hard', or something similar. But there it was, so plainly stated as to leave no room for hope: I was doomed. The scalding tears ran down my cheeks (as far as I recall, there was no one else in the kitchen at the time). I was broken and finished, all washed up at the age of eight or nine. I would go...I did not know where, perhaps a dark place, no further definable than that (and how, as a child, I feared the night-time dark!).

I cannot say how long that painful situation lasted, the boy on the big couch (which no longer gave him any comfort), looking through tear-filled eyes at the familiar fire (which no longer gave him any cheer): not, I think, more than a minute or two. I am less clear about the conclusion of the episode than I am about its core moment; but I think that when the doctor had departed, as he soon thereafter did, my father came in to see if I was all right and quickly realised that I was very upset. I think that he did manage to elicit my faltering revelations that I had overhead his chat with the doctor about someone dying, and that I had thought that they were talking about me; that he quickly set the record straight, and made it clear that they had been referring to a married man (unknown to me) who was dying of cancer. I imagine that he laughed and teased me a little, and set about getting me out of the dumps – a process later completed, I suspect, by some judicious attention from my mother (possibly she had been out at church, or visiting a good friend not far away). So I recovered my spirits, and experienced a great sense of relief that I was not, for this time at least, to get the chop. And, doubtless, as day followed day and I recovered and picked up the old routines, the episode ceased to have any resonance. But it lasted long enough to enable me now to recreate it with some sense of immediacy, though I cannot know for certain whether the experience left an indelible mark, even from that very early time, which in some way shaped my subsequent attitudes.

Was it the case that in that moment, as I am sometimes tempted to believe, I underwent, far too early, far too young, a painful initiation into the kind of consciousness that should have been reserved for a much later date? Had I, in fact, tasted, however briefly, the wormwood of essential and perhaps irreversible loneliness, when the soul unhappily falls away from all stay, from all relationship? Yet something in me rejects that possibility as far too melodramatic. If such an early experience was, indeed, formative, it has since been countered and overlain by numerous other experiences that left a different kind of aftertaste. There is, after all, no simple clew to lead us through the labyrinth of our existence.

*

I seem always to have been fated to be (as the Italians say) *amletico*, particularly as an adolescent – that is to say, brooding and introspective, like Hamlet. While it is certainly the case that with the advancing years I have left most of that behind me, I suspect nonetheless that throughout much of my childhood and adolescence, my self-preoccupation and moodiness were a source of concern (if not anxiety) to my mother. (I say this all the more readily, having now, at this late stage, been through the trials and tribulations of parenthood myself.) Highly introverted as I was, I had a lot (far too much) going on inside my head; and when I look at the photographs of myself as a child, I see an intense little atom, often solemn and serious, or even stern, with a hint of grim determination in his stance. I had, no doubt, my joyous moments and my childhood glee; but what strikes me forcibly about the child in the photos is the air of adult sobriety he sometimes conveys.

It was probably for reasons such as this that my mother seems to have determined to encourage in me whatever signs of extraversion and spontaneous capacity for fun she discerned. I cannot otherwise explain the moment, so vividly etched on my memory, when she put on one of her most positively smiling expressions, and told me with a beaming face that I was a 'jolly little fellow'. I describe her here as having 'told me'; but my recollection is that there was an element of persuasion in it, as if she meant to convey to me that this was the way I *ought* to be. It may also be the case that she needed to persuade not only me but indeed herself in that regard.

Twice in my early life, in a state of emotional turmoil, seething against some injustice or set of injustices which I cannot now recall, I ran away from home. I must have been eleven or twelve on both occasions, on the verge of adolescence. Once I ran away from the house in Newry, having carefully penned a note to explain why I was doing so (it may have contained nothing more definite than a statement to the effect that I could 'take no more'); once I ran away from the house in Warrenpoint (where we habitually spent the month of July), and walked a long, long way, in what seemed to be a volcanic state of emotion, along the seafront road towards Rostrevor. In due course I ceased to seethe, and in any case was growing hungry; perhaps, too, the night was just beginning to draw in. So back I went; and on neither occasion was there any major recrimination. Many years later, in one of the most disturbed periods of my life (some time after the death of both parents, when it seems that I had some leftover grieving to do), I wrote an appalling poem (one of many such) which begins by describing my departure from all hope of domestic security:

Windward, a thousand miles from bliss,
And callow-hearted into night ...

It is only now that it strikes me that this kind of utterance may have been an instance of the 'return of the repressed' (as Freud has it), a reliving (admittedly under very different circumstances) of some of that early childhood hurt.

Yet what in fact was the nature of that childhood pain? Why did I then so acutely feel that I was the victim of injustice? For it is in terms of injustice, however obscurely felt, that these incidents of wilful self-alienation from the family present themselves. I can only imagine that, as the youngest of three boys, I had a struggle to survive the rough and tumble of physical competition and collision. I was not only the youngest, but small and slight; and certainly the elder of my two brothers, Peter, was physically much stronger. I can remember all too well some of the pains and indignities to which he (not vindictively, I think, but thoughtlessly) subjected me; and, in particular, two incidents at the seaside in Warrenpoint, where we went on summer holidays.

On one occasion he held me under the water, by superior force, for what seemed an unendurable length of time. I arose with lungs ready to burst, feeling (I imagine) like a man who has been keelhauled. For a short period thereafter I developed a fear of the water, though in due course I came to terms with that. Far more dramatic, however, especially in its immediate consequence, was the other example of Peter's capacity to inflict hurt.

We were far out towards the distant edge of the beach, the tide having retreated to its farthest point. There were rockpools to explore, and various exoticisms, including crabs and shellfish, to be sought out or turned over and perhaps collected. Peter found what seems to have been a hefty fist-sized piece of blubber, a gross fatty mass which smelled in the rankest way of rotten fish. We both examined it as an unusual curio: not least among its attributes was the fact that it stank to high heaven. What urge then possessed him I do not know; but he seized and held me, and smeared the disgusting mass of greasy fat all over the back of my neck. As usual on an occasion such as this, I was powerless; his superior age and size made him invulnerable to my comparatively puny attempts to retaliate.

I was filled with a great surge of anger and utter frustration. I could do nothing but retreat, carrying with me my sense of baffled impotence. So all the way up the beach I stalked, a distance of some two hundred yards, and all the time, in my puny frame, the great rage seethed without diminution. Like the woman in Burns's poem 'Tam O'Shanter', who waits for her husband to return from his drinking spree, I nursed my wrath 'to keep it warm'. On and on up the beach, up the steps to the road, across the road to the house, into the house, a creature of fury I stride, seeking to vent my rage and frustration on any suitable object that comes my way. I am carried almost unconsciously down the corridor from the front door.

I see the frosted glass panes of the kitchen door in front of me. I strike outwards with maximum force against malicious fate itself. Perhaps I am directing my great anger (though I have no conscious thought of this kind) against what Hardy in *The Woodlanders* calls the 'intangible Cause' which is 'too elusive to be discerned and cornered by poor humanity when in an irritated mood'. My right hand shoots forward palm outward, and, the force of the blow matching my vehement feeling, I smash in one swift movement one of the two frosted panes.

Was it following this event that I decided to run away from home? I cannot be sure. But I can recognise what the motive for running away would have been. Unjustly victimised by my brother, I may have felt doubly victimised (whether I was physically punished for my outrageous act or not) by being exposed as the villain of the piece (it was after all I who had been spectacularly destructive, not my brother; and whereas his spiteful deed had been committed far beyond the confines of the house, mine had been enacted criminally close to the hearth itself). In my uncontrollable anger, I had wantonly thrown away the role of innocent victim, and assumed instead that of chief culprit. There was an inevitable logic in this, but my soul could not accept it as just.

On more than one occasion my short temper got me into hot water at home. Once, when I was in my early teens, I fell asleep curled up on an armchair. My father, in a playful mood, could not resist the sight of my rump invitingly vulnerable to slap or 'skelp'. He duly woke me up out of a deep sleep by lightly smacking me. I awoke in an instant rage, saw to my right one of our best dining-room chairs, flailed viciously at that with my boot, and saw an entire chair-leg fly off into the kitchen. General outrage followed; while my mother (God bless her!) did her best to defend me: 'It was an accident, I'm sure! It *was* an accident, wasn't it?'

She pressed me for an answer. But it has always been one of my perversities that I insist on telling the truth in situations where the truth is really not what is required. I felt, moreover, that I was deserving of punishment; whatever the mitigating circumstances, I knew that what I had done was wrong. And I was dismayed and guilty at the destruction I had wreaked on the good chair. I refused the escape-clause she was offering me.

'No,' I insisted on replying (perhaps still with a trace of lingering defiance in my eyes, which I did not mean to refer to my response to her question), 'I did it on purpose.'

There and then my mother gave me a number of almighty wallops with her hand on my exposed upper legs; and for some time afterwards I bore the marks. I do not recall that, either at that time or at any period since, I bore the slightest sense of resentment against her. I had sinned and confessed; I deserved the punishment. I have often thought of the incident subsequently (partly because it is the only occasion I can remember when she chastised me in that way). I now feel that it was, in a real sense, a loving punishment; for she could not accept that I, for whom, as her youngest, she may have had a particular fondness, could so disastrously fail both her expectations and his own better self.

*

It is natural for me to situate my mother, in the first instance, at the centre of our domestic life; and I hope that I do her no injustice if I say that she seems, in retrospect, to have been remarkable for her ordinariness. She had a great love of music, but she played no instrument and did not sing; and her taste was middlebrow – Handel's 'Largo', Puccini, popular short pieces by Elgar, the Luton Girls' Choir singing 'The Nuns' Chorus'. She liked to read whenever she found the time, but was not interested in the classics. Her favourite author was Irish and sentimental, and is now almost forgotten, even in Ireland: Annie M. P. Smithson. But she did not always have the leisure to read. She was not just a housewife and mother, but, in spite of a busy routine, a daily communicant; and was, in addition, as fully involved in the business of the bar as circumstance required.

She was fortunate that, in the midst of so many demands, she had constant home help. It is a matter of some astonishment to me to recall that throughout my childhood and adolescence we always had a maidservant in the house, with her own bedroom and a fixed set of duties. I am astonished because it is utterly inconceivable that I myself in my own family should ever have employed a 'maid' in this way (indeed, we have never even come close to having an *au pair*). It is not just a case of not being able to afford such an arrangement: it is more a case of total recoil from the class division such an arrangement suggests. Yet my parents were not particularly wealthy, nor were we in any sense close to being upper class (by my reckoning, at this distance, we were barely middle class, and I sometimes looked enviously at those sons and daughters of doctors, dentists or solicitors, who occupied large detached houses on the outskirts of the town, on the Belfast road or, classier still, the road that climbed up the hill to Cloghogue at the start of the route to Dublin).

But times were different then, and it was much commoner than it is now to have a live-in maid. A succession of figures came and went, some staying for only a brief while; but the most vivid personalities in the pantheon (both of whom stayed long enough to be a real part of the family) were Maggie (who eventually left to get married, leaving the family moist-eyed at her departure) and the wonderfully spirited Minnie (who in the end astonished everyone by going off to become a nun, and leaving us all even more desolate than we had been when Maggie departed). It was the convent's great gain when she brought her loyalty and devotion to their service.

So, thanks to Minnie and the others, my mother had welcome support in the midst of her busy routine. Yet she made the most of the opportunities she had; and perhaps her apparent ordinariness was a conscious achievement on her part, a remarkable assimilation of the varied facets of her existence into a seamless integrity of character. One of the greatest tributes I can pay her is that she was equally at home in church, home and public bar; was always the same person, the same firm reality, no matter the context in which she found herself. For her there seemed to be no division between these different roles, and in all of them she managed to be consistently herself. She not only helped my father to do the accounts (usually on a Sunday evening, a task that at a later date was shared by various members of the family); she also worked regularly behind the bar counter, in an environment which, if not exactly coarse, was no place for either a shrinking violet or a 'holy Josephine'. Yet she was never compromised by her involvement, remaining her usual self and retaining her habitual integrity; nor, on the other hand, did she make the customers feel uneasy by introducing a 'false' element of misplaced piety or gentility.

She was a warm-hearted and generous woman, spontaneous in her concern for others. A customer would have over-indulged, and be very much under the weather, so she would appeal to my father's better side: 'Joe, that man has had too much to drink. He looks in a bad way. Could we not give him something to eat? A ham sandwich? Or maybe a cup of Bovril?' (the cure-all on these occasions).

My father would be readily persuaded, and the steaming cup of Bovril and the sandwich would be placed, not in the hands of the drunk (for he was in no state to hold anything with any constancy), but on the counter before him. And there he would stand, swaying slightly and breathing deeply, and sporadically venturing to sip from the cup. Alas for my father, his only reward would be to endure the drunk's incessant repetition of his thanks and appreciation.

'You know what, Joe? You're a lovely man . . .'

A sceptical lift of the head from my father, who is in the process of serving another customer.

'Joe! Joe!' The insistent drunk again.

'What is it now?' (My father is a busy and therefore impatient man.)

'C'm 'ere, Joe.' (Gesturing with a loose and floppy hand.) 'Joe, c'm 'ere... till I tell you . . .'

My father reluctantly travels the length of the bar to hear what he has to say.

'Joe. Joe!' A deep breath and loud exhalation. 'Did anyone ever tell you you were a lovely man?'

'Drink up your Bovril and get home out of this to your wife!'

'Ah, Joe... Ah, Jasus, Joe, don't be cross... Because do you know what it is? You're a [burp!] lovely man . . .'

And if you were to look across at Joe at that point, he would have a shrugging smile on his face; even if, the next minute, he was urging the drunk to get on about his business in what sounded like the tones of genuine anger. My mother, in the background, had the quiet satisfaction of knowing not only that the right thing had been done, but that her husband shared in that satisfaction.

She was forthright and principled, but in the bar at least she never came close to anything like preaching. In fact, I cannot remember her ever preaching much, in any context, and it seems that as far she was concerned, actions always spoke louder than words. Yet I do recall one exchange she had with a male customer which left none who heard it in any doubt as to where she stood. Both Art, the younger of my two brothers, and myself had won scholarships to help us go to university, and the customer in question, in a waggish mood, wanted to know whether it was from herself or Joe 'that the boys got the brains'. I can still recall my mother's reply, and the promptness with which she gave it:

'They got them from the Almighty.'

Given that kind of background, it is perhaps not surprising that I recurrently acknowledge, however reluctantly, the challenge posed by the parable of the talents: whatever abilities we possess are in the nature of gifts, and we are obliged to make the most of them.

On one occasion in our bar when my mother was present, my vile temper got me into trouble once again. I was about sixteen or seventeen, and I was leaning over a newspaper just behind the counter, absorbed in my task, and oblivious to my surroundings. One of our customers, who had had a few drinks and was, as the saying is, 'in good form', decided he would play a prank. He was a cattle-dealer and a regular customer; and I suppose he was amused by my intense absorption, perhaps also feeling that, in any case, a teenage youth is a fair target for a man whose spirits are high. So he raised above my head the remains of the Guinness in his glass; perhaps held it there for a second while I remained oblivious to what was going on; then, to complete his joke, tipped the contents over my head. I saw the black drops spatter the paper I was reading, and simultaneously felt the cold liquid in my hair. When I glanced up, it was clear what had happened; and the perpetrator was showing his yellow teeth in a wide guffaw.

I was utterly furious, and wanted to use the full range of foul language at my disposal to tell him so. But my mother was present, and I could not freely indulge my urge to bespatter him with the worst terms of abuse I could devise. Instead of calling him a fecking shite, I had speedily to adjust my rage to strike verbally (that being the only form of retaliation I had); so I settled, as a compromise, on what I took to be the milder expletive, 'bugger'; which I enunciated with all the plosive force and venom I could muster. My mother took it pretty well, though she must have been alarmed at the vehemence of my response. My sister Harriet, however, who was a stickler for high morality and severe good conduct, took a rather different view when she heard about the episode.

'What did you call him?' She had taken me aside to obtain confirmation from me, so that, once the truth had been established out of the mouth of the miscreant himself, the judgment could be delivered.

I was doubtless a little surly in my reply. 'I called him a bugger. And he deserved worse!'

Her face was a study in shock and horror.

'You could hardly have called him anything worse! If you only knew what that word meant, you would never, *never* let it pass your lips! If you only *knew!*'

But I didn't know; and her extreme emphasis, while summoning the spectre of unrealisable horrors, did nothing to enlighten me. Some years later, when a major scandal broke about homosexual activity in the nearby town of Lurgan in County Armagh, I was fully apprised of the precise meaning of the word 'bugger'. But I had applied it to the cattle-dealer in much the same spirit as the Australians use the word 'bastard', in which there is no intention to impute illegitimacy; and I, likewise, was far from imputing sexual unorthodoxy to the cattleman, who was a butch heterosexual bastard, if ever there was one – as well as a fecking shite.

*

I gather from the family folklore that, before I was born, it was assumed that I would be a girl, probably because, after the arrival of my two sisters, the next two children had been male, and the odds favoured a female again. I don't know if the appearance of another boy occasioned disappointment in either of my parents; nor do I know why they called me Brian. My second name is Dominic; and the reason for that reveals something further about my mother. I came into the world with a full head of black hair (rather more, I fancy, than I at present possess), and as I lay wrapped in a cream-coloured blanket, the black and cream colour scheme suggested a fanciful parallel to a female visitor: 'He looks,' she said, referring to the colours of the order's garb, 'just like a little Dominican.' My mother readily took the hint, and Dominic became my second name. I have never known whether she hoped that this incident represented a divinely revealed indication of my future fate, nor whether, if such were the case, she was disappointed in my failure to fulfil the promise.

By the time I reached the age of sexual awareness, my thoughts were in any case very definitely turned away from celibacy; and I come now to one of the most vividly registered formative moments in my life, which in addition directly relates to my mother. I must have been fifteen or sixteen, and went to the cinema with her and my brother Peter. I cannot recall what the main feature was, but I do remember with exceptional clarity that the trailer for the coming attraction starred Lena Horne. I was looking at this in the casual way one does when waiting for the main feature, when suddenly my entire attention was seized by the svelte figure of the star in the very centre of the screen. She was wearing a tight, body-hugging, off-the-shoulder dress, and gyrating slightly as she sang.

It will seem extravagant if I say that at that moment my soul went out to her; but in any case she magnetised my attention, and in the same moment I knew, instinctively, that this was a turning away from my mother. I felt not the slightest guilt about it; it did not seem like a betrayal. I was to be, of natural necessity, divided from her in a gentle and inevitable 'sundering'. This is, in fact, the word used by Stephen

Dedalus in *A Portrait of the Artist as a Young Man*, in a sequence in which he reflects on the way he has had a difference of opinion with his mother as to his possible priestly vocation: 'he was made aware dimly and without regret of a first noiseless sundering of their lives'. I too seem to have accepted this division between my mother and myself in the same fatalistic way.

What haunts me as a major and perhaps unresolvable question, though, is whether or not this division was also a self-division; and one to be undergone, moreover, not just by myself but by the sexualised male in general. In his *Three Essays on Sexuality*, Freud tells us that in the course of a development 'through which all human beings ought to pass' we must unavoidably 'withdraw' our affection from our parents. Freud calls in fact for a 'complete' withdrawal; and therein may lie the problem. For it does not seem to me (and I am speaking here specifically of the heterosexual male) that, even if the sexual drive takes over and directs him away from the family tie, his affection can ever be completely withdrawn from the mother. The question then is whether the 'sundering' I speak of is not just inevitable, but also leaves in its wake a tragic self-division. It may leave the adult male with a permanent discrepancy between the erotic drive, in its full indefeasible urgency, and the loving-kindness associated by him with the mother, who has now of necessity been relegated to a different realm.

This problem the male struggles to transcend, and is, or at least can be, successful in so doing. But if we define the problem in the terms just employed, we may, perhaps, come closer to understanding a source of inner male conflict than is possible through Freud's own much-vaunted notion of the 'Oedipus complex'. It seems to me absurd to suggest that (even at the deep level of the unconscious) all or most men wish to 'possess' the mother. They wish to possess their female partner, but have to relearn or reacquire the tenderness that they are in danger of leaving behind when they escape from the experience of maternal affection. And they have to learn to integrate that tenderness into the sexual encounter. We should, perhaps, be less surprised than we are to learn that the original title Lawrence had in mind for *Lady Chatterley's Lover* was *Tenderness*.

*

Further fragments of memory, the details sometimes vague.

What age was I when I accompanied my mother on her shopping expeditions along Hill Street? Was I not yet at school? (Certainly not at primary school, though perhaps I was in the Infants' or Senior Infants' class at the Convent of Mercy.) Or it may be that I was at school, and the shopping was done on a Saturday morning. I am particularly fond of Irwin's bakery, where the smell of fresh bread and of sweet confections is delightful, and where the woman behind the counter gently teases me by calling me 'Blackie'. She cannot resist, perhaps, provoking in this affectionate and light-hearted manner one so small and young and yet so solemn-faced under his fringe of black hair. Perhaps she keeps it up until the sober and watchful child gives her a smile. Whether I show it or not, I am doubtless delighted with the woman's attention.

Another favourite shop was the chemist's known as 'The Steps to Health'. I must have visited this place with my mother also, though how young I was I cannot recall. The owner was a tall balding man with a well developed professional courtesy of manner, a white coat of the kind hospital doctors wear, and a thin Ronald Colman moustache that looked as if it might have been drawn over his upper lip by a make-up pencil. Later, when I had become a frequent visitor to the cinema, I began to see him as a petty gangster who probably wore a fedora when he was off duty and was really working for a mobster who existed somewhere behind the scenes. The shop was obviously just a 'front'. On the other hand, that Ronald Colman moustache might be enough to make him a good guy, so perhaps he was an undercover G-man.

By the time I had learned to read, I was able to appreciate the ingenuity of the shop's title. There were in fact four steps up from the ground-level of the street into the interior of the shop, each bearing a separate word in large writing, but with the sentence running from the bottom up:

HEALTH

TO

STEPS

THE

As a child I thought this was as clever as one could be. The 'Steps to Health' were not just words but real steps! Even now, I find it difficult to express how delightful it was to discover this precise correlation between language and reality.

Another memory of my mother. We are walking along the Well Road in Warrenpoint, on a fragrant summer evening in July, the sun just beginning to move down towards the western horizon. The hedges are about to pocket the darkness, but there is a while to go yet before their dim leaves fade. Mother is saying in a very light-hearted way that she is fed up with her situation. I do not think she really means it, but would like to be sure. So I ask some basic questions, and finally this one:

'What are you going to do?'

'Ach,' she replies, with a familiar expression of mock-exasperation on her face, 'I'm going to run away with a soldier.'

I am certain now that she is codding, and the smile in her eyes when she returns my look of inquiry confirms it. I am aware again of the fine fragrant evening in July.

Another time Mother enters my brothers and myself in a fancy dress competition. We are the 'Three Wise Men', complete with flowing robes of exotic colour and fabric which have a peculiar and slightly stuffy smell, and each carrying a prop that serves as a gift of the Magi (boxes and caskets). It is decided that one of the Wise Men must have been black, so someone has to do an Al Jolson and black up with burnt cork (since my father bottles his own stout, there is no shortage of corks). No prizes for guessing who the victim is. We win a prize, and my mother has a studio portrait taken by Newry's leading photographer. Out of that photo there still gaze, robed and crowned, two white older brothers and a smaller black boy, looking serious and Caucasian beneath his dark veneer. I was never meant to be an actor.

But the prize was wonderful, and made all the trouble seem worthwhile ('Brian, don't wipe your face! Don't, please don't scratch your nose!'). It was a snowhouse, the first I remember seeing, and in retrospect seems to have been very large. I do not know if these are still on sale, but a snowhouse consisted of a cardboard shape lavishly covered with pure white cotton-wool, with chimney, doors and windows carefully added. Inside was a veritable treasure-trove of gifts, and part of the fun was rummaging in the interior of the house and unearthing all kinds of surprises. Far more exotic in its appeal to that dark little pagan was this snowhouse, more wondrous by far, than the Magi from the East and their precious offerings to our Saviour.

*

Christmas Day, late in the evening. It was one of the few days in the year when we made use of the 'drawing-room', upstairs on the third storey of the house. It was a special room, with a thick carpet and impressive sofa and armchairs, draped in their genteel covers. It also contained a baby grand piano; and it was rumoured that John McCormack had been accompanied by that very piano when he had given a recital in the Town Hall (the recital may have been part of the farewell tours made by McCormack in 1937–38). The story was that the piano had been supplied by the dealer, McAreavey, for the great occasion, and that my father had subsequently bought it.

The fire is sinking in the grate, and beneath the ash only the faintest red glow is visible. I raise my eyes to look along the room, and see, scattered on the carpet, the orts and fragments of the earlier festivities. Strewn around are torn pieces of Christmas wrapping paper, the multicoloured remnants of crackers, the peelings of a mandarin orange. Under the piano are heaped some of the presents which have yet to be gathered up by their owners. The thin green pine-needles are beginning to accumulate under the Christmas tree. I hate to admit it, but Christmas is over. All that splendour comes down to this!

I have only in my memory similar fragments to offer when I try to recall my ordinary-extraordinary mother. So much is omitted, because not adequately recognised at the time. She was too close to us, too much a presence that we took for granted, a fount of ready sustenance that we thought could never fail. She affirmed her reality below the level of our conscious or analytical thought. It was only after I had left my childhood days behind that I learnt some basic documentary facts about her: how she had been educated at the Ursuline Convent in Sligo, had been before her marriage a post office employee, and how it was that, while she was working in a post office in Cookstown (opposite the entrance to my father's 'back bar'), she and my father had struck up a relationship. But these objective facts, belonging to a world and a time prior to the existence of the family and her role as 'mother', seem even now to have little connection with the familiar presence I so unthinkingly, so subjectively regarded as the immutable centre of the household.

So much unrecorded, then, because in a sense unrecordable. I accepted without question, as a natural given, the affirmative energy she brought to our lives. I was like the speaker in Hardy's superb poetic epiphany, 'The Self-Unseeing', who recognises, too late, the bounteous and privileged existence he and others enjoyed as children:

> She sat here in her chair,
> Smiling into the fire…
>
> Childlike, I danced in a dream;
> Blessings emblazoned that day;
> Everything glowed with a gleam;
> Yet we were looking away!

CHAPTER THREE

Church

There were two choices of church for a Catholic in Newry: you could go to the Cathedral in Hill Street, or to the Dominican Church in Dominic Street. Since we were within easy walking distance of the former, there was never any doubt that we would turn out to be 'Cathedral Catholics'. My mother walked to daily mass there nearly all her days; my father and my two brothers and myself went to the Confraternity meetings every Tuesday night, and of course we all went there to mass on Sundays and holy days. During Holy Week we were there for both Holy Thursday and the Stations on Good Friday. My brother Art and myself were, moreover, altar boys for some time, which meant that we were in the church for morning mass on weekdays.

Being an altar boy proved to be a highly profitable experience whereby we managed to combine successfully service to both God and Mammon. For after you had established yourself as a reliable member of the cohort, you were assigned to midweek weddings, and were paid for your trouble (sometimes handsomely) by the best man. After the service was over, all four of us altar boys (or, in the case of a really posh wedding, six) would troop into the vestry, and stand there with the self-consciousness of youth; while the priest might, none too subtly, give the best man his cue. ('The altar-boys did very well, what? Very well. Sure how would we manage without them?') After that there was the formality of the handing over of the pound note or (for those with a higher sense of style) the more discreet envelope, passed to the most senior figure in our little group. We would then leave the vestry as rapidly as decency permitted, and joyously divide the spoils.

We quickly got to know the individual priests and their foibles. Some would make you more nervous than others, because you sensed (or had good reason to be acquainted with) their impatient nature. An altar boy had a number of complicated little rituals to follow, and you had to get your timing right, for instance in the ringing of the bell at the consecration of the host, or in the minor example of choreography when, at the end of the mass, all those involved, the priest included, genuflected in unison before leaving the altar. Some priests said the mass more slowly than others; one man was notorious for the speed and dispatch with which he got through the ritual, and was known (affectionately) as 'Flash Harry' for his fifteen-minute mass on weekdays (Sunday mass had to include a sermon, so no possibility of a world record there).

Most people were grateful to Fr Harry for his no-frills approach; he was also regarded with some affection because at the Confraternity, when prayers were added at the end of the rosary, he always growled 'For Ireland', and proceeded to say one Our Father, one Hail Mary and a Glory Be to the Father. But it was hard going sometimes to keep a straight face when you sat as a member of a packed congregation at that Tuesday Confraternity. The major provocation to merriment was provided by poor Francie, who was not, to put it charitably, right in the head, and insisted, not only on always turning up, but on beating everyone else to the punch with his own all-purpose version of the response. Thus, during the Rosary, the priest in the pulpit would say the first part of the Our Father, up to 'as it is in heaven', and the congregation would be expected to respond with the remainder ('Give us this day . . .'). Similarly, the Hail Mary would be said by the priest as far as 'the fruit of thy womb, Jesus', and the congregation would take it up at 'Holy Mary, mother of God'.

But Francie would always leap in long before the priest had finished his stint, and whether it was Our Father or Hail Mary or Glory Be, there repeatedly and tirelessly arose like a solitary mockery the one voice proclaiming audibly throughout the church 'Giddy giddy giddy giddy Holy Ghotht Amen'. If you did manage to stifle your giggles at that, you could pose a further test to your self-control by looking over at the owner of the offending voice. If Francie was within eyeshot, you would catch him, across the many male heads in the congregation, carefully picking what appeared to be a flea or other minute instance of parasitic life from his grey, close-cropped hair, and holding it between index finger and thumb before dismissing it, with a jerk of his head, from his attention, so as to make sure he uttered (on his own cue) his cannily mistimed 'Giddy giddy giddy giddy giddy Holy Ghotht Amen'.

I am not sure if we learnt anything from this experience. What we might have come to appreciate was that the kingdom of God is all-inclusive and recognises no distinction between high and low, rich and poor, clever and feeble-minded. I suspect that my devout mother suggested this interpretation to us. But we found it difficult to get beyond the comedy of the situation, either to that inclusive vision of the Church, or (be it said) to any sense of tragedy in the wasted life that Francie so conspicuously flaunted before us.

*

Young Catholics growing up nowadays have a very different kind of education from the one people of my generation received. Some of the changes have undoubtedly been for the better: they have been spared much of that wounding sense of guilt which neurotically afflicted many of my age, and have a less fearful sense of God, who for most of us had been a harsh and punitive figure, setting impossible rules of an absolute kind and waiting for you to trip up so that he could pounce with a kind of divine 'Aha! Gotcha!' It was much later when I came upon the radical Protestant thought of William Blake that I recognised, in his Satan, the false image of God that had been instilled in me earlier. Blake saw Satan as the (falsely worshipped) God who was deemed to rule the world, and part of his role was to act as the Accuser; that is to say, when someone 'fell' and sinned, then the evil accuser was at hand to indict the imperfect human person, inducing a crippling shame. We are well rid of that psychological condition, which has nothing to do with the liberating 'good news' of Christ.

Yet if there have been major improvements in the way children are taught about God, there may have also been very serious losses. I do not think that children nowadays are given any real sense of the meaning of the sacraments, of their central importance in Catholic tradition, and, most important of all, of the operation of grace through the sacraments. True, there was a suspicion of scholastic sophistry in the distinction between Actual Grace and Sanctifying Grace (the former was given to you in order to help you out of a sinful condition, the latter was the condition of the soul in a sinless state); but at least these formulas not only kept before you the notion that there was an available redemptive power, but made it clear that such redemption was purely a gift (as the Latin word *gratia* signified) which God in His transcendent goodness generously bestowed. In other words, you could not 'earn' grace, any more than you could 'earn' redemption. Hence (according to this view) the resonance of that phrase in the liturgy, *O nimis caritas*, 'O exceeding love' (of the Most High), that He should care for poor humanity.

For Catholics, it used to be the case that the two sacraments which meant most to them in terms of the weekly routine were Penance (that is, going to confession) and the Eucharist (receiving Holy Communion). I say that this *used to be* the case, because certainly in these days confession has lost all its centrality (for me and others of that generation, it was a weekly event), and I doubt very much if Holy Communion has the same meaning for young people now as it once had for us (schooled as we were in the doctrine of the Real Presence, which we took very seriously). It is perhaps in keeping with the two versions of God which are evident in the preceding paragraphs (God as punisher, God as exceeding love) that Penance and the Eucharist constituted for me a similar duality, one negative, one positive. While confession usually induced a deep feeling of anxiety (it is emphatically *not* easy, in spite of what some Protestants seem to believe, to lay your shameful deeds before another human being in the confessional box), the reception of the sacred host in Communion inspired an even deeper sense of joy and, on occasions, something which might have been called euphoria were it not for the profound tranquillity which accompanied it. And this pattern was established very early on, in my case at least, inasmuch as my first confession was an occasion of much anxiety, while my first Communion was (like Napoleon's, we are told) a gala day.

It should be said at once, however, that my anxiety over my first confession was not then, as it often subsequently was, because I had some horrendous sin to reveal, but rather (oh innocent days!) because I could not think of any sins to tell. I remember with painful vividness standing in solitary anticipation in the long school corridor in the Abbey primary school, looking towards the door of the office behind which the priest awaited to hear my first confession. I had time – too much time, I think – to ponder on what was imminent, because I had to wait until the boy before me came out. So there I stood, aged seven (the age of reason, according to scholastic reckoning), rehearsing all the formulas ('Bless me father, for I have sinned; I was disobedient x times, I forgot to say my night prayers once' – and so on, down to the moment when I made my act of contrition – and please, please, God, don't let me forget the words!). But the huge problem for me was this: that as far as I could remember, I had *not* been disobedient, and I *had* said all my night prayers (no wonder that in later life one of my undergraduate colleagues at Queen's University was to dub me 'the wise virgin').

So I remember going back a few long paces to the Christian Brother who was in attendance, and saying to him: 'Brother, I can't think of anything to say. I don't know what to confess!' He must have been a very patient man (though I have no clear recollection of him), for I repeated this performance at least three times, as, with mounting anxiety, up and down that inhospitable corridor I went ('But Brother, I just can't think of anything to tell'). I can only compare it to the kind of 'dribble-itis' that sometimes afflicts us before a nerve-wracking ordeal, when we can't stop going to the toilet. After all that fuss, the confession itself was anti-climactic in the ease with which it passed off: I knelt on a great bulky cushion, covered with some coarse cloth, and allowed the very kindly priest (who was fully visible in the daylight of the office, unconcealed by any intervening barrier) to draw me out, to my satisfaction and to his. Then the act of contrition, and the final blessing, and I was a free man. I emerged from the room with a great sense of relief, feeling within my breast a sense of uplift which I took to be the potent operation of grace, and walked away from that particular rite of passage.

I spare the reader details of my later experiences of the confessional when, far from having nothing to tell, I often seemed to have far too much. Worst of all was the onset of adolescence, when you had to guard against looking at 'dirty' pictures (alas, in the biochemical condition that then afflicted a teenage male like myself, even the black and white drawings for the corset ads in the daily newspaper, as earlier the nude statues reproduced in our copy of Arthur Mee's *Children's Encyclopaedia*, were a major turn-on); beware of entertaining 'bad thoughts'; and above all refrain from 'touching yourself'. The consequences of failing to maintain these impossibly high standards meant the kind of self-abasement so superbly described in Stephen Dedalus's visit to the confessional in Joyce's *Portrait of the Artist as a Young Man* (though some of us might envy the extent of Stephen's Luciferian commitment, and the fact that among the usual sordidities he could include some genuine spectaculars). The strain of all of this was made even worse in that you had to distinguish between grave or 'mortal' sins (which entailed eternal damnation) and 'venial' sins (which merited a spell in Purgatory): though you could take some comfort, at least, from the fact that once you got that far you were assured – eventually – of salvation. Purgatory, as Dante has it in the first Canto of *Inferno*, contains

> souls in fire and yet content in fire,
> knowing that whensoever it may be
> they yet will mount into the blessed choir.
>
> (*John Ciardi's translation*)

Mortal sin was assessed according to three criteria: grave matter (it had to be a big one), full knowledge (did you know or realise what you were doing?) and full consent (did you positively assent to, or even will, the fatal act?). The last criterion offered the best possibilities for self-defence, particularly to anyone of a casuistic or legalistic turn of mind: for you could always argue that an inexorable thrusting on had overturned the restraining will of the reason, and that, at the very least, you could not possibly wish, in a positive sense, to commit grave sin. But as far as self-analysis went, your own cool reason did not always (or often) hold sway; doubts of the most nagging kind insinuated themselves, shame in its most irrational guise contaminated your very being, and it was usually safer (given the high – the inordinately high – stakes involved) to plead guilty before the inner tribunal of the self. After that, you went off to confession and 'took it like a man'.

In fact, the scrupulous self-examination you felt obliged to undertake before confession, far from acquitting you in your own eyes from the imputed guilt, usually had the opposite effect: you began, with a neurotic zeal, in a manner akin to obsessive-compulsive disorder, to unearth worse and worse aspects of your case. It is no wonder that Catholics of my generation use a term which is foreign to non-Catholics and, indeed, to Catholics of more recent vintage: we acknowledged the possibility that, if you weren't careful of being over-careful ('Lord, what fools these mortals be!'), you could end up in the unacceptable state of 'scrupulosity'. It was one thing to be 'scrupulous' or to 'feel a certain scruple' about doing something: but once you had slipped into the more extreme condition known as 'scrupulosity', you could end up in a state of religious mania from which only a professional might be able to rescue you.

To this day I approach the confessional (rare as my visits to confession have become) with, at best, very mixed feelings. But far other were my emotions in the reception of Communion, and even now, in this later period, I am still deeply grateful for the sacrament of the Eucharist. As a child, I truly accepted the doctrine of the Real Presence: God as Christ was fully present in the host, and to ingest that was to allow the divine itself, whole and undiluted, to enter into your soul. The 'proof' of God's presence was evident in the expansive glow that subsequently filled your breast. This was the energising and also strangely tranquillising presence of God himself within you; this was your direct access to that category that lay outside normal everyday existence, the Sacred. And the old rituals whereby the Church impressed upon you the symbolic meaning of this sacrament greatly aided in the effect: you walked in reverence up to the altar rails, knelt down in submissive patience, and, most telling detail of all, folded over your profane hands the white altar-cloth until the priest reached you. Then, as the altar-boy held the paten or silver plate beneath your chin (for fear any fragment of the sacred host would fall to the profane ground), you received the host, head back and eyes closed, into your mouth.

Times have changed, and no thinking Catholic can, on balance, lament the innovations brought about by Vatican II. Yet not all the changes have been for the better. As one watches the members of the congregation casually line up to receive the host into their own hands, not at a fixed and symbolic location such as the altar rails, but at various locations throughout the church, chosen on the basis of mere convenience and accessibility, it is hard not to feel that something of importance has been lost. What the altar rails symbolised was the well-nigh unbridgeable divide between the secular and the sacred: to kneel at those rails and in such proximity to the Holy was a privilege, and, if taken in the right spirit, was conducive to an attitude of reverence. But the very word 'reverence', along with its cousins 'sacred' and 'divine', is in grave danger of disappearing entirely from the lexicon of advanced Western civilisation. We shall soon inhabit a fully secularised 'infotech' world, where the buzz and hum and flicker will put paid to any notion of a transcendent order. I for one am happy to think that, luckily, I shall be long gone before the worst excesses of such a world have made themseves obvious. In his writings on archaic cultures, Mircea Eliade noted that, for primitive peoples, the 'Real' and the 'Sacred' were equivalent categories: what hope for us, who are soon to be reduced to mere 'virtual reality' in what may at last come to be a technological wasteland? Looking back a couple of centuries, I have considerable sympathy for that servant of the Brontë family in Yorkshire, Tabitha, who complained that the fairies had all disappeared because the 'factories' had driven them away.

John Henry Newman, having changed his allegiance from Anglicanism to the Roman Church, was deeply affected by the emphatic centrality of the doctrine of the Real Presence; it meant, for him, that no Catholic church where the sacred host was lodged in the tabernacle could ever convey a sense of emptiness, or of the absence of God from His own holy place. If there is one reason for preferring to have been educated in the Catholic faith rather than in an alternative Christian tradition, it is perhaps above all to be found in the bold claim of the Real Presence. I am grateful, too, that the early tranquillising joy felt in the reception of the Eucharist not only ushered me into a realm of experience I should otherwise never have known, but has remained for me an important criterion in the measuring of inner happiness. It was partly at least because of that early experience that I was subsequently able to enter with such imaginative sympathy into so much of the poetry of Wordsworth; not just the 'presence that disturbs me with the joy of elevated thoughts' in 'Tintern Abbey', but numerous passages in *The Prelude* in which the poet describes (or attempts to describe) sublime moments of deep and tranquil insight. Alas, like the ageing Wordsworth himself, I can remember but not relive my own moments of elevation as, alone in my study, I pored over the pages of *The Prelude*, and allowed my mind to enter deeply into the imaginative experience described. Yet, even if I could relive them, what words would serve to reproduce them? What is involved is a highly elusive or evanescent experience, and the mind thereafter finds it difficult to recall exactly what transpired. So Wordsworth speaks of how the 'soul',

> Remembering how she felt, but what she felt
> Remembering not, retains an obscure sense
> Of possible sublimity …

In Melville's *Moby-Dick* Ishmael is more confident in his celebration of this inner joy and tranquillity when he acclaims, in ecstatic terms, the possibility of a continuing access to the deep calm of the spiritual self: 'Oh, grassy glades! oh, ever vernal endless landscapes in the soul; in ye, though long parched by the dead drought of the earthly life, – in ye, men may yet roll, like young horses in new morning clover; and for some few fleeting moments, feel the cool dew of life immortal on them.' It has frequently been my experience to attain something like that sense of tranquillity and self-possession in the act of reading, perhaps in the context of a library, where monastic silence reigns.

In recent years, I have enjoyed the annual opportunity of spending a week or two in the south of Spain. Perhaps the closest I have come to the deep tranquillising sense I speak of has been on those occasions when, on a Spanish beach on a rich summer evening, while the sun has some time to go before its setting, I have sipped my cheap wine and, from time to time, raised my eyes from my paperback to admire the indefatigable, unchanging, everchanging motion of the sea. It is, of course, a crucial detail that the wine be cheap, since what is important is the human capacity for creative response, not the material occasion of that response. Since we live (or try to live) in a late capitalist world of 'designer labels' (each as fatuous as the next), stifled by a ubiquitous consumerist economy, there is a positive duty to refuse false luxury and practise a measure of judicious asceticism, if only in order to keep our priorities right. In any case, if there is a heaven for me (and I hope that Keats is right when he claims in one of his letters that in the afterlife our earthly joys will be repeated but in 'a finer tone'), it will have to include wine, a paperback, a Spanish beach that retains its lingering warmth under a multicoloured sunset, and the sense, no longer to be dismissed as mere illusion, of genuine insight.

*

For the majority of Northern Irish Catholics of my generation, religion was, from the dawn of consciousness, an integral and crucially important feature of life. When I reached what I must (with some embarrassment at the tardiness of my development) term my late adolescence – that is, in my early twenties – I began to find Catholicism intolerably oppressive and claustrophobic, and resolved to throw it off. I remember a moment when, on a retreat personally undertaken at a monastery north of Aberdeen (where I had my first university appointment), I informed the abbot with undue candour that I had 'decided to lapse'. He was appalled at what he took to be my misuse of language. 'But you don't *decide* to lapse,' he protested. 'It either happens or it doesn't!' But, from that point on, the die was cast.

The reasons for my disaffection were the obvious ones and may be briefly stated. I could not reconcile Church teaching with my developing sexuality, and, in addition, felt (though vaguely) that the Church was not sufficiently concerned with social justice. I had, besides, considerable trouble (and still do) with the doctrine of the Assumption of Our Blessed Lady into Heaven. It semed to me that the Resurrection and

Ascension into Heaven of Christ were unique events, and the attempt to promote a second ascent of an unblemished physical body strained credulity.

Thus for some time I became an agnostic (though emphatically not an atheist). I simply no longer knew whether there was a God or not, and I tried to control any drift into that absurd (but humanly understandable) condition attributable to a writer like Thomas Hardy: hating God for not existing. I came back to Christian belief very gradually over a period of many months, for reasons that I find difficult to put into words. I felt, let me simply say, a need to pray – not, be it said, in order to petition for help, but rather because that attitude of creaturely dependence and reverence seemed to me deeply rooted in my being.

So I forgot all about the Assumption and the Virgin Mary, and read as much as I could of those theologians (such as Hans Küng) who stressed, in the first instance, the *humanity* of Jesus (Küng speaks of the Christian God, in a phrase I treasured, as 'the god with a human face'). Since I saw no reason not to admire Jesus, I began at night to say the prayer which, according to biblical scholars, can be authentically attributed to him – the Our Father. And around that habit there gradually grew what I hoped was a more considered acceptance of Christian belief. I was not, at any point, persuaded by the mere force of argument to change my ways; and doubtless an orthodox Catholic would say that I recovered the 'gift' of faith.

Belief in God has always for me had more to do with profound instinct than with logical argument in favour of His existence. I do not feel that you can either 'prove' or 'disprove' God's existence ('How few things can be demonstrated!' exclaims Pascal); and I warm to Newman's relegation of logic in the matter of belief. At one point in his *Apologia Pro Vita Sua* he cites Saint Ambrose: 'Non in dialectica complacuit Deo salvum facere populum suum' ('It was not through logic that it pleased God to save His people'). Newman goes on to refer to his personal dislike of 'paper logic', for in the development of his own faith 'it was not logic that carried me on; as well might one say that the quicksilver in the barometer changes the weather. It is the concrete being that reasons; pass a number of years, and I find my mind in a new place; how? the whole man moves; paper logic is but the record of it.' This awareness of the limitations of logic recalls Pascal's curtailment of the powers of reason: 'Reason's last step is to recognise that there is an infinite number of things which surpass it.' What makes Newman's relegation of logic so telling is that he himself, in a prose that is lucid as well as impassioned, sustains his argument with such a consistent regard for consecutive reasoning. Newman, in other words, reveals the power of that very logical process to which he finally assigns a secondary place.

At school, in our Christian Doctrine classes, we duly learned the 'proofs' of God's existence, adapted and simplified (as far as I recall) from Thomas Aquinas. The leading argument was, of course, the argument from design: the whole idea that the universe, in both its cosmic and microcosmic order, 'reveals' an intelligent designer. From the stars in their sidereal courses, wheeling in their appointed paths, to the minute and intricate beauty of the snowflake as seen under a microscope, all things speak of intelligent design or pattern. Indeed, in its most enthusiastic form, the argument invokes the idea of God as artist (an idea present in Saint Augustine, and one which influenced Joyce), generating the beauty of the world.

I must here confess that I have found it increasingly impossible to find much comfort in this argument. In the wondrous patterns of the snowflake (or, as set forth in Michael Behe's remarkable book, *Darwin's Black Box*, the irreducibly complex structures at the biochemical level), Nature can be said to reveal an intelligent artist-designer, but not necessarily one that is benevolent. Is it not rather the case that, if we consider Nature realistically and in its totality, it suggests the opposite? How can we argue that a benevolent God is indicated by tigers, tornadoes, sharks, earthquakes, poisonous insects, and all those numerous features of the planet which work (actively, it sometimes seems, as Thomas Hardy might insist) against not just human welfare but human survival? What kind of deity could be imagined as happily revealing his benign attributes through an economy of eat or be eaten, where 'the survival of the fittest' is the one rule that we dare not forget? Is it to this 'benevolent' deity that we are to refer the appalling and widespread waste of life, as beast preys on beast, often in the most savagely destructive manner?

Neither can I accept that the gazelle that is being torn to pieces by the ravenous lion does not feel pain as we feel pain. Those who offer that facile escape from realities should reread the end of one of Beckett's best-known stories, 'Dante and the Lobster'. In spite of Belacqua's misgivings, his aunt proceeds to put the lobster into scalding water to be boiled alive. The story concludes with a famous contrapuntal sequence, as first Belacqua, then the narrator give their succinct versions of the event:

> Well, thought Belacqua, it's a quick death, God
> help us all.
>   It is not.

I applaud Alec Guinness when, in his autobiography, *Blessings in Disguise*, he confronts the specific difficulty of reconciling the 'horror' of the ichneumon-fly with the notion of a 'benevolent God': 'No one had been able to satisfy me about the necessity, in creation, of the ichneumon-fly; and they still haven't. It is an unpleasant little creature which pierces the body of the charming, rotund, prettily-decorated puss-moth caterpillar, depositing its unwelcome eggs which, when hatched, eat their way through their living host.' Guinness does not say so, but he seems to be taking his cue here from no less an authority than Charles Darwin, whose similar awareness of the ways of the ichneumon-fly pushed him, further than Guinness, not into problematic doubt but gradual loss of faith. 'I cannot,' he wrote, 'persuade myself that a beneficent and omnipotent God would have designedly created the Ichneumonidae with the express intention of their feeding within the living bodies of Caterpillars.'

No, the ways of 'Nature' do not bear too close an examination, and certainly cannot be said to reveal a 'benevolent' deity. Those who insist on adhering to such theological naivety should be obliged to read Melville's *Moby-Dick*, one of the most honest, most earnest investigations of the problem of reconciling savage (or 'demonic') nature with a benign creator. In the chapter entitled 'The Shark Massacre', we have a confrontation of the problem in its starkest form. The huge carcass of a whale, moored to the side of the ship, provokes a feeding frenzy among the rapidly congregating sharks, who then begin to prey on one another. 'They viciously snapped,' we are moreover told, 'not only at each other's disembowelments, but like flexible bows, bent round, and bit their own; till those entrails seemed swallowed over and over again by the same mouth, to be oppositely voided by the gaping wound.' There is a degree of insistence here which suggests exaggeration; but, at the same time, such exaggeration hardly invalidates the summary judgment delivered by the watching South Sea islander, Queequeg: 'Queequeg no care what god made him shark…wedder Fejee god or Nantucket god; but de god wat made shark must be one dam Ingin.'

We may or may not agree with Melville's suggestion that the sharks in their blood-lust are a manifestation of 'the demonism in the world' (or at least we may decide not to take that literally). But at the same time we can hardly refer the sharks to a benevolent deity who has created them as part of an acceptable 'design'. The sharks (along with many other creatures) imply (to put it mildly) that all is not well in the natural order. We may not wish to go all the way with a writer like Richard Dawkins, who sounds rather too categorical, or even strident, in his (atheistic) assertion that in the universe at large 'there is, at bottom, no design, no purpose, no evil and no good, nothing but blind, pitiless indifference'; but the least acknowledgment we owe is that any argument based on the intelligent design of nature is fraught with difficulties.

There is, therefore, much to be said for the conclusion drawn by Tennyson, who lived through both pre-Darwinian and Darwinian investigations into the nature of Nature, and was compelled to consider whether Nature offered any sense of meaning or purpose (particularly after the sudden and pointless death of his closest friend, Arthur Hallam). Tennyson felt that Nature offered no proof either way as to the existence of a benevolent deity. A passage in the 1897 *Memoir* by his son Hallam Tennyson (named after the poet's friend) presents the young Tennyson in 1833, along with Arthur Hallam (some months before his death), looking through microscopes at 'moths' wings, gnats' heads, and at all the lions and tigers which lie perdus in a drop of spring water'. Tennyson's view was that it was strange 'that these wonders should draw some men to God and repel others. No more reason in one than in the other.'

These are large and serious issues, with which, perhaps, non-theologians should not casually meddle; but to refuse the argument from design is not necessarily (in spite of Richard Dawkins's inference) to abandon orthodox Christian belief. It was, after all, no less a figure than Newman who, in one of the most eloquent passages in the *Apologia*, noted that the tokens of 'a superintending design' in the human experience of the world are 'faint and broken', and spoke of 'evolution' as 'blind'. His conclusion is that the world and the beings in it are 'implicated in some terrible aboriginal calamity'; in other words, whatever traces of divine order might once have existed have been blighted by original sin. Consistently, in *The Idea of a University*, Newman argues that an intelligent Being is not manifested in an orderly world, but is rather found 'behind the veil of the visible universe'. In this regard Newman again approximates to Pascal, for whom God is the *deus absconditus* (or hidden God) of Isaiah.

Does it not in any case make more sense to seek the manifestation of God in the human scale rather than in the non-human (or inhuman) processes of Nature? No matter how much proof a scientist might offer for the rationality of the natural order, or how much the poet or painter might rhapsodise over Nature's beauty, Nature must finally repel us because we have, as one of our unique human attributes, what Nature conspicuously lacks: that is, a moral sense. That, in turn, can be regarded not only as a mark of our uniqueness, but (perhaps) as a pledge of our high destiny.

Surely, then, we may more wisely seek God in humanity (or even human aspiration), rather than in the amoral vastness of Nature. The collective human adventure might ideally be seen as a journey towards self-realisation, in which God is implicated. Nietzsche tells us that man is the 'not yet determined animal', evolving towards an unforeseeable terminus. The Christian would add to this the Jewish tradition of God's involvement in human history; and, as Norman Cohn reminds us in *Cosmos, Chaos and the World to Come*, the Jewish view of their god, Yahweh, as 'lord of history' led a number of adherents to an expectation of millennial fulfilment. Thus they began, in a radical break with previous world-views, 'to look forward, impatiently, to a glorious

consummation when all things would be set to rights'. Such an anticipation of an apocalyptic end to history permeates Christianity, with its
desire for 'the coming of the kingdom'; and, indeed, in the foundational
moment of Christianity, the Incarnation, we find the most vivid sym-
bolisation (and, for the believer, realisation) of the intimate involvement
of the divine in human history.

We may or may not accept the presence of God in the progressive
human adventure, and events like Auschwitz or Hiroshima mean that
there can be no easy or unthinking acceptance of such a belief. Graham
Greene was surely justified in his antipathy to facile Victorian notions
about the inevitability of human progress. But if we accept that there is
such a thing as human development, however sporadic and broken such
development may be, and that the numerous cultural forms in which
this is manifested have therefore their own intrinsic importance, then
we may discover another valid reason for the importance of literature.
For literature is the invaluable and irreplaceable record of human experience throughout the civilised ages. As Newman puts it in *The Idea of a
University*: 'Literature is to man in some sort what autobiography is to
the individual; it is his Life and Remains.' In spite of the ravages of anti-
humanism, we still read literature in part to acquire some more precise
insight into the nature of the species to which we belong, and the various contexts in which we are expected to function. I would always wish
to believe that literature is a continual and open-ended attempt to define
the meaning (or incalculably full range of meanings) of the word
'human'.

*

Institutions in general, including the Catholic Church, might be
regarded as a necessary evil. The problem with the institution is that,
because its emphasis is on efficient organisation and the common rather
than the individual case, it is not sufficiently sensitive to the nuances of
the particular situation or to the qualities of unique personhood. In this
respect, Catholicism has something to learn from the individualistic
tradition of Protestantism. Yet, on balance, the institutional Catholic

Church may be the best safeguard we have against the loss, through manifold dilution, of the essential meaning of Christianity: and to speak in these terms is to invoke the great central idea of Tradition, as a guarantee of continuity. To put it figuratively: we need a strong ship (or ark) to carry the Christian message across the turbulent waves of history; or, we need the assurance of a still centre at the heart of the human cultural adventure (though ideally, one adds, that still centre should be sufficiently flexible to accommodate whatever aspects of human meaning or human self-definition the cultural adventure reveals). Perhaps we should evaluate the Catholic Church in a way similar to our judgment on democracy: it is far from perfect, but the available alternatives may be worse.

In Chapter 5 of the *Apologia Pro Vita Sua*, Newman argues that the infallibility of the Church is essential as a 'breakwater' against 'fierce wilful human nature'; in particular, his argument is that sacred truth must be preserved against 'the all-corroding, all-dissolving scepticism of the intellect in religious enquiries'. Newman's discourse at this point runs the risk of becoming unattractively authoritarian, but a balance is maintained. He recognises that 'freedom of thought' is 'one of the greatest of our natural gifts', but, in a striking phrase, insists that such freedom of thought needs to be rescued 'from its own suicidal excesses'.

We have every reason to acknowledge the possible justice of such a warning in a radically sceptical 'postmodern' age which would have us believe that no access to foundational truth is possible; and whether we are to see the spirit of postmodernism as 'suicidal', or destructive of the bases on which civilisation has traditionally rested, there is no disguising its excessively Dionysiac intoxication with the 'the all-corroding, all-dissolving scepticism of the intellect'. Indeed, it is essential to acknowledge in this context the undue emphasis on 'intellect'; for the indulgence of unfettered intellectual 'play' in postmodernism has been at the expense of our deeper emotional selves. The result has been that while much of what postmodernism 'argues' is logically or intellectually irrefutable, it remains disturbingly 'untrue' in terms of what the widest range of our experiences tells us is deeply or richly relevant (even if we are unable to find the exact words with which to express such experiences). In this way we are in danger of enshrining a culturally endorsed schizoid state – by which I mean that our culture is one that may encourage us to keep our emotional and intellectual functions separate, the split between the two arising from the undue dominance of intellect.

That kind of polarisation allows for no creative interaction between passion and intellect, and our emotional selves beat in vain against the wall of intellectual 'discourse' (how one may come to hate these buzz-words!), in a futile attempt to gain entry to the debate. How much more positively interactive, to revert to Newman, is his sense of the creative polarisation of Church and individual, 'Authority and Private Judg-ment', engaged, as he sees it, in an 'awful, never-dying duel'. Both his concluding rhetoric and his image reveal a generosity of vision which is sadly absent from so much present-day commentary on our culture. 'Catholic Christendom' is seen as 'a vast assemblage of human beings with wilful intellects and wild passions, brought together into one by the beauty and the Majesty of a Superhuman Power'; it is 'a moral factory, for the melting, refining, and moulding, by an incessant, noisy process, of the raw material of human nature, so excellent, so dangerous, so capable of divine purposes'. Perhaps it is only those who can place at the centre of their awareness the passionate realities of human nature who can feel the urgent need for ethical enlightenment or salvation.

Most of us accept, in any case, that, whether or not we acknowledge what Kant called the 'categorical imperative' (that is, an inner sense of moral obligation), we have a high and serious duty not just to refrain from evil but, if possible, to do good. The question then arises as to whether we can *be* good and virtuous on the basis of our *ethical* aware-ness only (deriving that awareness, say, from Aristotle in the *Nico-machean Ethics*, or from the aforementioned Kant); or whether we can be good and virtuous only with the additional assistance of religious belief. Partly as a result of a Catholic upbringing (though not only on that account), I have a deep belief in human imperfection (understood, in theological terms, as the doctrine of original sin); and, correspond-ingly, an acceptance of the notion of grace, whereby our highly untrust-worthy natures are enabled (occasionally) not just to perceive the good, but (perhaps) to act as we should on that perception. The perception of the good is infrequent enough; so rare, as well as transient, are our highest insights, so quickly do they melt away into the flux of our daily experience, that we may come to feel that we require the assistance of a power outside ourselves to keep us in touch with our better selves. Moreover, even if we do have the correct perception, there is no guarantee that we can rise above habit or routine (or sheer passivity and inertia) and put what we know to be good into practice. It is possible to find, outside the Christian tradition, not just succinctly worded acknowledgments of our flawed human nature, but recognitions, in particular, of our difficulty in doing what we feel we ought to do. One of these recognitions, from Ovid's *Metamorphoses*, I memorised early on: *Video meliora, proboque; deteriora sequor* ('I see the better things, and approve of them; but I follow the worse' – a sentiment which strikingly anticipates the similar statement by the Christian Paul in his Epistle to the Romans (7.19): 'For I do not the good that I wish, but the evil that I do not wish, that I perform').

One of the most dramatic instances of such moral failure in our recent history concerns the appalling passivity with which so many, in France, Poland and elsewhere, accepted the maltreatment of Jewish members of the community by the Nazis. They clearly knew (whatever rationalisations they provided, either at the time or subsequently) that what they were witnessing was morally repugnant; yet they failed to act. Rather than sit in judgment, however, on those who did not intervene when their consciences called loudly for them to do so, we should reflect on our collective human inadequacies, and above all recognise this: that there are recurrent situations where the pure ethical gesture is called for and where ethical awareness alone is unlikely to supply that gesture. It is only a transcendent sense of value, to which the individual would be willing to surrender, if need be, his life, that might motivate an act of moral intervention in the face of imminent self-destruction. To put it in even starker terms: what force for good is strong enough to make us actively oppose evil on such a scale, and where the danger to our own well-being is so horrifically evident?

It is above all, perhaps, according to the criterion of consistency that any claim to a virtuous life is to be judged; by which I mean not only a kind of stamina in the pursuit of the good, but a sustained commitment to virtuous proceeding at many different levels (personal and familial, social, public: there is not much point in saving the starving people of Africa if you are insufferable to your fellow-workers, or surly and unsympathetic towards your partner or children). There is a sound basis in the Christian tradition for believing that the energy that moves us in a consistent or sustained way towards generosity, forgiveness, compassion – as these manifest themselves in *action* - is grace: the implication in our lives of the divine, so as to establish a condition of cooperation, whereby our otherwise frequently misplaced strivings achieve direction, purpose and practical fruition, usually over a period of time in which consistency of application is necessary.

It would be wrong, of course – indeed, it would be an instance of narrow fanaticism – to claim that only conscious Christians are capable of truly virtuous acts. My knowledge of the great German Catholic theologian Karl Rahner is severely limited, but I am very taken with his notion that those who are apparently non-Christian may still be described as 'Christians' of an 'anonymous' kind. His general argument is that, since it is God's will that all humankind be saved, then 'every man who comes into this world', whether avowedly Christian or not, 'is pursued by God's grace'. The 'pagan', therefore, is not to be regarded as someone 'who has not yet been touched in any way by God's grace and truth', but rather as 'someone who must already be regarded as...an anonymous Christian'. If such a person is subsequently converted to Christianity, all that is then happening is that his or her 'anonymous' Christianity, up to that point *implicit* in his or her being, is *explicitly* realised or declared.

Yet although many may do good and be saved without any conscious knowledge that they serve Christ, the life of the *saint* is hardly to be explained except in terms of the individual person's *conscious* cooperation with that power beyond himself or herself. The supreme instances of such cooperation are those wherein the individual transcends his or her usual imperfection, not just in a moment of choice or decision, but in the creative acceptance of the consequences of that transcendent choice. One thinks of Maximilian Kolbe, who not only 'took the plunge' in deciding to substitute himself for a fellow prisoner and die in his place in Auschwitz, but thereafter, up until his death, behaved in a consistently selfless way in the company of those who were to die along with him. The moment of decision was a *coup de théâtre* which ushered him onto the stage, and gave him a role to play; but thereafter there was the more prosaic business of getting his lines right and (as the Noël Coward saying has it) not bumping into the furniture. It is in the totality of his behaviour, perhaps, that he appears as that strangest of human phenomena, 'the saint'; and the saint is one who, while remaining within the orbit of human comprehension, profoundly troubles us by acting as an index of something beyond our ken.

CHAPTER FOUR

Imaginary Worlds

I seem to have been blessed (or cursed) from my earliest years with an extremely lively imagination. As far back as I can remember, I was an avid reader; and among my earliest memories are waking up on Christmas morning (sometimes at an ungodly hour), rummaging around at the foot of the bed in the poor light of a struggling winter dawn, and unearthing from the bundle of things left by Santa Claus my copy of the *Teddy Tail* annual.

Teddy was a well-dressed and larger-than-lifesize mouse (not at all like Disney's cartoon character, Mickey, who was 'cute' in a way Teddy was not); and, as you read, you tended to forget that he was supposed to be some kind of rodent. In some ways I preferred the *Rupert* annual which my older brother, Peter, received at Christmas; and I am still haunted by those idyllic English landscapes through which Rupert Bear and his animal friends pursued their adventures. Those sylvan scenes, so timeless in their essential recreation of woods and hills and fields, were my introduction to the idea of pastoral, and are blended in my memory with the fresh smell of the annual's recently printed pages. But although I had a slight preference for the *Rupert* annual, I knew that I would in any case be allowed to read it eventually; so I was happy with the *Teddy Tail*.

As far as I can recall, though, it was that annual that introduced to me the idea of witches; and the piece in question was colourfully illustrated with drawings of hook-nosed females in pointed black hats, complete with broomsticks and cauldrons. From that time on I was afflicted in my dreams by witches, and often cravenly sought the refuge of my parents' bed. Once there, I felt safe, snugly lodged between my mother and father: even though I knew that I might still suffer some nightmare visitation in my sleep. One of the worst dreams I had while in my parents' bed was one of those nightmares in which you dream that you wake up and *then* undergo the dream-experience. So it was that once I dreamt I woke up in that way, and saw, just at eye-level across from where I was lying, the head of Superman, heaving, as it were, into view. But suddenly the features changed, the nose became elongated and sharp, and it was no longer Superman, but an ugly witch close to the side of the bed! At that point I woke up (really woke up), and the horror was dispelled; but I still remember the details to this day. I cannot pretend that I suffered anything like the visitations undergone by Samuel Taylor Coleridge; but there is a passage in one of his letters of 1797 which I can read with a degree of fellow-feeling. Coleridge recalls how, as a child, he said the prayer 'Matthew, Mark, Luke and John', with its reference to 'four angels' protectively 'round me spread'. He then adds: 'This prayer I said nightly, and most firmly believed the truth of it. Frequently have I (half-awake and half-asleep, my body diseased and fevered by my imagination) seen armies of ugly things bursting in upon me, and these four angels keeping them off.' It is not just because I too was familiar with the prayer of which Coleridge speaks that I sympathise with his experience.

One of the most afflicting consequences of my seeking refuge in my parents' bed was that it laid me open to the charge of acting like a 'baby' or (worse still!) a 'cry-baby'. Older brothers, in particular, feel it incumbent upon themselves to remind you of such unacceptably regressive behaviour. I cannot remember how long the dreams of witches continued, but eventually I experienced some alleviation; so that even if they did come back, they did so with much less frequency. I began in due course to extend my reading, and probably found enough fodder in that reading to keep my hyperactive imagination well exercised and quiet.

I would in some ways like to be able to claim that either my mother or my father introduced me to Shakespeare, Milton and Dickens and other great 'classics' from an early age; but, upon further reflection, I thank God that this was not the case. We did have, like many Irish families of that era, a complete set of Dickens, which, in my recollection, had a musty, leathery smell and the appearance of rarely having been opened.

The volumes of Dickens were certainly never opened by me (even though, once, my brother Art made a valiant start on *The Pickwick Papers*, so that for a brief while we happily imitated some of the better known speech mannerisms of Sam Weller). No, most of my early reading was of two kinds: weekly comics, and boys' adventure and school stories.

In this context, as in many others, I must pay due tribute to the tolerance and generosity of my mother (and presumably, beyond her, my father, since he was the financial provider). The local newsagent was a short walk away, and on practically every day of the week (excluding Sunday) we would pick up from them one or more comics (which were charged to a weekly bill). At one point we were the recipients of around fifteen different publications each week, all of which were eagerly seized upon and read more or less from cover to cover. My mother sometimes sighed and raised her eyes to heaven when it came to settling the account, but she did not seriously attempt to cut back on the list. These weekly comics were all British publications, and we had everything from easy-to-read comic-strip publications such as *The Dandy* and *The Beano* up to the more challenging publications, such as *The Rover*, *The Adventure*, *The Wizard* and *The Hotspur*, which engaged you in serious and sustained reading. For these were not 'comics' as the term is understood nowadays, in that their illustrations were sparse (one black and white picture at the head of the story), and the pages were covered with small print that required an earnest commitment of comprehension.

It was in the print-congested pages of these British comics that we read about ingenious sleuths, World War II flying aces, star soccer players, exceptional cricketers, and the preternaturally gifted athlete known as 'Wilson'. In the soccer stories my favourite was the goalkeeper in the 'Nick Smith of the Rovers' series, Joe English. Joe's judgment was so extraordinary that he would refuse to make an attempt to save the ball because he *knew* instinctively that it was going to hit the crossbar or the post. The fans were not always capable of appreciating his exceptional sang-froid, but Joe was the eccentric-as-hero and stuck to his guns. The context of many of the stories was English working-class, and perhaps in such a context it was only in the guise of blatant eccentricity that an individual like Joe English could display that aristo-cratic nonchalance which I was later to identify as *sprezzatura* (so dear to the heart of Yeats).

But by far my favourite character of all was Alf Tupper, 'the Tough of the Track', another supreme individualist who, as part of his indepen-dence of spirit, flaunted his North of England working-class origins. Alf was one of the best middle-distance runners in the business, but, what-ever the degree of his success, he never forgot that he was a welder by trade. He took pleasure in annoying the 'toffs' whenever they crossed his path, and the proud emblem of his lowly origins was his insistence on fuelling himself, no matter what the occasion, with his favourite meal of fish and chips.

My affectionate regard for Alf was one of a number of influences which complicated my inherited Irish Nationalist feelings of antipathy towards the British. In my own mind I began, however vaguely, to dis-criminate between the working-class English from the North of Eng-land, who did not quite fit the image of arrogant Anglo-Saxon rulers of empire, and the upper-class English with their posh Home Counties accents who had been to public school and would treat others (includ-ing a Paddy like myself) with lofty disdain. Alf had a broad human appeal which almost transcended national difference – almost, but not quite, since the world in which he moved was obviously that of a differ-ent culture. When later on I began to take an interest in cricket, includ-ing the county championship, it seemed natural to me to support teams such as Yorkshire or Lancashire rather than Surrey or Sussex. English-men from those northern regions were more representatively human, it seemed, than their southern counterparts.

In his autobiographical work, *An Only Child*, Frank O'Connor pro-vides an account of his early reading that is both similar to and yet strik-ingly different from my own. He tells us how, growing up in the city of Cork in the early decades of the twentieth century, he began by reading the English 'penny weeklies' such as *The Gem* and *The Magnet*. What he eventually came to feel, however, was that there was an unbridgeable gap between the world depicted in the weeklies and his own immediate cultural circumstances. He was rescued from this dilemma when one day he managed to borrow from the public library a book by another Corkman who was personally known to him: Daniel Corkery's *A Munster Twilight*. This revelation that there was an alternative national (or even local) literature 'settled the hash of the English boys' weeklies', for 'henceforth their creations would be less real' to him than Corkery's. 'And one day,' he concludes, 'I woke to find the Invisible Presences of my childhood departing with a wave of the hand as they passed for ever from sight. Not angrily, not even reproachfully, but sadly, as good friends part ...'

O'Connor here maintains a fine balance (as he again so superbly does in one of his finest short stories, 'Guests of the Nation') between the conflicting claims of English and Irish culture: he manages to be pro-Irish without becoming stridently anti-British. Yet he does bid a final farewell to the 'Invisible Presences' that came to him from the English penny weeklies. In my case, such a definitive farewell was never entertained. Even when, as the years passed and I grew away from the childhood experience of English comics, I left Joe English, Alf Tupper and Braddock, V.C., and all the others behind, they were not replaced by something more Irish. But then the cultural situation in which I found myself was rather more complicated than O'Connor's, in that, while I might satisfy myself by affirming my Irish identity, I had from the beginning to come to terms with a state which was defined as British, and one in which the majority thought of themselves as such.

*

One of the most glorious experiences of my childhood, when I would have been about nine or ten years of age, was arriving home one afternoon after school and being presented with a huge pile of brand-new American comics. They must have arrived, by post, from our American cousins in Boston, some time earlier; but for one reason or another they had been held in reserve until this moment. American comics had a glamour that British comics could not match: they were always in full colour, printed on paper of rather better quality, and wrapped in glossy covers. I was so overwhelmed by this treasure trove that for some time I could not bring myself to read them, but rather, like a miser fingering his gold, I counted them up, and rearranged them in different piles, working out how many Gene Autrys there were, how many Roy Rogers, and so on.

What this memory clearly reveals is that American comics were a much less constant feature of the childhood reading experience than the more available British weeklies. It is doubtless for that reason that they seem to have had less cultural influence. Nonetheless, I read as often as I could get hold of them those comics that featured Batman and Robin; Spiderman; Superman (for whom I had a particular fondness, since, like myself, Clark Kent wore glasses, yet was certainly no weakling, as I too hoped not to be); Captain Marvel and Captain Marvel Junior (Mary Marvel never, I must confess, made the grade as far as I was concerned, and I would risk a breach of political correctness if I were at this point to explain why). I memorised those ancient names whose capital letters provided Billy Batson's magical call which, in a bolt of lightning, transformed him from a weak mortal into the mighty, the indestructible Captain Marvel. The magic cry was 'Shazam!', derived from the first letters of Solomon, Hercules, Achilles, Zeus, Atlas and Mercury. On odd occasions when I found myself on my own, I too uttered the cry, only half-believing (but still hopeful) that some dramatic change might occur.

Yet the truth is that I tended to identify much more readily with Captain Marvel Junior; was I not after all the 'junior' member of my family? Moreover, the transformation that occurred in the case of Freddy Freeman, the newspaper vendor, when he called out, not 'Shazam!', but 'Captain Marvel!', was even more remarkable than in the case of Billy Batson. Freddy was lame, and moved about on crutches; but once his magic call was uttered, he became a slimmer version (dressed in blue, where Captain Marvel wore red) of his senior mentor, just as invincible, just as powerful (or almost so).

My favourite memory of Captain Marvel Junior concerns an episode in which he was almost outwitted by the evil gangsters who planned to take over once they got rid of him. They persuaded him to accept a wager that he could not fight his way out of a bag. The hero duly allowed himself to be placed in a large bag, securely tied at the top, and was then to prove his strength by liberating himself through his own exertions. Too easy, surely! But there was a major catch: the ingenious 'baddies' had provided a bag made of *rubber*, so that every time Captain Marvel Junior threw a punch, it simply rebounded, making no impression. Again and again he punched and kicked and threw himself against the yielding rubber, but to no avail. So here he is in close-up, wild-eyed, sweating, close to despair! Meanwhile, the gangsters are taking over, chuckling evilly over their own ingenuity. What is to happen?

Captain Marvel Junior matches the cleverness of the baddies by an ingenious ploy of his own. He calls out 'Captain Marvel!'; there is a bolt of lightning; he is changed back into crippled Freddy Freeman. But, look, the lightning has seared a large hole in the bag! Now all he has to do is call once more 'Captain Marvel!', and turn into Captain Marvel Junior again. Then he exits through the hole made by the lightning-bolt, and sets about the baddies in the usual way. That story affected me so much that years and years later I wrote a poem about it (like most of my poems unpublished and unpublishable) called 'Little Boy Blue'. I genuinely do not know whether the 'meaning' of that poem has to do with a son-figure empowering himself by calling on a father-figure, nor what this might reveal of my own psychology. But in this context I should perhaps also take note of the fact that one of the characters in the movies with whom I most closely identify is Michael Corleone in *The Godfather* (Parts 1 and 2). Like me, that character (so memorably created on screen by Al Pacino) is the youngest of three boys; but, more to the point, he fulfils his destiny (a tragic one) by identifying with his father. I cannot see that my own career has in any way been tragic; but perhaps I am responding in the Corleone saga to the fantasy of winning a father's total approval.

Besides the action-hero comics, we read more indiscriminately any American comic we could get our hands on (often through the process of 'swapping'). One of the series I remember was called 'Crime Does Not Pay', and featured dramatic instances of criminals who thought they had got away with it only to be brought to justice at the end. There were also a number of horror comics, with bizarre tales graphically illustrated in extravagant line-drawings and lurid colour. One of these I read in my second year at secondary school, when I was eleven or twelve. A man attends a fancy-dress ball and meets up with a woman who is wearing a witch-like mask. During the encounter, when, by agreement, neither removes the mask, they find that they have a lot in common and get on very well. Quite quickly, they decide to get married; the woman, though, insists that she be allowed to keep her mask on, and the husband agrees. But that night he has a dream in which it is suggested to him that her mask is being used to conceal something. Roused from his sleep, he confronts her with this possibility, and begs her to take off the mask. She pleads with him not to insist; but he refuses to take no for an answer. Finally, he pulls brutally on the mask to tear it off; he removes it; and finds himself looking at a bloodied skull-face. Her 'mask' had been her real face – a fact that comes home to him as she lies, dying, in front of him, her teeth ghastly in the bloodied visage.

I do not recall whether or not I tried to interpret this horrific story, to save it, as it were, from mere sensationalism. I perhaps understood it as a cautionary tale, whereby the male is warned to accept affectionate female companionship on its own terms, and not seek for satisfactions that are beside the point. The truth may be, though, that I read these stories simply to enjoy, with mingled feelings of disgust and fascination, the frisson I got from them.

Another grotesque tale concerned a sailor who is thrown by his enemies into the deep Atlantic to drown. Apparently murdered, his insane will refuses to accept that he is in fact dead. So he urges himself to keep walking along the ocean floor, determined to wreak vengeance on those who assaulted him. As he makes his way along the sea floor, small predatory fish begin to nibble his clothes and body; so that by the time he climbs out of the ocean on the other side of the Atlantic in North America, his flesh and his clothes are in tatters, and portions of his skull and bones are visible. But he persists in pursuing his enemies; he cannot be stopped. He has become one of the living dead – he is a zombie!

I mention these grotesque horror comics to emphasise just how omnivorous and indiscriminate my reading-habits were. Perhaps (in view of the present state of Western culture, where serious reading is said to be in a state of decline) I am trying to persuade myself that one can ingest decadent rubbish and not be permanently harmed by it. Or perhaps these bizarre tales did indeed, in some sense, develop or 'educate' my imagination. Yet I am more inclined to believe that I could *afford* to read such sensational and trivial tales because I had acquired better reading-habits elsewhere. My imagination was well ballasted by solid books before I ever came to such lurid productions.

My brothers and myself, year after year, read all kinds of storybooks, and in so doing accumulated a huge number of volumes. To remind myself of the extraordinary number of books we eventually possessed, I have only to picture in my mind's eye how my brother Peter took over a spare bedroom upstairs, and lined the books up in rows against the four walls. We had all the usual favourites: Enid Blyton, especially the 'Famous Five' stories (though in due course, as a matter of connoisseurship, we awarded the palm to Blyton's 'Adventure' tales, *The Castle of Adventure, The Mountain of Adventure*, and so on); Richmal Crompton's William books (and during my 'high' William phase, I was a willing imitator of William as far as that was possible, down to the telling sartorial detail of wearing one stocking down and the other up); and, of course, a vast Biggles collection (we had just about every Biggles story ever penned by Captain W. E. Johns, from the era of his risky flights in the Sopwith Camel up to World War II and after).

One part of our book-hoard exercised a particularly potent spell over our imaginations. This was the whole series of stories dealing with English public schools at different times down through the first half of the twentieth century. It seems to me astonishing that we should so readily have fallen under the spell of tales which were set in a culture that was obviously far removed from our own. We were all day-boys at the Christian Brothers' school in Newry; so how could we identify with youths who were boarders in a public school system of which we knew next to nothing? Had any of us ever come even close to participating in a midnight feast (with lots of 'tuck') in the 'dorm'? Or why should we (or indeed how could we) care about which of the 'houses' at school won the annual cricket match?

There are doubtless a number of factors, and these, though sufficiently complex, are not beyond analysis. What immediately appealed to
us was the fact that we were reading about boys of an age similar to our
own, operating, however 'realistic' the style and setting, in the appeal-
ingly liberating realm of fiction. Moreover, these characters were at one
and the same time familiar (like them, we spoke English, and we readily
understood the group dynamics of the school situation) and yet curiously exotic (their English was peppered with slang of a kind we had
never heard before, and with other odd locutions such as 'I say, old
man'; while the games they played were so unlike our Gaelic football).
They were at one and the same time both like us and not at all like us;
and therein lay part of the fascination.

Be that as it may, we willingly allowed our imaginations to carry us
into the alien world of the English public school. The names of the
books that I can recall still remain powerfully evocative: *Day-Boy
Colours*, *The Luck of the Lennites*, and, from earlier in the century,
Pepper's Crack Eleven. The first of these was a moral tale, and centred on
a senior boarder known as 'Drift' Marriner (I don't think that at the time
of my first reading I picked up on the full implications of the nautical
terminology, so dear to our neighbouring island-race and so charged
with imperial and other associations). Marriner had been both an outstanding scholar and a gifted 'rugger' player, but had let things 'drift'
(one of his favourite phrases, nonchalantly delivered, was 'Let it drift').
He is at last saved from his ingrained habit of irresponsibility by his
friendship with a younger day-school boy, who sets him an example of
effort and commitment. I am certain that if I were now to read the story,
I could not fail to be aware of its homoerotic aspect; but in those early
days of blissful absorption in the book, such a perception would have
been unthinkable.

The central sport in the other two stories was cricket, and indeed it
may be the case that my lifelong fascination with cricket dates from the
time of reading books such as these. Both stories climax, as far as I can
remember, in a crucial cricket match which must be won against the
odds, and both are very much in the spirit of the famous opening stanza
of Sir Henry Newbolt's 'Vitaï Lampada':

There's a breathless hush in the Close tonight –
Ten to make and the match to win –
A bumping pitch and a blinding light,
An hour to play and the last man in.

In both school-stories the team captain shows sterling leadership ability in the face of unusual adversity, and the cricket teams they lead are triumphant. I cannot quite quote from memory the last sentence of the Edwardian *Pepper's Crack Eleven*, but it went something like this: 'If the sun should ever set upon the British Empire, it will be because the schools and playing-fields of England no longer breed young men of the character of Pepper.' Being good Northern Nationalists, we had our inevitable chuckle over that; yet mingled with the dominant irony, I suspect, was a vaguely positive sense of the rhetorical assurance with which the claim was delivered.

*

Two or three years ago, at a book launch in Dublin, I met a woman from my home town of Newry who was a contemporary of my sister Majella. She recognised me before I recognised her (it had been most of forty years since we had last met); but what brought me back across the years with a shock of belated acknowledgment was the very first thing she said. Recalling my family, and what in particular had singled me out, she remarked: 'Ah yes! You were the one who would have gone to the cinema every night of the week.' I had always recognised that I had been a frequent visitor to the pictures; but I was at first taken aback to learn that it was precisely with reference to this one habit that she should choose to characterise me after all the intervening decades. On reflection, though, I had to grant the justice of her version of my younger self. I was hooked on the cinema from way back, and it was in that seductive cave of fantasy that so many of my attitudes were shaped.

In fairness to the cultural richness of my home town, I should make it clear that I was not confined to the cinema for dramatic entertainment. There has always been in Newry a strong tradition of amateur

drama, and a thriving musical society. But partly because these productions *were* amateur, I have in general retained (scandalously, for one like
myself who lectures on dramatic as well as other texts) a preference for
film over live theatre. I have, though, happy memories in particular of
an amateur production in the local town hall of the musical *Lilac Time*
(which freely adapts some well known Schubert melodies in a format for
which 'popular' is perhaps too lofty a term). What made the show a success, apart from the quality of the music, was the spirit and energy with
which the players and singers entered into the performance. The Newry
Musical Society was fortunate indeed to have a soprano of the calibre of
Nuala Neary and a natural stage-comedian as gifted as Charlie Smyth.

For this presentation (which ran for a week) I had the good luck to be
asked (along with a pal of mine, both of us aged about sixteen) to operate the spotlights from either side of the balcony. We were very uncertain
with our timing and focus to begin with but, under pressure to get it
right and not spoil the performance, we quickly became, if not adroit,
then error-free; and, as a bonus, by the end of the week we could hum or
sing just about anything in the show, or re-enact the most dramatic
scenes. For us the highlight of the performance, which delightfully challenged us every night not to burst out in inappropriate laughter, came at
the end of a turbulent love-scene. A central character in the piece is
Schubert himself, tortured with a love that his female acquaintance feels
unable to reciprocate. In a scene set in a café, he declares his love, is
spurned, and sings passionately to its climax the song 'I want to carve
your name on every tree'. He ends fortissimo on a note of extreme des-
peration, claiming in song, in spite of the rebuff, 'Yours is my heart!
Yours is my heart!' And then rushes off the stage.

It was at this point that we would brace ourselves against the onset of
anticipatory giggles. The preceding scene had already gone 'over the
top'; but enter now, to compound the mischief, a waiter who, in the
aftermath of Schubert's painful passion, is given a deliberately inappropriate choric comment on what he has just overheard. But to make
matters worse, the waiter was played by a local man, who was not only
somewhat effeminate but was rumoured to have a preference for the
boys over the girls; and, in his case, the words he had to utter were

fatefully allocated (I try to recreate the intonation): 'He's a queer faylo! I wonder what he's up tew?'

Yet however gifted the local actors were, the plays and shows they put on were comparatively infrequent, and cinema offered a more consistent source of entertainment. There were three 'picture-houses' in Newry in the early 1950s, of rather different character. The most opulent was the Savoy, which stood opposite our house across the Clanrye river and the closely parallel Newry Canal: from the upper storey of our house you had an uninterrupted view of its red neon sign and its imposing front. The Savoy had a genuine foyer, which created a sense of occasion, sharpening the feeling of anticipation and providing a real liminal space between the workaday world and the technicolor fantasies of the big screen. It was also the only one of the three cinemas to possess a balcony, and the flight of steps up to that was a further initiation into imaginative possibilities. The Savoy was the 'class' place you would bring your girlfriend to, when you were old enough to have one: two balcony tickets and a box of Black Magic could lead (with luck) to major developments.

Not far away along The Mall was the Imperial Cinema, where, it now seems to me, I saw mostly musicals (most memorably *Singin' in the Rain*, 1952) and some at least of the Hitchcock movies (such as *The Man Who Knew Too Much*, the James Stewart and Doris Day version of 1956). My recollection is of a longish, narrow space, not at all as big as the Savoy; yet it was well worth a visit, as they got some of the big movies on first release. Some of my most vivid cinematic memories from those years are associated with that long, narrow channel which left you nothing else to look at but the screen. When the new cinema technologies came in, the Imperial for a brief while led the way with Vistavision (Paramount), until the Savoy easily surpassed that rather feeble cinematic enhancement with Cinemascope (Twentieth Century Fox, to begin with) and stereophonic sound. I can still recall all the ballyhoo surrounding *The Robe*, starring Richard Burton, the first Cinemascope production.

The least prepossessing was the third cinema, the Frontier (because of its proximity to the Border, Newry is known as 'the frontier town'). It was long and wide, and, unlike the smaller Imperial or the plush Savoy, often played to a sparsely populated house. I seem to have seen a lot of westerns there (for some reason I think automatically of Glenn Ford and William Holden as the stars of one or more of these); though it may be that the very title of the cinema has led to some confusion in my recall. It is certainly the case that if, as a child, I had heard someone refer to 'the James family', it would then have meant Jesse and Frank, and not, as now, William and Henry.

The Frontier must have occasionally put on movies that had been released some time before, for it was there that I was deeply moved (as I repeatedly was at the movies) by the 1948 film *The Babe Ruth Story*, but not as early as 1948. I was especially affected by the scene in which Ruth (a somewhat saintly icon as portrayed by William Bendix) casually says a big hello to a crippled boy in a wheelchair, and the young lad, responding to such magnificent charisma, slowly and miraculously, as the soundtrack music swells, stands up – cured as by magic after all hope for him had been abandoned! It was also at the Frontier that I saw that weepie to end all weepies, *Magnificent Obsession* (Rock Hudson and Jane Wyman, 1954), which then and there (I was thirteen) I *knew* was the greatest movie ever. The ancient critical treatise on the sublime, attributed to Longinus, encourages us to believe that the greatness of literature is to be measured by its emotional impact. Even in my most unformed state I was an instinctive Longinian (and to some extent have remained so), inasmuch as, happily ensconced in the liberating dark of the picturehouse, I judged cinematic art on the basis of its ability to arouse the most intense feelings. In spite of temptations to dismiss it as a 'fleapit', I had a soft spot for the Frontier because I could (depending on which route I chose) pass by it on my way home from school. It was a pleasure to linger outside, looking at the display case full of 'stills' from the week's offerings, and remind myself that there were (or might be) other, more exotic, worlds.

I was, in general, happily indiscriminate in the movies I chose to go and see. Frequently I would seek out the gross stimulus of the horror movies, including that spate of sci-fi films about invaders from outer space which Hollywood produced in the Cold War period, as if to satisfy the national paranoia in America about the possibility of a takeover by aliens of a different sort, the 'Commies'. It became a test of nerve to see if you could keep your eyes unflinchingly on the screen while the sound-track music signalled some climactic and intolerably inhuman revela-tion, in the form of creatures from an alien dimension. Yet of all the horror movies I saw, it was not a science-fiction but a classic tale that inspired the extremest terror: *Dr Jekyll and Mr Hyde*. What I saw was not the Fredric March version so beloved of film critics, but the less highly rated Spencer Tracy remake of 1941 (again, the film was being recycled in the fifties). Yet it was good enough to put the wind up me.

When I was still only ten or eleven, a gang of us were able to gain spe-cial (and otherwise forbidden) access to X-rated movies. The woman who sold tickets for the front stalls (the cheapest seats) in the Savoy would admit us once the lights had gone down. Thus it was that I saw the Spencer Tracy *Dr Jekyll and Mr Hyde*, and paid sorely for my trans-gression by being subjected to harrowing nightmares for three succes-sive nights. One scene in particular seeped into the core of my being, partly because of a musical 'hook'. Jekyll vows that he will never again take the elixir and allow Hyde his destructive freedom. He walks through a London 'pea-souper' fog and in due course sits down to rest on a bench in a public park. In the background, and throughout the entire sequence, a distant band plays the jaunty (and once well known) tune, 'See Me Dance the Polka' (a Victorian music-hall song, written by George Grossmith). In a stillness filled only by that distant sound, the camera rests in close-up on Jekyll's face. Slowly, at first almost imper-ceptibly, his features begin to change – the eyes sink back into the head, the lips thicken, the teeth elongate, the face grows dark and hirsute. Mes-merisingly, the camera holds its fixed point of view as Hyde slowly but inexorably emerges – and all the while the sprightly tune sounds innocently in the background. For years afterwards, whenever I heard that tune I relived the scene, and that same tune evokes, even today, a vague sense of unease and excitement, the jaunty air forever overlain by a more sinister tonality.

In interpreting this film and my response to it, I can make out some of the obvious meanings (so obvious, perhaps, as to be banal). Jekyll – a medical doctor, after all – is the reliable and rational authority figure, and Hyde is the disturbingly irrational alternative, which we fear may be present somewhere in all of us; and it is precisely in those who are most evidently in positions of authority that we most fear his sudden emergence. From the punitive father or teacher to the callously repressive dictator, recurrently reappearing in the guises of Stalin or Hitler or Pol Pot, Mr Hyde seems to be an ineradicable part of our social and political structures.

Perhaps, though, the film disturbed me because I had some reason to be aware of the Hyde not only in others but in myself. As a schoolboy, I was utterly appalled to hear stories of boys of my own age inserting a straw down a frog's throat and inflating the creature until it burst into shreds. Yet if I examine my own conscience in this regard, I myself appear far from blameless. It shocks me still to recall how on one occasion, in some cool frenzy of sadism, I cornered a young cat we had, and again and again threw the animal sadistically against the wall in our back yard. What monstrous urge was at work in me then? The cat survived, but not before its piteous mewings had fallen repeatedly on my wilfully deaf ears.

Or, again, how often at the seaside in Warrenpoint did I declare war on all crabs, and, having caught one with an open mussel-shell tied to a fishing-string, then another and another, bash them to pieces, exulting in a mounting obsession as their mushy yoke-yellow or orange interiors splattered the promenade? True, I feared their inhuman shape and movement, and regarded them as my enemy (they would nip and hurt me); but what disturbs me even now was the unholy zeal with which I exterminated them in great numbers. Were these denizens of the sea-bed, operating out of sight beneath the surface, perhaps the half-recognised symbols of the irrational and frightening impulses of the self, likewise hidden in the deeps of the mind? Shakespeare's *Macbeth*, like many texts, fascinates because it so vividly dramatises the usurpation of the civilised self by an upsurge (or insurrection) of 'black and deep desires' – Macbeth himself becoming fatally mesmerised by the dark excitements which 'make [his] seated heart knock at [his] ribs', until clarity of moral perception is 'smothered' in a shapeless miasma of eruptive evil.

It would be too much to claim, though, that my youthful experience of the melodrama of *Dr Jekyll and Mr Hyde* was fated to lead to *Macbeth*. I remained as indiscriminate in my picture-going as in my promiscuous reading of comic-books and popular tales. True, I acquired some basic standards of judgment. I realised in due course that a forthcoming Hitchcock was one not to be missed (*Rear Window* came out in 1954); and I had advance notification (because of the publicity) of the significance of blockbusters such as *Shane* (1953). But my random hit-or-miss approach paid huge dividends when I unexpectedly came across a masterpiece. It was in that way that in 1957 I stumbled upon Sidney Lumet's *Twelve Angry Men* in which Henry Fonda (supported by a superb cast whose names, of course, meant very little to me at the time) gives one of his finest performances, as the one just and conscientious man on a murder-trial jury.

But two of the most memorable movies that I saw in my teens not only arrived in our local cinema (the Savoy, in this case) unheralded, but were offered as mere supporting features (for this was the era in which you would often have two films for the price of one). The first was *The Ox-Bow Incident*, adapted (as I was to learn a long time afterwards) from the novel of the same name by Walter van Tilburg Clark. The movie was released in 1943, and its subordinate position as supporting feature is readily explained by the fact that when I saw it in the 1950s it was being recycled. As he was later to do in *Twelve Angry Men*, Henry Fonda plays a humane figure who in this instance opposes the lynching of a suspect gang which, on the most slender evidence, a rabid group seek to perpetrate. This time, however, his voice of reason goes unheard, and the lynchings are carried out, not horrifically, but in sufficiently vivid cinematic terms. Subsequently, evidence emerges to prove the innocence of those who have so horribly died, far from kin and civilisation (the events take place on the open range); and the lynchers are exposed to the full impact of what they have so mistakenly done. I walked out from that one shell-shocked, but exhilarated by the passion for justice which (like *Twelve Angry Men*) it left behind.

The other great film which I saw as a second feature (one that I think would have to be included in my top ten of all time, but was on that occasion inexplicably relegated to a supporting role) was Stanley Kubrick's *Paths of Glory*. I refer to it now as 'Stanley Kubrick's', but at the time I saw it (shortly after its release in 1957), it was, in my eyes, Kirk Douglas's and Adolphe Menjou's movie; for in those days the name Kubrick meant nothing to me, and continued to mean nothing until a good deal later when I saw *Doctor Strangelove*. From start to finish I sat enthralled by *Paths of Glory*. Never before had I had such an insight into the horrors of trench warfare; and I was lost in admiration at the images of desolation that the director conjured up in the depiction of no-man's-land. I feel certain that Kubrick's movie was a major stimulus (even though the effect was delayed until some years later) in my subsequent appreciation of the war poet Wilfred Owen; and like those war poets of whom Owen was one (others include Isaac Rosenberg and Siegfried Sassoon), *Paths of Glory* confirmed me permanently in an instinctive revulsion against war or violence in any form.

Like the two Henry Fonda movies, *Paths of Glory* was morally earnest, tautly focused on a small core of strong personalities (which allowed for tense dramatic interaction), and wholly gimmick-free: by which I mean that the special effects department was only minimally involved, or else involved (as perhaps in the creation of Kubrick's desolate war-landscape) in a way that was subordinate to the larger issue. It is perhaps a symptom of their artistic seriousness that all three films are in black and white. Like the classic western *High Noon* (1952) or some of the better *films noirs*, they stand or fall on the solid merits of the story and dialogue, the quality of the acting, and a severely disciplined cinematography. I am not alone in thinking that the recent advances in cinematic technology, breathtaking as they doubtless are, are a very mixed blessing. In a newspaper interview in 1998, no less a figure than Robert Redford deplored the fact that films 'have now become so driven by effects and the technology of the industry' that 'the humanistic side of filmmaking' is being ignored. 'Films,' he added, 'that have strong narratives, intelligent scripts and real, well-developed characters are getting harder and harder to find.' Directors and producers, it seems, now take the easier option, bombarding the spectator trapped in the cinema-seat with vicarious sensations, hyper-enhanced by special effects and stereophonic (or 'senssurround') sound. Might it be the case that, for all their undoubted cinematic genius, directors like George Lucas and even Steven Spielberg will be harshly judged by future historians of the cinema, not just for what they themselves created, but for the imitators they spawned?

Here I run the risk of sounding too severely judgmental in my evaluations; I owe it to myself to set the record straight and adjust the balance by countering the Puritan in me with the Longinian, and recalling my own youthful appetite for emotional excess and, indeed, sensational stimulus. This youthful bias was to remain with me. At the age of nineteen, I belatedly saw for the first time, on television over the Christmas season, that greatest of all sentimental classics, Frank Capra's *It's a Wonderful Life*; and I fell for it immediately. (By the same token, I regret to say, Orson Welles' *Citizen Kane* leaves me cold – admiring but unmoved.)

In earlier years I was a sucker not only for such extravagant 'three-hankie' weepies as *Magnificent Obsession*, but for the tear-jerking musical *With a Song in My Heart* (1952), the Jane Froman story starring Susan Hayward. I had no idea before I saw the film who Jane Froman was, but I am still profoundly moved by those songs with which the richly emotive voice of Froman held me spellbound in the highly charged darkness of the Imperial. It was then, aged ten or eleven, that I heard for the first time 'Stormy Weather', 'Blue Moon', and, most memorably of all, 'Embraceable You' – the possible beginning of a lifelong admiration for the music of George Gershwin.

Even less than books were films consciously regarded as a source of knowledge or 'education'. All I can say is that the imagination was stirred and activated in the cinema, and in ways which did not conflict with, but rather supplemented, the early-established habit of reading. The movie-house in particular was a means of escape, a path into a world of fantasy that could be savoured in the companionable darkness. At that time I had not the slightest notion that the cinema was or could be a serious art-form, and even when I sat enthralled by the work of Sidney Lumet or Stanley Kubrick, it remained a matter of 'entertainment'; so that when, at Oxford in my early twenties, I saw my first Bergman movie (a lucky choice, in that it was *The Seventh Seal*), I was stunned by the recognition that film could indeed deal with grand themes in this most rigorously artistic way.

But my early experience of the cinema was as often as not a grateful and uncritical plunge into a colourful world of costume-drama and glamour. Gene Kelly swashbuckled with a dancer's finesse and timing in *The Three Musketeers*, and John Derek as Robin Hood lived and fought alongside his larger-than-life companion rogues in some never-never technicolor Sherwood Forest. I sailed the seas of impossible blue with Burt Lancaster and his buccaneers in *The Crimson Pirate*, and, along with Sabu, happily entered the Arabian Nights world of marvel and magic to which Sinbad had dangerous access. In addition, in these imaginary worlds that had no counterpart in actuality, a host of female icons smiled and beguiled and teased the imagination. So it was that the cinema was the royal road to a fantasy-world that contained both the exotic and its near neighbour (in both sound and sense), the erotic.

When I consider the number and quality of the films that came out of Hollywood in the fifties, I cannot but be grateful that that was the period of my deepest fascination with the cinema. Uncritical in my tastes and enthusiasms as I was, I was still well catered for by a movie industry which, while it paid due attention to the box-office and the making of substantial profits, nonetheless produced work of the highest quality. I would never exchange my *Rear Window* or *Twelve Angry Men* or *Shane* for all the episodes of *Star Wars* that human ingenuity could devise.

CHAPTER FIVE

Summers in Warrenpoint

We were fortunate as children in that every summer my father went to the expense of renting a house, usually on the seafront, in the nearby seaside town of Warrenpoint. It was all the more generous of him inasmuch as he benefited not at all from the arrangement; for while the rest of us enjoyed the month of July in happy proximity to the sea, he was tied as usual to the bar-business, and in fact was inconvenienced by my mother's absence, since it meant that he had to provide all his own meals while keeping an eye on the pub. He was not the type of man who knew his way around a kitchen, and he would, perhaps, eat out for lunch; but for his tea each and every evening he would boil himself an egg, coping as best he could throughout the month with that lack of culinary variety.

For the duration of our stay in Warrenpoint we saw him only late at night and early (and briefly) in the mornings. Every day, except Sunday, he travelled the six miles up to Newry on the early bus and returned to Warrenpoint that night on the late one. Sunday was his one day of rest, and he might treat us all in the evening to knickerbocker glories or peach melbas in the ice-cream parlour in the big square in the town, a pleasant fifteen or twenty minutes' walk away. I never heard him complain about an arrangement which left him to fend for himself most of the time; nor do I ever remember the slightest feeling of guilt on my part that he should be excluded day after day from the seaside party.

There was one house in particular on the seafront that we habitually rented for a number of consecutive years. Whenever I return to that spot, I am struck by the magnificent view the situation commands, straight ahead, of Carlingford Lough. From the left-hand side the

Rostrevor Mountains sweep down towards the Carlingford Mountains which extend in an even more massive prolongation from the right. The two mountain ranges fail to meet, and the gap between them offers a distant view of the horizon and a path to the open sea. How often as a child I sat and watched Fisher's coal-boats, black below and ruddy in their upper quarters, move slowly past the Carlingford Mountains on their way to the open sea, diminishing very gradually in size, until they disappeared over the horizon. And even then you could trace them for a brief space of time by the plume of smoke that hovered in the air. Later on in my geography schoolbook I came across a series of sketches designed to demonstrate that the world was round, and that the sea curved downward beyond the line of vision. They showed a ship disappearing gradually over the horizon until nothing but the smoke from its funnel could be seen – Fisher's boats there and then memorialised in an otherwise dull textbook.

But the most singular feature of the mountain-scene across the lough was (and still is) to be found on the top of the Carlingford range. If you look carefully as the mountain reaches the sky, you can see clearly a head with forehead, nose and chin; a small declivity followed by a rising chest; and a further extension of what seems to be the rest of the torso. I learnt early on that this was the grave of one of the greatest of early Irish heroes, the giant Finn MacCool. This was the same Finn who built the Giant's Causeway off the Antrim coast as an unfinished bridge, by which he had meant to travel to Scotland, and in one gigantic exploit created both Lough Neagh and the Isle of Man. For, taunted by a rival giant on the other side of the Irish Sea, Finn had scooped up a piece of Northern Ireland and thrown it at his enemy, only to see it fall short. The hole left by the scoop was filled with water and became Lough Neagh; the giant clod that fell between Ireland and Britain was the Isle of Man.

Living in that house across the road from the seashore, you were within sight and sound and smell – and easy reach – of the sea. You walked across the narrow (but sometimes busy) road, down the stone steps, and there immediately in front of you was the beach with all its promise. When the tide was in full, and especially on a stormy day, the waves would hurl themselves over the low stone wall and right onto the road: if you were not familiar with the ways of the sea at that point, you could be soaked through in an instant. But when the tide had retreated to its farthest distance, the scene was magically transformed: your eye could travel over what seemed an immense space to the sea's edge, now removed to a distance of some two hundred yards. With the sea thus withdrawn, there lay exposed a large tract of land densely covered with a seaweed that seemed to have been growing there for decades. This primeval tract was known as 'Maggie's Island': and it was the strangest of sensations to walk across that squelching surface, negotiating with care the uneven terrain of wet and slippery seaweed, especially if you allowed your imagination to dwell on the fact that, when the tide was in full, this same tract of land on which you now made your way would be fathoms under water. It would be an exaggeration to say that you might feel like the Israelites walking on the dry sea-bed, while the power of their God stayed the Red Sea to each side of them in walls of water; but something of the experience of walking 'Maggie's Island' probably fed into my cinematic encounter with that spectacular scene in Cecil B. De Mille's *The Ten Commandments*. And sometimes, at that time a young and timid swimmer myself, I would look on from the safe haven of the shore, while those of our party who were gifted swimmers, an older brother or sister or older friend, would swim far out at full tide to where one could imagine 'Maggie's Island' to be submerged beneath them, and tread water above awesome depths that dizzied my imagination to think of.

In the earliest years of our sojourns in the favourite house at Warren-point, the place had an additionally exotic appeal in that the lights were not electric, but gas. It was often the case that, as you sat reading at night by their humming light, you were readily transported from that deep domestic calm to another world; until, raising your eyes from the book, you again took in the little sitting-room and its unusual cushions, with one cushion, which was circular and made up of multi-coloured seg-ments, particularly vivid – another small (and exciting) reminder that you were in a different place. Or sometimes, on a wild and stormy night, when the proximity of the sea made its elemental fury more palpable, you could look across Carlingford Lough to the black mass of the mountains, time and again jaggedly split by the vicious flash of forked lightning, and thank heaven that you were sufficiently removed from that violence.

Warrenpoint is the locus, or one of them, for my experience of what T. S. Eliot in *Four Quartets* calls the moments in the rose-garden: that is, the haunting memories of childhood in which a special kind of beauty is revealed to the dawning consciousness. But these memories are, for me, so faint and evanescent that they have no definite shape. What age was I when I first registered the peculiar sweet perfume of a flower? This is associated in my mind with Warrenpoint, if only because there were more opportunities in that situation for experiencing an immediate pastoralism, either in the gardens of friends or acquaintances on lovely summer days, or in walks along the Well Road (at that time lined by hedges and banks where we would hunt, sometimes successfully, for tiny wild strawberries), or in the fields around about, where we 'haked' orchards or paddled in the Moygannon river. But I cannot anchor that sweet smell, more vivid now in memory than in any available current experience, to any particular occasion. All I know is that there are certain passages in poetry, especially poetry that sets out to be highly evocative of sweet odour, which trigger in me a memory so deep that it refuses self-definition. It is with that sense of subtle invasion that I find myself reading some passages in Shelley, as, for instance, the speech of Panthea in *Prometheus Unbound* when she informs her sister Asia that

> my wings were faint
> With the delight of a remembered dream,
> As are the noontide plumes of summer winds
> Satiate with sweet flowers.

How can I describe the effect on my imagination of that word 'satiate'? Can I even be sure that that is indeed the word in which the power of the passage is invested, especially since on a rereading the suggestiveness begins to fade, and the words turn back to the banality of mere descriptive prose, losing the fleeting magic that they seemed to possess? The 'magic casement' which appeared to open now irreversibly closes, and one accuses oneself of folly and self-deception. Yet it is often this elusive feature of poetry which we are obliged to pursue – though, alas for that ambition, the kind of criticism which prevails, and for some time has prevailed, in the academy gives short shrift to any such hopes. What we used to call the 'aesthetic' properties of the poem (which the Latin poet Horace appositely terms the 'sweet' or *dulce*) disappear under the weight of political analysis, whether the politics be those of feminism, cultural criticism or post-colonial concerns. In a wide waste of strewn aesthetic blooms, rudely forced to yield 'deeper', more authentic political meaning, Ideology stands dominant, like the colossal monument in the desert in Shelley's 'Ozymandias', around which 'The lone and level sands stretch far away'. Had I been forewarned that such would be the barren landscape engendered by literary criticism, I think I would have studied accountancy, perhaps made some real money, and devoted my spare time to an uncontaminated amateur enjoyment of great writers from Dante to modern times, learning to relish in my own way the densely evocative Henry James, or D.H. Lawrence and Virginia Woolf, or the poetry of Thomas Hardy or Robert Frost.

Many of my memories of Warrenpoint can be reached only across the frontiers of blank intervening time, and seem now, in some instances, to have the remoteness of the mythic. It is in some such terms, for example, that I recall the lighthouse beam that faithfully, rhythmically, silently reached across the bay to our seafront house. Beam, beam, beam, three times; then darkness; then the light, again; again; again. It was probably to that rhythm that I sometimes fell asleep, lying in one of the upper bedrooms facing the mighty dark of sea and night and mountain-mass. Yet the experience was so integrated with the consciousness that then was mine that I can hardly now lay hold of it at all. Indeed, it is easier for me to relive it vicariously, by reading some of the pages of Virginia Woolf's *To the Lighthouse*, in which I find subtly and elusively inscribed so much of my own seaside family mythology. I can recall vividly my first encounter with Woolf's novel, reading it, in my twenties, on a train between London and Holyhead, and sinking so deeply and imaginatively into it that I was almost bewildered when I raised my eyes from the book and had to take account of my immediate circumstances.

In this regard, I was probably the ideal reader that Virginia Woolf herself seems to have required; I was similar in my reading to Mrs Ramsay in that novel, who, peacefully absorbed by the sonnet in her book, sinks deeper and deeper, becoming more and more thoroughly immersed in the text until she seems 'like a person in a light sleep'.

What precisely it was that so engaged me in that novel it is hard to say: but beneath its elegant and graceful prose are the firm contours of the archetypal – the Mother, the Father, the Family, and the Lost Gardens of early childhood. No wonder that Virginia Woolf should more than once return in her later years to the real scene of these childhood experiences, Talland House overlooking St Ives' Bay in Cornwall, and, hidden by the darkness, gaze grief-stricken on its garden-space, seeking in vain the irrecoverable past, which is, as we have learned to acknowledge, 'another country'; and one for which we possess no certain passport. Something, I think, of that nostalgia touched me, in however minor a way in comparison with Virginia Woolf's, when I first read *To the Lighthouse* and thought of long-vanished summers in Warrenpoint.

How distant, too, seem the 'pierrots', the very name evoking a bygone age! These offered their summer shows for free (though they did pass round a collection-box) on the bandstand in the public park, an octagonal structure erected in the early years of the twentieth century; and what they provided was an odd blend of comedy and glamour. Clever Jock and dupe Alec (or was it the other way around?) went through their familiar routines in their markedly British accents (one was, I think, Scottish), adding that vague touch of the exotic to the proceedings. On reflection, I think it was Jock who was the 'wise guy', kitted out as he was in tartan cap, plaid jacket and (if memory serves me right) plus-fours; while bespectacled Alec was more soberly dressed in dark jacket, waistcoat and trousers, looking perhaps like an accountant who was finding himself in an anomalous situation.

ROUTINE ONE: Jock Proves that Alec Is Not There
Jock: I bet you ten shillings that I can prove that you're not here.
Alec: You can prove that I'm not here? Of course I'm here! Isn't that right, boys and girls?

(*Mingled murmurs and other outbursts of agreement from the audience.*)

Jock: But *I* say that I can *prove* that you're not here.

Alec: Well (*not without sarcasm*), we have to see this, don't we? Show us your money, then. (*Both produce ten-shilling notes and place them at their feet at the front of the bandstand stage.*) You go ahead then and prove I'm not here.

Jock: Right. Are you in Belfast?

Alec: No.

Jock: Are you in Dublin?

Alec: No!

Jock: Are you in London?

Alec: NO!

Jock: So! If you're not in Belfast, or Dublin, or London, then you must be somewhere else?

Alec (*a little impatient with this demonstration of the obvious*): Of course!

Jock (*exultantly, and to the delight of the audience*): Well, if you're somewhere else, then you're not here!

(*Jock triumphantly sweeps up the two ten-shilling notes while a disgruntled Alec, hands on hips, looks exasperatedly on.*)

ROUTINE TWO: Jock Hides the Matchbox

Jock: I bet you ten shillings that I can place this matchbox where I can see it, everybody in the audience can see it, but you can't see it.

Alec (*his delivery obviously more directed towards the audience than towards Jock*): You are saying that you can place that matchbox where you can see it, everybody in the audience can see it, but I can't see it?

Jock: That is correct.

Alec: I don't believe *that*, boys and girls, do you?

(*Mingled shouts of 'Yes!' and 'No!', mostly the former.*)

Alec: Do you really think he can? Well, let's see then.

Jock: Ah, the bet – don't forget the bet. Ten shillings, please!

(*Alec, in tetchy humour, hands over his banknote, and looks on suspiciously, and to titters from the crowd, until Jock belatedly whips out his ten-shilling note and places the two notes on the bandstand floor as before.*)

Jock: So, I will place this matchbox where I can see it, everyone in the
   audience can see it, but *you* can't see it!
Alec (*impatient*): Go ahead, then!
(*Jock, after the slightest of pauses, places the matchbox squarely on the top
of Alec's head. Laughter and applause. Alec more disgruntled than ever, as
Jock once more sweeps up the ten-shilling notes.*)

Banal as these routines were, we were content to watch them, standing in the crowd on a fine summer evening. It was an unthinkingly
accepted part of the entertainment known as 'the pierrots': you did not
question the conventions, but took them for what they were. Richer in
memory, though, than this rather pathetic comic entertainment was the
rhythmic prancing of the dancing-girls, with their short skirts and long
and (so it now seems) perfectly shaped legs. Vividly made-up, with red,
red lips and heightened features that profited from the bandstand foot-
lighting as the sun went down, they filled the dull air of many a mundane summer evening with vague erotic promise, all the more thrilling
for its very vagueness. Perhaps one would need some of Fellini's evocative skills to do justice to such scenes as these, and the early images of the
Fascinating Woman that they conveyed. Yet such a self-consciously
artistic treatment as Fellini's would rob them of their essential innocence, and fail to do justice to the child's acceptance of their magic as a
thing not really out of the ordinary.

*

I was a confirmed smoker by the age of six (stealing the cigarette butts
out of the pockets of my father's heavy overcoat as it hung on the round-
topped banister at the foot of the steep stairs in the house in Newry).
Blame it on my two older brothers, for once I had seen them at it, I felt
it incumbent on me to go through, as soon as possible, that male rite of
passage (for so it seemed). I might also claim that I was an habitual gambler from a very early age, but would have to add that such a claim is not
as dramatic as it might at first appear. All it means is that I joined in the
games of poker and pontoon, where the stakes were pennies and

halfpennies; and that I occasionally, at the age of nine or ten, backed a horse or two, usually sixpence each way. (Women and booze – to complete the list of activities which traditionally ruin many a good man – came much later.)

Warrenpoint is associated in my mind with a number of these pursuits. We seemed there to have more time and freedom to smoke, for example, going off to 'hideaways' in the fields, or else smoking on the beach when we were by ourselves. There were, in addition, two welcome sources of cheap cigarettes. Every so often the family (excluding my father) travelled across Carlingford Lough on one of the large motorboats that were regularly available, and my brothers and I were able (while my mother turned a blind eye) to buy cheap fags in Omeath in the Irish Republic (or, as we insisted in calling it in our unreconstructed way, 'the Free State'). Omeath in my recollection was seedy but exotic: you made your purchases (Omeath rock, Cleeve's Irish Toffees, not obtainable in the North, and the cigarettes) among a clutter of crude wooden stalls near the jetty; or else, if you had the patience to contain yourself, bypassed those and entered the town proper.

I always felt a thrill of excitement when we stepped into the boat on the Warrenpoint side. It would sway as it took the weight of the passengers, and you realised that however big and solid it was, it was never fully stable. Yet you were trusting your life to it for the duration of the trip! You paid for your ticket; then the motor would burst into life. You were on the move, and the familiar shore of Warrenpoint began to slip away. I would trail my hand in the water, if I were close enough to the side to do so, and look ahead to the distant shoreline of Omeath which all the time came more and more into focus. Halfway over, and you could frighten yourself with dangerous fantasies: what if the boat overturned, at just this point where you were at the farthest distance from both shores? Would my feeble breast-stroke be adequate in the face of the waves, which were now lifting roughly against the side of the boat? Would I have the stamina to swim and swim and swim? My breath threatening to fail, desperate gasping, panic, the slide under the waves…I looked down at the thin boards which were the only thing between us and the alien element of the sea, perhaps feeling, in my own small way, something of the insecurity that the first astronauts felt as they gauged the thinness of the metal shell or glass window that interposed between them and the inhuman vastness of space.

But already we are out of the Maximum Danger Zone, and the jetty on the far side is visible. We have left the dull old familiar world of Warrenpoint behind, and ahead is the exotic prospect of a barely familiar region. The engine is cut, and we drift, drift, steered quietly at the end towards the new world. I am all impatience in these last few minutes, the slowest in the whole journey; I have time to note the rainbow-coloured oilslicks on the water, and the increasingly noticeable smell of the diesel as we make our way in. My rising excitement beats in vain against the necessary restraint. I finger the coins in my pocket, and am eager to spend them on the unfamiliar packs of cigarettes (Sweet Afton and others) which are unobtainable in Warrenpoint. Then as my feet touch solid ground again, I am ready to run off to the stalls, but the voice of my mother or of a brother or sister calls me back; so I must fret and fume for a little longer. But then at last we are indeed launched forward into our adventure, and ahead is the full panoply of what Omeath has to offer.

One other cheap source of cigarettes was less certain, and involved a great deal of luck. Up the town in Warrenpoint, away from the seafront, was an amusement arcade. Among the slot-machines were a number in which the prize for a combination of skill and chance was a cigarette. You put your penny in, and a silver ball was released; if you managed to propel the ball upwards into one of a series of holes, with just the right amount of force, the cigarette was yours. You needed the luck, but there was a canny element of judgment in the way you pulled the little hammer back to shoot the ball upwards. And if you were successful, you had the satisfaction not just of a cheap fag, or even the sense that you were, for that brief moment, favoured by fortune; you could also congratulate yourself on your skill and judgment, in getting it just right. Can you doubt, then, that when you smoked that particular cigarette it was with a keener pleasure than usual?

Warrenpoint was also the locus of much of my experience of gambling. It was in the front sitting-room of the house there that we played our poker-games or games of pontoon, my two brothers and myself along with other lads in the neighbourhood. I quickly discovered that I was not a born gambler; I hated to lose, and found intolerable the fickleness of Fortune, which could have you winning over a pound at eight o'clock, yet send you penniless and distraught to bed two hours later. I am sure I must often have fought back tears at the injustice of it all, and it is not surprising that I should have ended my poker days before I was out of my teens. It became clear to me, also, that I had no skill at bluffing in poker; I was always a bad actor, and could not commit myself to the sustained charade that bluffing requires.

My experience of gambling on the horses was intense but also short-lived. I was never the kind of full-blooded gambler who chooses his favourite and goes for broke by backing it 'straight' (to win only) in an all-or-nothing gesture. That is the way of the true devotee; but my own instinct was to look for an outsider that I could back each way at generous odds. If it won, bonanza time! If it came second or third, I still got back two or three times my bet. I had one bonanza I can never forget: the horse's name I cannot recall (and in that detail I reveal my lack of gambler's credentials), but it was ridden by Jimmy Greenaway, at that time an apprentice (claiming seven pounds). I congratulated myself on my astuteness; for had I not worked it all out, that, with the going heavy, a seven-pound allowance would make all the difference? Picture, then, an eleven-year-old with a fag in the corner of his mouth, a shrewd customer, one of the boys, and never more so.

The most vivid memory that I have of the bookie's in Warrenpoint, however, has nothing to do with the horses. The bookie's shop was up the town, in a laneway off the main street. His name was Jack Campbell. I think that we frequented it because it was the one nearest to us, though it may also be the case that its location off the main thoroughfare made for a sense of security (we were not exposed to incidental parental scrutiny). For it was, of course, part of the ritual that we smoked as well as gambled. One of our group, and in many ways the closest friend we had in Warrenpoint, was Eddie, who had a number of remarkable attributes. I pass over here his prowess as a swimmer (once, that is, he had been taught by my sisters), and his skilful reconnoitring manoeuvres prior to our raids on local orchards. No, Eddie's most entertaining feature was his astonishing maximisation of the sound and the effect of the burp (or 'rift', as we called it). It was a precious act: he would call attention to the imminent performance by setting his very ample mouth theatrically awry. Then he would pause for just the right amount of time for dramatic impact, before releasing a very loud and sustained rift that seemed in its prolongation to move up and down through several gradations of sound.

One day as we congregated outside the doorway of Jack Campbell's, the divine afflatus came upon Eddie, and he let fly with devastating effect. But immediately, as if in a spirit of planned antiphonal reaction, came an answering burst from no less a figure than Jack himself, as *he* let fly, loudly and abundantly (to borrow a phrase from Orwell's *Nineteen Eighty-Four*) from what we may politely term 'the other end'. Wind sang to wind in unforgettable antiphony; yet this was not at all planned (for neither party could have known of the other's intention) but was the felicitous product of mere happenstance. We all collapsed in a knot of hysterical laughter outside the doorway; and I doubt if at that time or even subsequently we reflected, as good gamblers might have done, on the odds against such a happy conjunction of inspiration, such a rare instance of spontaneous dialogue.

*

Et in Arcadia ego: words attributed to a skull or death's head. 'Even in Arcady, even in the sweet days of early innocence,' says Death, 'I am already present.' My memories of Warrenpoint are overshadowed by two major tragedies. One of these was sufficiently remote not to trouble the imagination unduly. A wealthy local man (who made his living as a bookmaker in Newry, I believe) was out in a motor-launch in Carlingford Lough with a group of friends, when a sudden squall arose. It seems that the boat was not of a draught deep enough to withstand the force of the assault. It was overturned, and, while there were some survivors, the bookmaker and his wife perished, far from 'all effectual aid'. For days afterwards a pall of depression seemed to lie across the bay.

But far, far worse, and the worse for being so close to us, was the tragic death of a toddler, aged only two or three, in a road accident. He was the son of the people who owned the sweet shop on the corner just yards from where we lived. Year after year I would go to that shop to buy my bullseyes, aniseed balls, brandy balls, or rhubarb rock; at first, in the years after the war, carefully husbanding my sweet coupons to do so. The family were called Cole. Harry was a big man, not much given to small talk, rather taciturn, but unfailingly patient when, having entered the shop and rung the little bell above the door by the act of entry, you saw him emerge from the domestic quarters to serve you. His wife was also larger than the norm: big-boned and handsome, with a pleasant smile. For years they had but one child, a daughter, and we got to know her very well, for she would be in and out of the house where we stayed. She was, I think, close in age to myself. Then, to their joy, when the daughter was seven or eight years of age, a late pregnancy produced a son. Harry and his wife were congratulated all round; their family was complete.

But one day the daughter, then perhaps only nine or ten, was left in charge of the toddler. Somehow or other, through no fault on her part, he got away from her charge, ran heedlessly out of the door, and across the busy seafront road. A heavy truck was passing at speed. The toddler was obliterated. It was a pure devastation. The family was never the same thereafter.

Now when you entered the shop, the doorbell tinkling behind you, you were more usually served by the distraught mother than by her husband. It may even have been the case that he was psychologically incapable of working in the shop. Mrs Cole was older and greyer looking, and her air was a good deal more abstract than before. I cannot recall how I responded emotionally to this; perhaps I took, eventually, the coward's way out, and started to buy my sweets elsewhere. At night I lay in bed and heard the wind buffet and rattle the 'No Waiting' signs, and perhaps imagined the rain washing clean away all trace of the child's innocent blood. In truth, though, the scene of devastation had been swiftly cleared by the time I knew the accident had happened. Yet somehow some horrific details filtered through, and haunted my imagination. So small, so vulnerable the child; so vast, by comparison, so insensate the juggernaut that destroyed him!

I visited recently the scene where the accident happened. A barrier is still in place where the child rushed out across the road, but, alas, was erected only after the event, far too late to bring that child back to a bereft family. The site where the shop stood is now derelict, and the bell that tinkled above its door is heard no more. The parents of the toddler are both dead. I stand on a Saturday in mild autumn weather across from the magnificent sweep of the mountains down to the lough, and think of Wordsworth's poem 'The Ruined Cottage'. Perhaps here too the 'secret spirit of humanity' counters the 'oblivious tendencies' at work, and survives the desolation of the site; but I am not convinced that such is the case, and find myself looking only at a painful vacancy.

*

Unlike Newry, which was predominantly Catholic (and sometimes fiercely Nationalist), Warrenpoint was a 'fifty-fifty' town, with a substantial Protestant representation. Because we spent the month of July in Warrenpoint, it meant that we were always there for the 'Twelfth' celebrations; and, on every Twelfth of July (savage little Nationalists that we were) we devoutly hoped it would rain (it never seemed to, a fact which gave rise to a fleeting suspicion, not finally accepted, that God was in reality a 'Prod'). Often the Orange parade would pass along the seafront, right outside the door of our holiday home; and among the walkers was Dougie Grahame, usually one of our gang (we might plunder orchards together), but on this day subsumed into tribal propriety. So we made a point of looking out for him, and as he was sighted, would chant, unheard by him and from the safety of our sitting-room, 'Yella-belly buckteeth big fat Grahame!'

It pains me now to think how bigoted – indeed, racist – we were: for the purpose of the 'yellow-belly' slur was to to point up the physical differences between Protestants and ourselves. As far as I recall, the myth was that Prods had smoother and more jaundiced skin than us taigs; in any case, by various ethnic indicators (the boast was) you could 'tell one of them a mile off'. We were as ethnophobic as that appalling little bigot of a narrator in the 'Cyclops' episode of Joyce's *Ulysses* – he who at one point, when assessing the way the dog Garryowen starts sniffing the Jewish Leopold Bloom, imparts the received wisdom that 'those Jewies does have a sort of a queer odour coming off them …'. In our case, the Prods were the hated Other; and we, as children, however generous or morally sensitive in other ways, imbibed the shibboleths of the tribe. So, too, we seized on opportunities to vent our spleen against the hated 'Them'; though when I think now of this ensuing instance I am still inclined to laugh.

In our own home in Newry, we did not possess a telephone, but the house we rented in Warrenpoint did have one, and, if we watched our opportunity, we could make secret and forbidden phone calls. It was well known that Douglas Grahame's father was the master of the local Freemasons, and we had his number (perhaps felt that we had it in more senses than one). So what we would do was dial that number, let the phone at the other end ring, wait in breathless anticipation until it was answered, and then shout down the line, 'Orange bastard!' Kinks of laughter followed, and mild hysteria – and we had the satisfaction not only of playing, as we thought, a great prank, but of proving our Nationalist credentials. Croppies lie down? No way!

There is an obvious question to be asked at this point. How did it come about that, in spite of the tolerant attitudes evident in the way my father ran his pub, we could be so instinctively, so unthinkingly, bigoted? The answer has to be that there were numerous other influences at work in the culture which militated against tolerance. Most important of these was the schooling, both in terms of the system and the pedagogic content. We were, to begin with, forever segregated from 'the other side' at school, never meeting them even on sporting occasions (since we played Gaelic football, while they played what some of our teachers would denigrate as 'foreign' games such as rugby, cricket or soccer). And the way we were taught, especially in our history classes, exacerbated in us the sense of victimisation and exclusion, first by an unjust Britain, then by a rotten political system, clearly identified as 'British', which allowed the uncompromising Unionists to hold on to power indefinitely. What history told us was that all our woes stemmed from British interference in Irish affairs; and that the most lasting damage, that most visible in our immediate circumstances, had been done by the Protestant plantation of Ulster in the seventeenth century, which had dispossessed the native Irish, namely us (in my own family there was a tradition handed down orally that we had once been prominent Catholic landowners in County Tyrone, and had been forcibly evicted by Protestants; the legend turned out to contain a core of truth, though the dispossession occurred not, as we at first thought, in the seventeenth century, but in the 1790s, a particularly turbulent period, remarkable for an even higher than usual degree of sectarian conflict).

In this reading of history – one that became increasingly sectarian in its obsessions – the Protestants, the Unionists, the Orangemen, the Apprentice Boys, the Freemasons all tended to become interchangeable appellations for the one Oppressor, who defiantly paraded his oppression in the most triumphalist way on the Twelfth, marching behind that hated British flag which functioned as the symbolic guarantee of his invincible position. It would be difficult to convey, to a British readership in particular, how alienated one felt from the Union Jack and the other trappings of Britishness; the Union Jack was the diametric opposite of everything we held dear, the most extreme and intensely focused image of the hated Other. Even now, it is easier for me to accept it as merely one flag among many in a panorama of European insignia than to see it elevated to solitary prominence in even the most mildly celebratory context. Some atavisms, alas, die hard, and perhaps all one can do with those is bring them to the highest level of consciousness and confront them (as Seamus Heaney repeatedly counsels in his prose essays) with the persistent (if often unheeded) voices of reason and civility.

*

According to ancient legend, as relayed by Hesiod, Aphrodite (or Venus) emerged from the ocean (as depicted so spectacularly in Botticelli's great painting *The Birth of Venus* in the Uffizi Gallery in Florence). D. H.

Lawrence (who devoted some of his most extravagant prose to the figure of Aphrodite) reminds us that she was 'born of the sea-foam', and adds that, in contrast to the Virgin Mary, she is 'the queen of the senses'. In my own case, the seaside is vividly associated with at least two rather different experiences of sexual awakening. One of these should properly be placed under the aegis of Aphrodite Pandemos (the goddess of sexual lust, as opposed to Aphrodite Urania, who is associated with a higher kind of love); although, in truth, the episode is of such a minor nature that Aphrodite might not deign to acknowledge it at all.

With regard to an interest in the opposite sex, I needed little prompting (but was in dire need of (a) information and (b) opportunity). Even in infants' class at school (and I mean even before I had progressed to Senior Infants), I can recall dropping my pencil or pen on the floor so that, in the act of going down on hands and knees to pick it up again, I might have the chance to look up the girls' skirts and catch a good close-up look at their knickers. Are all men, I wonder, condemned to be instinctively voyeuristic? So again it was to prove on this later occasion.

I think I must have been in my early teens, and found myself, late one evening, on an almost deserted beach. Almost deserted, but not quite; for in addition to myself there was a youngish mother (perhaps in her thirties) and child. It must have been a mild evening, for all three of us were still in swimsuits. The mother was absorbed in the activities of the child, a toddler, and stooped frequently to help him (or her) as the child stumbled along, pausing now and then in desultory fashion to dig up the sand or explore the mysteries of the beach. What I very quickly realised was that the woman, who was wearing quite a low-cut swimsuit, revealed in her constant stooping a generous portion of her breasts; and these now became for me a focus of obsessive interest. But I would, of course, be cunning and escape observation even as I, a willing if inexperienced 'Peeping Tom', indulged in observation of my own.

So up and down the beach I walked, passing on each transit as close to her as I could safely do without detection, seizing every opportunity to gaze and take my fill of the fascinating cleavage. God knows how many times I passed her, obsessed in my adolescent voyeurism as I was. It was in truth, as Wordsworth says in dealing with quite a different experience of youthful guilt, 'an act of stealth and troubled pleasure'; for I am sure that I was conscious that I was feeding on forbidden fruit. I doubtless told myself it was only a venial sin – 'only looking' from a distance, after all, not involved in the intimacy of touching. But I must have been uneasily aware of the compulsive nature of my behaviour, and of the sweet and subtle riot in my breast which banished rational self-possession.

Coleridge says somewhere that a sin is 'an evil which has its ground or origin in the agent, and not in the compulsion of circumstances'. I was, certainly, under no outward compulsion, and could have turned my steps in a number of alternative directions across the expanse of the beach. Yet the behaviour remained, in some sense, compulsive, as if I could not but succumb to the temptation. I fancy that if Dante Alighieri had been watching me from on high, and was in need of one more exemplar for inclusion in his gallery of sinners in the Second Circle of Hell (reserved for the carnal), he might have found in the given components of the scene the infernal landscape in which I might be eternally placed: a barren beach, in increasingly doubtful light, and the sinner circling obsessively around one particular object which wholly precluded him from any wider and more generous perception.

*

A very hot day. The entire week preceding had been building remorselessly to this culmination. The green paint on the front door and doorframe was blistered all over, and from the seafront across the road there was not a breath of air. If you raised your eyes, you saw a blue sky, cloudless, with a fiercely burning golden orb. We ran around all day in swimsuits, back and forth across the road to the beach, barefooted, as wild as Red Indians, and, from the ravages of sunburn, more truly 'redskinned' than they. I was nine or ten years of age.

My mother had to work as usual in the kitchen, using the range cooker. In there, the heat was oppressive, especially for a woman like herself who, though not notably overweight, had still an ample figure. She did not often go into the sea, partly because she had never learnt to swim – a point on which she could be sensitive. When she did take a dip (and that would usually be in the evening, when the beach was pretty much deserted), she would 'jouk' down in the water and move her arms in front of her as if she were doing the breast-stroke, all the while resting her feet on the bottom. We used to tease her about it, perhaps implying that in acting thus she was guilty of 'cheating', and so failing to honour her own high moral standards.

On this day she had suffered so much from the heat that she decided she would have to cool down in the sea. Nor would she wait for the evening. So across the road in her beachwear she went, and plunged gratefully into the waves. I think I must have been busy about my own affairs, and did not see her come out and return to the house. Absorbed and happy, I swam or roamed the beach, looking for mussels or crabs, and did not return to the house until some necessity impelled me to do so.

It is only when I enter the house that I learn from my sister Majella that 'Mammy isn't well'.

What's wrong?

The problem had arisen, I gathered, from the heat which had raised her temperature, followed by the sudden coolness of the sea.

So what effect…?

'She's lost her memory.'

Mammy was sitting on a couch in the sitting-room, with my second sister, Harriet, on one side of her and one of my brothers (Art, I think) on the other. This was ominous. All the members of the family (my father excepted, since he was working in Newry) were now in anxious attendance. Mother's eyes were blank and puzzled, and she seemed to find it difficult to speak. It was clear to me that when she glanced at me, she failed to recognise me. I was shocked by her air of total bewilderment. The room was unnaturally still and quiet.

When I leave the room to follow my brother Art, he turns on me a gaze from which he is trying to clear the cloud of worry.

'She'll be all right. It'll wear off. The doctor's been sent for.'

Sure enough, she did recover by the evening, and we were all able, eventually, to laugh at it. It still took her a while, however, to come to terms with the fact that a span of her life, however small, had been wiped clean from her memory; for she did not ever, as far as I know, recover the period of hours during which she was affected. Sturdy, strong and active, it irked her that she should have been diminished in this way by circumstances outside her control. So she was not after all invulnerable. The father that I knew could, on rare occasions, disappear under the irrational assault of alcohol. Even my mother was not, it now seemed, immune to the irruption of unforeseen and destructive forces. It was a disturbing revelation; but I was obliviously carried onward through a succession of sunny days by the sequence of happy holiday activities that followed.

*

My most severe visitation from Aphrodite while on holidays at Warrenpoint came like a bolt from the blue. Even now, I struggle to come to terms with it, and wonder if it is material for psychoanalysis. It has to do with the visit to our family home of Geraldine, then aged thirteen or fourteen, about the same age as myself, though perhaps, if not a little older, then more mature and developed for her age than I was. All I can recall of her appearance is that she had long fair hair, fine-spun gold I am now tempted to say, as if at this distance she is more myth than reality. But real she certainly was, the daughter of the owner of the Frontier Cinema in Newry, though why she stayed under our roof in Warrenpoint, or even how long she stayed, I cannot now recall.

What I most wonder about is this: was it her appearance and general demeanour that so affected me, these being rare and cherishable in themselves, or was I in addition subtly influenced by my knowledge that she was from a wealthy family, so that this awareness helped to establish her mythic status as a 'high-born maiden'? Was I moreover intrigued by her association with that temple of fantasy (however tawdry in some of its aspects), the Newry cinema where I had seen so many images of female glamour in Hollywood movies? Why was it that she so affected me, even during a stay that must have been brief?

However it was, her presence plunged me into a condition that can

best be described as feverish; and even though I had had very little contact with her, she became a deep source of infatuation, eventually provoking in me behaviour that can only be characterised as manic. For I
remember that on the day of her departure, I lay on my bed, and, under
a compulsion I had no way of understanding, kicked my legs repeatedly
in the air, throwing my body recklessly from side to side, in an ecstasy I
could not control. I should make it clear that what I felt was not the pain
of loss (the fear that I should see her no more), but rather a sense of initiation into the mysteries of what the ancient Greeks called *ate* (trans-
latable as 'divine infatuation').

I do not recall that I ever met Geraldine again; and only a couple of
years ago I learned from a casual meeting with her elder sister (a nun),
whom I had not known previously, that she had died of cancer less than
a dozen years previously at a comparatively young age. I think of those
lines with which Alexander Pope concluded one of his greatest poems,
The Rape of the Lock, in large part a tribute to the beauty of his central
female character, Belinda. In closing he addresses her in terms that move
rapidly from teasing gallantry to deeper recognitions, complimenting
the beauty of her eyes, but envisaging a time

> When those fair suns shall set, as set they must,
> And all those tresses shall be laid in dust.

So Geraldine of the golden hair is no more, and has entered a stillness
and peace far removed from the fever which she once generated in the
veins of a very immature teenager.

CHAPTER SIX

Lislea

When I was a Schoolboy I though[t] a fair Woman a pure Goddess . . .
– I have no right to expect more than their reality.

(John Keats, letter to Benjamin Bailey, 18, 22 July 1818)

I seem to have spent a lot of my time trying to come to terms with the opposite sex, in their many manifestations. Since my first school was a convent school and I was taught to a large extent by nuns, it was there that I had one of the earliest opportunities to see females who were not family members. Given that the females in question were women who had devoted their lives to celibacy and were heavily enshrouded in the ample and old-fashioned dress that nuns then wore, it was highly unlikely that anything of an erotic nature would transpire. Nonetheless, these anti-Eves or anti-Delilahs were doubtless a formative influence in the way I came to envisage women in general: and in retrospect, they divide, for me, into two archetypes.

On the one hand, there were motherly and humane figures; on the other, severe and punitive authoritarians. The former was typified by Sister Celestine: kind and (as it now seems) elderly, she was the most obviously maternal of the entire company. In one of her most genial performances, she would rummage around in the deep pocket of her gown, and finally produce a large, cherubic apple for the lucky recipient (which, happily, was sometimes myself). Things in those early days, of course, tasted differently: this was a sweet prelapsarian apple, bearing no association with or trace of the Fall.

The other side of the coin was severely represented by the tall, imposing, and (I am tempted to add) metaphorically dark figure of Sister

Bertram, a rigid disciplinarian who rarely, as I recall, yielded to the temptation to smile. It is with this darkening presence that one of the most vivid episodes from those years is associated. There were, as far as I remember, no urinals in the school (since the institution was, apart from the infants' classes, for girls only); which meant that the boys had to pee over the toilet-bowl in one of the cubicles (though of course exercising that inalienable male prerogative of remaining standing while doing so). One day, and in total innocence (after all, we were five years of age), my friend Charlie and myself shared a cubicle for that purpose, with a view to hurrying up the procedure. I shall never forget the sudden irruption into the cubicle of Sister Bertram (who must have had, I assume now, the decency to wait until we had finished). She began to scold us for reasons neither of us could comprehend and, as far as I recall, induced in us not so much a sense of guilt or shame as of transient unease. In retrospect, I now realise that she was worried lest we might be engaged in something sexual behind the shut-over door of the cubicle. This all passed over our heads at the time: it was only after many years had passed that I realised what the problem was. It is the kind of incident that makes you appreciate the rightness of D. H. Lawrence's revision of an old dictum: 'To the Puritan all things are impure'.

Many of the other nuns, though, were wonderfully human. My favourite was probably Sister Anthony, whom I now envisage as youthful, clear-skinned, handsome, and possessed of a wonderful capacity for fun and laughter, usually betrayed by the twinkle in her eye. I well remember how, sitting on a bench along the high school wall, with the ample lawn just in front of her, she would take my hands in hers, hold me with her gaze, and encourage me tell her how much my brother Art (an inveterate gambler even at the age of seven) had made on the horses. This was done in a delightfully teasing way: she would make me, a solemn five-year-old, determined to show he could tell the truth and nothing but the truth, repeat, against her mock-protestations of incredulity, the exact amount that the brother had won. He did once, at that age, incredibly win £5 on the Grand National. Since £5 in the mid-forties was quite a sum for a seven-year-old like my brother, it is possible that Sister

The house at Clady, County Armagh; my father's birthplace.

My father (in the middle of the frame) as apprentice barman in his teens, c. 1907.

My father and mother (with an acquaintance, on the right) on their honeymoon in the Isle of Man, c. 1927.

My mother with her first-born, my older sister, 1934. It was typical of my mother to name her Majella, after the patron saint of childbirth, St Gerard Majella.

My father with two nephews (on my mother's side), 1934.

My mother (left) with her sister, Aunt Bella, and my two sisters, on Warrenpoint beach, 1938.

My father with my second sister, Harriet, at one of the 'breakwaters' on Warrenpoint beach, 1938.

My two sisters, Majella (left) and Harriet, on the beach at Warrenpoint, c. 1939.

We visit our relatives at Lislea, County Armagh, c. 1942. My Uncle Johnny is second from the left; my father in the middle of the back row, with my mother on his left.

My mother and father with my father's sister, Aunt Maggie (on the right), in Armagh, 1943.

The five of us (plus the dog, Spot): left to right, Peter, Harriet, myself, Majella, Art.

A saintly crew, c. 1947: the Infants' Classes at Our Lady's School (Canal Street), all in clerical or related garb. I am the solemn, dark-haired father-confessor – in what I think is a Franciscan robe – in the centre of the second row from the front. My two brothers are in the centre of the second-last row, Peter appropriately holding the papal keys, with Art on the right.

The Three Wise Cosgroves; we won a prize in a fancy-dress competition for this imitation of the Magi. The blackface in the middle is myself.

My father, in the middle of the group facing the camera, with his companions on board the Queen Elizabeth *on its way to the USA, 1947. He described the ship as an 'old bucket', but seems happy enough here.*

Self (on the left) and my two brothers, on the seaside wall in Warrenpoint, c. 1948.

My mother and one of her closest friends, Gretta, daughter of Aunt Maggie: in Royal Avenue, Belfast, 1949.

My mother with our fox terrier, Spot, outside the house we habitually rented on the seafront at Warrenpoint.

Our annual climb to the 'Clough More' (Big Stone), up the Rostrevor Mountain, summer 1949. The stone is to the left: I am looking out in the space between the heads of my mother and Aunt Bella, with brother Peter and my second sister, Harriet, to the right.

Myself and my brother Art, on the left, on an altar-boys' excursion to a seaside resort in the Republic.

I stand in front of my mother, who is flanked by my two sisters: Omeath, c. 1950.

Self and brothers (on a rather wet day) outside the lions' cage at Belfast Zoo. This was one of our outings with 'Fr Curtis'.

Happy days: my older sister Majella, mother, and myself, on a sunny July day at the seafront in Warrenpoint, probably 1951. In the background are the Carlingford Mountains; to the left is a 'breakwater', partly covered by an incoming tide.

A memorable beginning: Down defeat Armagh in the Ulster Gaelic Football County Championship, 1957; by the end of the decade, no-hopers Down are a force to be reckoned with. Interested spectators at the 'Marshes' football ground in Newry include my brother Art (second from right), self (fourth from right, back row), brother Peter (extreme left).

My parents in relaxed mode, at the wedding reception for my older sister, Majella, at Ballymascanlon Hotel, Dundalk, 1957.

Following a successful result in my final school-year examinations, I look forward to enrolment at the Queen's University, Belfast; photograph taken in Newry, 1958.

My mother poses beside the sweet pea in our backyard, summer 1959. The fact that she is wearing her apron means that she has just come from the kitchen where, as usual, she was baking or cooking. Cancer had already been detected; and within two years she was dead.

July 1960, prior to the trip to Kerry, my mother's last major outing: father, mother, self and two brothers.

Last throw of the dice: my mother flanked by father and cousin Kathleen (daughter of Aunt Maggie, and sister of Gretta), touring in Kerry in 1960. The man in the background is the eldest son of Uncle Johnny. Not long afterwards, my mother was confined to house and bed.

Anthony's incredulity was not entirely feigned; but in any case she made the most of the situation, playing it up for what it was worth, to the amusement of the onlookers, perhaps one or two senior girls, or one of the other nuns, such as the pleasant, delicate-featured Sister Patrick.

Probably, without being aware of it at the time, I was making important discriminations among these women, and being educated as to the different types of female they represented. In general the memories of their presences are fond ones; a number of them were sufficiently endowed with loving-kindness to function as an extension of my mother's protective care, so that they acted as substitutes for her while I was away from home. It was only much later, especially in my frequent visits to the cinema, that women were for me eroticised, and my imagination attached itself to this or that fantasy-icon. Even now, like multi-coloured gems, the images of these fantasy-females seen in the films of my youth pour forth profusely from the casket of memory.

Their names, however familiar (some more familiar than others), hardly seemed to be the names of real people – Joan Fontaine, Olivia de Havilland, Ida Lupino – and I felt privileged to be invited to share vicariously in their elevated existence. Like the speaker in John Donne's poem 'The Indifferent' (though utterly devoid of his cynicism), I could 'love both fair and brown'. Redhead, blonde, brunette – Rhonda Fleming, Virginia Mayo, Elizabeth Taylor – all were part of a pantheon that seemed endlessly plenitudinous. The pantheon was sufficiently accommodating to include everybody's younger sister, Debbie Reynolds; the ideal girl-next-door, the lisping June Allyson; the woman of the world, hardened by experience, Anne Baxter; or the exotic from another culture, such as Ingrid Bergman, whose voice, for all its glamorous strangeness of intonation, vibrated with recognisable human feeling, and seemed to rise from the deep warmth of a passionate heart.

The slim and fey or the buxom and tough, Audrey Hepburn or Jane Russell, all could find a place. There were those whose beauty was partly in their singing voice, such as Ann Blyth, or Shirley Jones; and those whose beauty was simply in the fact of their existence, such as Hedy Lamarr, or supremely, for me, Sophia Loren and (in a stunningly different way) Grace Kelly. Doubtless the response on my part was an erotic one, but it was not that of a fully sexualised consciousness. It was perhaps for that reason that Marilyn Monroe did not greatly appeal, since those breasts and hips could seem all too obviously sexual in their uncompromising physicality. But in general I was in thrall, in my imagination, to these enchanting female icons, and the endless indulgence they vividly (if vaguely) seemed to promise; so that I think of the Jack Lemmon character in Billy Wilder's *Some Like It Hot*, who, when he finds himself on the train in the midst of all the delightful females in the girls' band, attempts to describe his sense of infinite erotic possibility by recalling his childhood fantasy of being let loose in a sweetshop.

Probably, though, part of me knew that these screen-goddesses were indeed mere fantasies; for I cannot believe that even in my youthful days I wholly escaped the chill breath of my father's realism (often expressed in terms that would now be considered far from politically correct): 'If all the young women are so pretty,' I would hear him remark, 'where do all the ugly old women come from?'

Behind the harshness of the evaluation, I can sense now a degree of valid philosophical enquiry. And some time later I realised that my father's sentiments, somewhat crudely expressed, had been anticipated in a more sympathetic and generous vein in a poem by Thomas Hardy, called 'Former Beauties':

> These market-dames, mid-aged, with lips thin-drawn,
>   And tissues sere,
> Are they the ones we loved in years agone,
>   And courted here?
>
> Are these the muslined pink young things to whom
>   We vowed and swore
> In nooks on summer Sundays by the Froom,
>   Or Budmouth shore? . . .
>
> They must forget, forget! They cannot know
>   What once they were,
> Or memory would transfigure them, and show
>   Them always fair.

Hardy is not interested in speculating on the philosophical implications of his tragic recognition (and perhaps that is part of the poem's strength); but we may choose to believe that there are philosophical issues at stake. Thus, my father's stark observation might be rephrased, so that the question becomes not: 'Where do the ugly women come from?', but rather: 'Where does their beauty disappear to?' And more to the point: where did that beauty come from in the first place? In this way my father's caustic remark may have helped to sow the seeds of a later interest in Plato, preparing me, in however rudimentary a way, for a sympathetic interest in Platonic dualism. That there was beauty in the world one could not doubt; yet, at the same time, this beauty was not sustained in the world – was, in a sense, not 'at home' in it. It seemed to make sense, then, to locate the beauty elsewhere, in a realm of transcendence, where it could not fade; so that the beauty that we do actually see in our temporal world is but a fleeting shadow thrown on the 'passing shows of Being', a reflection (to change the metaphor) of that 'higher' beauty which exists outside of time. Yet what are the implications of such a view (to come back to the specific starting point) for an estimate of female beauty in particular?

Here, clearly, is a troubling division. Women are beautiful, but do not possess their beauty; they are, rather, temporarily invested with it. So that in a man's attraction to a woman, what he seems to be responding to is not *her* beauty, but a 'higher' beauty which 'shines' through her. Logically, then (as Dante felt with regard to Beatrice), there is an argument for bypassing the (mere) earthly manifestation of beauty in the woman, and seeking a more direct access to the 'heavenly' beauty of which she is the imperfect embodiment. Such division or dualism leads rapidly to a version of that conflict which is so central to our Western culture – a conflict between soul and body, spirit and flesh, with soul or spirit given priority.

One view would be that a proper sexual maturity in the male can arise only after he has achieved a degree, at least, of integration between these dualisms; he must, in a word, reconcile the sense of ideal beauty with the actual or 'mortal' version of that. One of those influenced by Plato, the Italian Renaissance neo-Platonist Marsilio Ficino, tries to restore the connection between the physical beauty of the individual woman and the 'heavenly' beauty of which her beauty is a 'lower' version. There are inevitably to be, he admits at the outset, 'two Venuses in the soul, the one heavenly, the other earthly'; but the accepted dualism is to some extent cancelled by the suggestion that these two forms of desire can operate harmoniously side by side. While the 'heavenly' Venus or desire in the soul is drawn to reflect upon 'divine beauty', the 'earthly' Venus (or, as it might be called, the erotic drive) seeks to generate that 'divine beauty in earthly matter'. The function of the erotic drive is to 'embody in a worldly creation' the beauty glimpsed by the higher desire of the soul.

Theoretically (and however abstract his argument may appear), Ficino's attempt to reconcile the two 'Venuses' has considerable appeal. In practical terms, however, it fails to provide any concrete illustration of this reconciliation, and, in addition, tends to impose upon women the need to be, in their beauty, something more than mere mortals. That way lies the extravagance of, say, Yeats's infatuation with Maud Gonne, which she rightly felt to be insupportable in its unrealistic expectations. Moreover, the truth is (whatever Ficino may argue) that very few of us are thinking of 'heavenly beauty' while engaged in the strenuous act of procreation. (Somewhat irresponsibly, I recall at this point a famous sketch by Peter Cook and Dudley Moore about the miracle of life. Pete undertakes to instruct Dud on how a human being is created. Chelsea win the FA Cup, your father starts in on the Green Chartreuse, invites your mother upstairs, and bingo! there you are.)

No, the integrations that are required need to occur in a fully realised situation. Like Keats, the maturing male must liberate the females to whom he feels attracted from their fantasy associations, and recognise, along with Keats, that he has 'no right to expect more than their reality'. In a word, he domesticates his strongest feelings, whether these be the feelings provoked by fantasy or the passions in his sexual nature. And one of the reasons I have such happy memories of my uncle's farm in Lislea is that it was in that context that I was privileged to experience the coming together into one sweet harmony of solid reality, domestic stability, and substantial (not fanciful) female beauty. Within that harmony, erotic response played a genuine but not a dominant or insistent role; it was but one feature of a more inclusive vision.

*

My father had, I gather, learned in his early years to drive, but I never saw him behind the wheel of a car. Following an accident, about which I have no information, he gave up driving, with the result that I grew up in a house where a family car was unknown. (Later, when I was learning to drive, I had to overcome inhibitions of a particular psychological nature, which arose, I think, from my sense that I was attempting to 'outdo' or surpass my father's achievements.) So when we were to pay one of our periodic visits to our cousins (and my father's brother and sister) in Armagh, we first travelled the nineteen miles to Armagh city, and subsequently the shorter journey to Lislea, in a taxi hired for the day.

It was always on a Sunday (the only day my father was freed from his work in the bar) that these excursions took place. The taxi was usually of the old-fashioned type known as a hackney; my father would sit in the front seat beside the driver, and the rest of the family would pile into the back, which was quite capacious, mainly because it had fold-up seats, besides the ample back seat occupied by my mother and sisters. As I recall those Sundays now (we left in the mid-morning), my memory is of dull Ulster sabbath weather, smoke wafting through the car from my father's cigarette, and a threatened headache or (worse still) vague and troubling intimations of car-sickness. It was perhaps only in that taxi that I ever came close to experiencing claustrophobia, though in a mild form.

The first stop was at Aunt Maggie's in Armagh. Maggie, a widow all the years I knew her, was my father's favourite sister. She and her husband Henry had had two daughters, both significantly older than any of the children in our family (in fact, one of the daughters, Gretta, was to become one of my mother's closest friends); the result was that there wasn't really anyone in that household 'to play with' while we were there. Some alleviation of the boredom was provided by the fact that the family owned and 'lived over' a sweet shop. So on invitation from one of the daughters (usually Kathleen), we would enter the shop, closed and shuttered on the Sunday, and in the twilit interior move freely behind and around the counter, feeling that we had privileged access to areas that would have been out of bounds on normal working-days.

But neither this privilege nor the possibility of free sweets could quite offset, for me, the sabbath *ennui*. The house tended to fill me with an indefinable melancholy; it was cluttered with furniture from a bygone age, which, in retrospect, strikes me as having been of a heavily Victorian kind. Perhaps the house had acquired something of the paralysis or stasis of Miss Havisham's, following, that is, the death of Maggie's husband. Whatever the reason, I found the visits there oppressive, and underwent that most excruciating kind of boredom known to the very young, when they are obliged to sit still and listen in on adult conversations in which they have not the slightest interest (because, in large part, they do not understand them). Sometimes, as a poor 'party-piece', I would sing a much abbreviated version of 'I'll Take You Home Again, Kathleen' (addressed, of course, to the daughter of that name); but that did not always succeed in raising my spirits. In fact, whenever I hear that song nowadays, I can be carried back in a vague melancholy sweep to a back yard in Armagh city, with a grey Sunday sky over my head, and the lingering reminiscence, as I stand in the sabbath silence, of an attack of car-sickness earlier induced by cigarette-smoke in the confined space of the taxi.

It was a relief for that bored little boy when my father stirred himself, and showed signs of continuing his pilgrimage on out through the Armagh countryside to my Uncle Johnny's farm at Lislea. The adults still lingered in a loose knot, talking; at the last minute someone would have forgotten something, and there would be a further delay; but at last we were all back in the cramped space of the taxi again (the taxi-man having gone off to amuse and feed himself in the interim). The taxi might feel somewhat claustrophobic, but at least we had regained our momentum and were leaving behind the dull and quiet house of my widowed aunt – a place where, as far as I was concerned, nothing happened. There was more life and action on the farm, partly because my uncle there had children (mostly and delightfully female) close in age to myself and my brothers. And there was more space, the possibility of walks through the fields, the sweep of the fresh air – always provided, that is, you were not overwhelmed by the strong (and excitingly unusual) stench of the festering flax.

*

   The hens stepped daintily about their feet, poking officious heads between them, and rushing out the door with a wild flutter and shriek when one of the girls hooshed them. Something timeless, patriarchal, and restful about it made Ned notice everything.

(Frank O'Connor, 'Uprooted')

Lislea (pronounced Liss-*lay*, with the accent on the second syllable) was my only experience of farm life, and was taken in small doses, over a number of four- or five-hour periods on a Sunday afternoon. It was, above all, a place remarkable for its hospitality. The taxi pulled into the farmyard in front of the house, and there standing in the door to greet us was Aunt Mary. She was petite and sprightly, with a ready smile and quiet manner, a light and gentle voice, and an accent that to my ears at least sounded rural and unusual. It was certainly the kind of accent you would rarely hear around the town of Newry.

   Aunt Mary was my uncle's second wife; his first wife (whom I cannot recall meeting, or even seeing in a photograph) had died early, after producing a family of three or four. The union with Aunt Mary had been more prolific, and she had had eight children, seven of them girls. The first family were on the whole significantly older than the children in our own family (though my sisters were close enough in years to have something in common with them); it was the second family that we got to know best, simply because they were similar in age to ourselves. The youngest girl in this second family would have been slightly younger than myself; the eldest girl perhaps ten years older. When I went there at about the age of ten, it meant that there were seven or eight attractive young women, aged from ten to twenty, in or around the house.

   My uncle's second marriage (I gathered from hints dropped and overheard) had been a little controversial. Mary had been his house-keeper while his first wife had been alive, and he had married her, after a decent interval, on the death of the first wife. The controversy arose, as far as I recall, because he had, as the unforgiving formula has it, 'married beneath him'. I know that I, who admired him anyway, admired him all the more when I heard that. He was right, I felt, to ignore the conventions, and to marry (as every outward sign seemed to attest) for love. In any case, I had a great affection for Aunt Mary, who belonged, in my eyes, to that special band of gentle and maternal women of whom the exemplar was my own mother. I had reason to believe, also, that my uncle had not forgotten his first wife. On one memorable occasion, I accompanied him (and for some reason it was only I) on a walk to his first wife's grave. The spring sunshine blessed our steps, as we proceeded in a silence that, in retrospect, strikes me as reverential; until we reached the grave and he lowered his tall form into a kneeling position. I joined him, hoping that my actions were worthy of the occasion. In the stillness that followed, the light wind stirred his hair as it stirred the grasses on the grave; and I could hear the sporadic calls of the crows, and once a sigh from the tall kneeling figure beside me. Then we returned the way we had come.

I can best describe my Uncle Johnny by saying that he was, in every feature, like an elongated version of my father – including his face. He was significantly taller, with an upright carriage and a patriarchal bearing; though I must pause here to ask what I mean by 'patriarchal'. He had, I suppose, an air of quiet authority, a self-possession which, it seemed, nothing could ruffle; and the authority was confirmed by his stature. His long gaunt face was earnest and surprisingly open, a little hardened by exposure to the weather, and in my mind peculiarly associated with the images I have seen of the long stone-carved faces of mysterious origin that are found on Easter Island.

He had the countryman's resigned acceptance of the uncontrollable ways of nature, but he was willing to provide, nonetheless, an eloquent commentary on the world around him. It was usually an interesting experience to go out walking with him, for he would keep up a running commentary on this or that as it presented itself to his view in the open fields. Once, for example, he pointed out a calf that had been born blind; it stumbled in its bafflement at the entrance-gate to the field, clumsily churning up the mud, a mute and uncomplaining victim of Nature. Uncle Johnny spoke of its plight with a countryman's detachment; and there was only the slightest regret in his voice when, removing the pipe from his mouth, he remarked: 'It'll be off to the slaughter-house in a month or so.' Then he put the pipe back in his mouth, and continued on his walk.

Yet he was no stoic, and the wide mouth often broke into laughter. He had a sly sense of humour, and loved telling stories which might end in a sudden revelation that caused him to share the laughter with his auditors. He spoke slowly and deliberately, as if he inhabited a different time-continuum from the rest of us, and was forever unhurried and unconcerned with the passing of time. It was this that contributed to the sense of his inner self-possession; and his large frame (though the impression may have been false) seemed never to have been shaken by ungovernable passion. I knew him, of course, only when he was already well advanced in age; so it is difficult for me to see him as anything other than a tranquil *paterfamilias*. As elder of the tribe, he took it upon himself to transmit orally much of the history of the family, in the form of vivid anecdote (it was he, for example, who relayed the story about the three Cosgrove brothers who had owned good land in County Tyrone, and been chased off it in the late eighteenth century in a Protestant takeover). He was both story-man and history-man, perhaps with something of the gifts of the *seanchaí*, or traditional story-teller, even though he had no acquaintance with the Gaelic tradition to sustain him in that role.

Around the kitchen range, after a brief lull in the conversation, when the silence was richly embalmed in the tobacco-smoke from his pipe and the only sound might be that of the soft shift and dislodgement of the coals in the range's grate, he would start off a story with the usual formula, 'I mind the time, many years ago now...'. Such an idiom ('mind' for 'remember') came naturally to him; and on one occasion he provided me, quite inadvertently, with a justification of one feature, at least, of the style employed by Synge in *The Playboy of the Western World*.

There had been an amateur drama festival in the Newry Town Hall, and among the performances was one of Synge's play, which (as much out of reverence for 'an Irish masterpiece' as anything else) I dutifully attended. I did not much care for what I saw and heard (and, in fact, still don't warm to the play, though I can find much to admire).

The following Monday we returned to school, and one of our most 'hobbyhorsical' Christian Brothers (a Cavanman, rabidly Nationalist, who always had a bee in his bonnet about something), decided on this occasion to take issue with the 'nonsense' Synge had inflicted upon us. It was, among other things, a reminder that those aspects of the play which had given rise to a riot on the opening night at the Abbey Theatre in 1907 could still prove a severe provocation to an Irish Nationalist of a particular stamp. The Brother focused his attack on the way 'ordinary, decent Irish people' were represented as speaking in *The Playboy*.

'"Till Tuesday was a week",' he quoted from the play in scathing tones. 'Where in heaven's name has anyone in Ireland ever spoken like that? Or' (with equally sardonic emphasis) '"*since* Tuesday was a week"! Did you ever in your life hear such words fall from the lips of anybody you are actually acquainted with? *Did* you?'

This was not a man you disagreed with, if you could at all avoid doing so. We all dutifully shook our heads. No, of course we hadn't! *Nobody* in Ireland spoke like that. But not long afterwards, on a visit to Lislea, I heard my uncle speaking about the harvest. The weather had been unusually dry and sunny. 'And,' he concluded, 'we had the hay saved since last Friday was a fortnight.'

I cannot help wondering if, in some sense, my affectionate regard for my Uncle Johnny constituted a subtle betrayal of my father. Should I plead guilty to the charge of transferring to my uncle the ideal father-image which his large and seemingly unshakeable frame more easily sustained? The case being, of course, that such an ideal paternity was so immediately attachable to him because he was an icon, seen from a distance, as it were, rather than (as my father was) an intimately known and imperfect human being. Yet I want to believe that there was room enough in my heart for both of them, and that, up to the end, it was essential that I establish a good relationship with my father.

It was easy to retain positive memories not just of my uncle (and aunt) in Lislea, but of the many experiences there. For we went to visit, after all, in holiday mood, on a Sunday outing, and their hospitality ensured that we were never disappointed. Besides the story-telling and the general 'craic', there was from time to time a female visitor who could read your fortune from the tea-leaves left in your cup (a tradition that has, alas, been almost abolished because, in the relentless march of progress, we now use tea-bags more often than not). My sisters and the other girls of marriageable or near-marriageable age would crowd round the gifted visitor, one of the main purposes of the interpretation of the augury of the tea-leaves being to discover what kind of man they would marry.

I cannot be sure that this display of female energy and enterprise was a significant and gratifying revelation of the nature of the opposite sex; though it may be that we males were at some level affected by the vague erotic excitement. What did certainly affect us, however, was the enveloping omnipresence of those youthful female cousins, all in their way striking or pretty, and illustrating in such variety the delectable nature of the female. Here, as almost nowhere else, do I despair of finding a language adequate to the experience.

In those less politically correct days, the daughters of the house in Lislea would attend on us at table while we, privileged as 'the visitors', had our evening meal in the large kitchen with the flagstone floor. Our appetites sharpened by an unusually sustained exposure to fresh air (we would have played around the farmyard, visiting some of the animals in the barn and elsewhere, or walked along the local lanes and boreens), we would sit down to the ritual of the evening meal, trying to resist the urge (such was our hunger) to spoil the sense of ritual by gobbling all before us. Sometimes, as I sat there trying to be patient, I would cup my hands over my mouth and nose, and smell the peculiar 'country smell' that those hands had somehow picked up in the course of the day – as if, on our walks through the countryside, the wind and grass and hedges had wooed the natural sweat, and had lovingly mingled with that their own vital life. The meal would be a kind of 'high tea', consisting of ham salad with a number of accompaniments (hard-boiled egg, potato salad), fresh brown bread and 'country' butter with its strong and salty flavour, and pots of dark hot tea.

The meal itself (the same kind of meal my mother would place before 'special' visitors, such as the parish priest) was particularly welcome, given our appetites; but nothing was more wondrous than to have that swirl of female solicitation for one's welfare all around as we ate, with soft voices enquiring as to our needs, and even softer hands doing everything to supply them. It was doubtless part of their appeal that their exotic femaieness (strangely and fascinatingly different for the male adolescent) was firmly rooted in the mundane immediacy of domestic routine, the ordinary rhythms of dining-room and kitchen. And if the presiding female deity at the seaside was Aphrodite, perhaps the substantial and attractive young women who moved around us with easy, instinctive elegance and such unselfconscious grace in the timeless country dining-room were avatars of some earth-goddess (whether from Celtic or some other pagan mythology, I am in no position to say).

We can all, of course, be betrayed by the idealising memory. I see these young women as rooted in domestic reality, but the backward look may be throwing upon them the glow of a glamorising imagination. If I find it difficult to find a language adequate to the rich depth of feeling such memories evoke, the problem may arise from the fact that I am attempting to describe something that, in a strict sense, never was (and perhaps never will be). It may be, too, that most Irishmen of my own and the previous generation are initially disposed in any case to idealise rural simplicity (and perhaps the English, though from a different cultural perspective, do something similar in their invocations of pastoralism in literature, especially in the Victorian age, and in their persistent evocation of the 'green hills' of England).

I do not here mean the deliberate or programmatic exaltation of the 'Irish peasant' we associate with Yeats and Synge and the Anglo-Irish Literary Revival, but something that is more deeply rooted in the Irish psyche. It emerges powerfully in Frank O'Connor's short story 'Uprooted'. Ned, a teacher and a city-dweller, returns to his rural origins from Dublin, and falls in love with the way of life which circumstances have led him to abandon. Unmarried, he sees in a local girl, Cait, a woman he might have married (or might still marry). But as the story's title suggests, he has been irrevocably cut off from his roots. To his brother Tom's earnest question, 'Why don't you marry her, Ned?' he can only reply: 'No… We made our choice a long time ago. We can't go back on it now.'

The story ends with Ned's recognition that in this simple rural existence 'a magical light' falls on everything; but it is a magic he must leave behind:

> Magic, magic, magic! He saw it as in a children's picture-book with all its colours intolerably bright; something he had outgrown and could never return to… It seemed as if only now for the first time was he leaving home; for the first time and forever saying good-bye to it all.

Yet I refuse to accept that my memory has played tricks on me where Lislea is concerned. Unlike the protagonist of O'Connor's story, I have no painful feelings of nostalgia for that way of life, but remain deeply grateful for the education it provided; and grateful in particular for the perspective those real-ideal young female cousins gave me on the nature of womanhood. For besides the fact that in their beauty they integrated, for me, the ideal and the actual (or, if you prefer, showed me the ideal fully anchored in the ordinary and the domestic), they also pointed the way towards a healing of that split between the erotic and the loving-affectionate which was to be threatened by my experience when I visited the cinema along with my mother – that episode, I mean, when I was so powerfully attracted towards the sensual image on the screen (the image of Lena Horne). The tendency in such a process (one that is inevitable, since the sexualised male must break away from the mother) is for a gulf to open up between such nascent sexuality and the loving-kindness associated with the now abandoned maternal figure. In the most extreme version of this sundering, sex becomes one thing, 'love' something else.

Four or five of the daughters of the house in Lislea were close enough in age to be in fairly constant social relationship with myself and my brothers; and I saw before me there young women who were erotically appealing yet attached to me by genuine bonds of cousinly affection. They offered, not fantasy-images as in the cinema, but real and immediate embodiments of female beauty in a multiplicity of forms, all in varying degrees fascinating and delectable; and, equally important, they generated the essential and integrated awareness that women were capable of both sexual appeal and loving-kindness.

Once in particular I found myself carried away by the appeal of the occasion; and the focus of my attention was the youngest girl, the one who was close in age to myself. We had already gone outside into the front yard, and should have been preparing to load ourselves into the taxi, when I was seized by an irresistible urge to return and say goodbye to her. I think that all I did was enter and take her hand in mine, there where she stood with her sisters in a row. The action was sufficiently unusual, however, to provoke murmurs and subdued teasing exclamations from her siblings; for it was clear that the gesture was on my part very deliberate. Perhaps, too, I gazed on her in a special way. She herself, the object of my attention, was probably both pleased and embarrassed to be singled out in this unexpected way; but they were all of them tolerant and amused, for I had already the reputation among them of being 'intellectual' (it may have been at the time of my last or second-last year at school, when I was fifteen or sixteen) and therefore 'a bit strange'.

I did not regret my behaviour as an act of folly, but retained in my memory the soft pressure of her hand in mine, my hold on that real and substantial warmth. Perhaps, like Mr Knightley in the famous scene in *Emma* when he visits Emma after he has reprimanded her for her behaviour at the Box Hill picnic, I half-meant to raise her hand to my lips, but then thought better of it. I had paid the price of self-exposure; but, although nothing was to come of it, I had at least established vital contact.

*

I remained, nonetheless, a slow learner where women were concerned. When I first came across that remark about women and goddesses in the letters of Keats, I clearly recognised my own tendency. In my first year at university, as a rather shy and nervous seventeen-year-old, I worshipped from afar a very pretty young woman called Jo; but of course could not bring myself to speak to her or even look her in the eyes. Instead, I indulged in absurd and private literary outpourings which did not merit the name of verse, let alone poetry. There was some excuse for that nonsense in the fact of my raw youth; but the truth is that even later in my undergraduate career I could still worship from afar a young woman from my home town and, when she appeared to 'spurn' me, again resort to a pathetic poetic outpouring, this time undertaken with something like masochistic relish.

But by the time I reached my late teens or the age of twenty, I had begun to deal more successfully in substance. I have on more than one level reason to be grateful to the God who made me for my rude capacity to enjoy (in spite of that stubborn and sometimes sullen Hamlet in my nature) the pleasures of appetite; and when I came across the term 'high animal spirits' in my reading of eighteenth-century literature, I had a good idea what was meant. I am grateful, too, for the education provided not by, but in, the cinema, especially in the 'back stalls'.

It was an established and accepted convention that the stalls at the back of the balcony, which were not overlooked by any of the other patrons, provided the best opportunity for a male and female to get to know each other (where the verb 'to know' does not quite carry its Biblical connotation, but is heading in that direction). Some of the cinemas had even thoughtfully provided 'love-seats', that is to say, a seat for two with no inconvenient barrier between the occupants. The back stalls, then, were the place where the 'coortin' couples' went, and if you managed to persuade a young woman to join you in that situation, you were (as the saying was) 'laughin', boy!'

When I was about twenty I was 'doing a line' with an attractive young nurse, and we seemed to be hitting it off. One evening I was indeed able to book two seats for us in the back row of the balcony in the Savoy, and from tentatively exploratory beginnings we ended up in a clinch (or series of clinches). As a very othodox Catholic who went regularly to confession, I felt obliged, the following Saturday, to tell all about it (or at least as much as was necessary) to the priest in the confessional. He plainly advised me not only that what I was doing was sinful, but that I should be careful in future not to put myself in such 'an occasion of sin'. Did I mean, he wanted to know, to see this girl again? Yes, I did intend to go out with her the following week. Then be careful, he repeated, to 'avoid the occasion'. Did I understand what he meant?

'Yes, Father, I do.'

'For your penance, say three decades of the Rosary' (a stiff sentence!).

There is a splendid sequence in Muriel Spark's early novel, *The Bachelors*, in which one of the young men, a scrupulous Catholic, is looking forward to a rendezvous with a young woman whom he really fancies. He fears, however, that he is entering into an occasion of sin, and consequently feels obliged to take precautions against a temptation that might otherwise prove too much for him. So he hits on the idea of eating raw onion in sufficient quantities to poison his breath and thereby render initial intimacies out of the question. He visits her in her place of residence, where they are, as he has known in advance, alone together. Her response to his oniony breath, however, is ironically just the opposite of what he had intended. It turns out that she has had in the recent past a boyfriend who used to eat raw onions and of whom she still retains passionate memories. The young man's carefully cultivated 'turn-off' proves to be a potent aphrodisiac, and his fate is sealed.

My own experience was not quite as ironic, but reveals in a different way what may befall 'the best-laid plans'. I was to take the nurse to the Savoy on the Friday evening following the confession, and I accepted that I must heed the priest's warning. So this time, while I did in fact book the seats in the balcony (the best seats in the house), I deliberately chose seats well away from the back, so that we would not be as readily exposed to temptation. The lights went down, our hands became entwined, we leaned towards each other, my arm went around her shoulder (the classic position) and our lips met. And met again. And again. The film we were supposed to be watching was (I can never forget the title) *North to Alaska*. To this day I have only the vaguest idea of what it is about; I was far removed from Alaska in that cinema-seat, and had entered a much more torrid zone. Later I was to reflect (in the coolness of retrospective appraisal) that by choosing to occupy seats in full view of other patrons I had not only *not* avoided the occasion of sin, but had compounded my guilt by 'giving scandal' (for, as I might now say with Matthew Arnold, 'rigorous teachers' had 'seized my youth', and, showing me according to their own lights 'the high, white star of Truth', had drilled these theological discriminations into me).

But I still have a great fondness for the song, 'North to Alaska', which was the only part of the film which broke through to my inflamed consciousness, and blended with our forbidden and blissful embraces.

North to Alaska, by the way, lasts over two hours.

CHAPTER SEVEN

School

I was educated by the Christian Brothers, at both primary and secondary levels, which means that, firstly, I was given an uncompromisingly Nationalist view of Irish history and of 'perfidious Albion'; and secondly was on a number of occasions the reluctant witness (though thank God rarely the victim) of sadistic punishment. Not all the Christian Brothers were rabidly Nationalist, though some certainly were, and all would have been proud of being Irish. They did their utmost to impart to us that pride in our national identity, and doubtless had some effect. Was it, I wonder, in part because of their influence that, when the time came for me to choose a Confirmation name, I deliberately decided on 'Patrick'?

The underside of this staunch Nationalism was rather less acceptable; and part of our essential education (and the challenge of 'growing up'), especially in our teens, was to learn to distinguish between a justifiable pride in being Irish, and, at the extreme end of that same spectrum, a xenophobic hatred of all things British (it was with considerable relish that our history teacher would quote that dictum borrowed from Jonathan Swift and handed down from one Irish generation to the next: 'burn everything that comes from England except their coals'). So we were subjected (and that, given our lack of authority in the classroom situation, is the accurate way of putting it) to a powerful and largely unthinking denunciation of the whole of British culture (except, perhaps, where occasionally there surfaced an Englishman who could be recommended as 'a good Catholic', such as G. K. Chesterton).

You were interested in soccer? (And in my late teens there was good reason to be so, given that one of the stars on the Northern Ireland soccer team – soon, in 1958, to distinguish itself at the World Cup finals in Sweden – was the Newry-born striker, Peter McParland, who played for Aston Villa.) That, we were informed in the most caustic tones, was a game for 'corner-boys', for effete and pasty-faced city-dwellers who were deficient in the manly athleticism of our own Gaelic footballers and, supremely, of our heroic practitioners of the ancient game of hurling, which went back to the dawn of Irish history, and had been played by no less a figure than the great Cuchullain. Rugby was dismissed as being 'neither one thing nor the other'; the idea of throwing the ball around! Did you ever in your life see such codology?

As for (and here the Brother in question seemed to have difficulty in bringing himself even to pronounce the word) *cricket*, well, God help us every one if that's a game at all! Could anyone who took time to sit down and think about it, devoting his entire ingenuity and energy to the project, come up with a duller or more tedious game? Hour after hour, day after day, and as much excitement as a maiden aunt's tea-party! Look at hurling, now, by contrast; if you wanted a sport that involved a ball and stick (or bat), where would you find the equal of hurling for speed and skill, the coordination under pressure – under *physical* pressure, mind, with your opponent ready to pounce and tackle – of eye and hand? But sure God love the English, they've never seen hurling. And cricket is just the kind of game for the cold-blooded race that tried – and tried in vain – to impose their petty will on the civilised world!

I see this now as an important part of our education; for we were forever being required to make intelligent discriminations and (under pressure to conform) to work things out for ourselves. Thus, it certainly was true that, once you had seen it, you had to admit that hurling was a great game; and we 'townies' had to restrain ourselves (given that we lived in the southern part of County Down, where hurling was practically unknown) from dismissing it as a sport for rustics in remotest Tipperary or Kilkenny. In fact, we learned to appreciate, for example, the legendary Rackard brothers, who played for Wexford, and about whose exploits we could read in the *Evening Press* (my father kept his bar well stocked with newspapers). But it wasn't necessary to dismiss cricket in order to enjoy hurling. They were very distinct games, with different kinds of appeal; and if you felt the appeal of cricket (which, somewhat surprisingly, given my Nationalist background, I early came to enjoy), you did not, on the other side, have to reject hurling. So in this way the enforced assessment of the 'either/or' mentality in sport, foisted vigorously upon us by our teachers, not only educated us away from narrow views in that particular sphere, but prepared us for a spirit of pluralistic acceptance in other matters as well. This, I am now inclined to believe, was one of the major challenges of growing up non-British in a predominantly British culture; and if you 'passed the test', so to speak, you could count yourself the beneficiary of the best that the liberal project of education has to offer.

A similar challenge to accurate or unbiased assessment was posed by further sweeping dismissals of the British and all their works and pomps. We would be assured, for example, in the usual dogmatic tones (which, in our later years at school, we clearly recognised as dogmatic, and among ourselves parodied as such), that the English 'had no sense of humour' ('Did you ever see them travelling on the London Underground? Not a peep out of any of them. They haven't, God help their wit, a word to throw at a dog! And when would you *ever* see Irish people behave in that inhuman and antisocial manner? Neither wit nor humour, the whole sorry lot of them!'). Yet perhaps that same evening (if it were a Tuesday) we would all go home and listen to the uproarious *Goon Show* on the BBC Home Service. Next day there would be the usual replays of what Bluebottle had said to Eccles, and Eccles's reply, with all of us trying to get the voices right (as, doubtless, our contemporaries were doing at the very same time on the neighbouring island). Obviously, the English *did* have a sense of humour; and this was one of many instances when, on the basis of our own independent experience, we had to learn to re-evaluate the anti-British bias of our schooling.

It is probably the case that, faced with these recurrent choices and discriminations, many of us developed a habitual detachment which functioned as a prelude to ironic awareness. If it is true that Northern Irish people (especially the often wickedly witty inhabitants of Belfast) have a peculiarly developed sense of humour, the explanation for that may lie in this: that one natural response to a fractured culture, in which the claims on one's loyalties are so incongruous and diverse, is ironic laughter at the unresolvable conflict. Certainly a number of my contemporaries, especially the more intelligent, developed an increasingly ironic sense of humour, especially as they matured towards the end of their schooldays. The irony was doubtless sometimes bitter (perhaps directed against the perceived inadequacies of the Catholic Church, which might appear to be out of touch with the 'real' world of modernity); but it also funtioned as a safeguard against the teaching of a Catholic religious order which had no compunction about resorting to a well-stocked legacy of political and, indeed, racist clichés.

Alas for some of my schoolmates, not all of us developed that self-protective irony which allowed us to distance ourselves from the raw propagandist rhetoric of some of our teachers. We had one history teacher in particular, the Christian Brother from County Cavan already mentioned, who derived from his origins in that region which is just across the border from Northern Ireland a Nationalist fervour which, at his most heated (which was most of the time), became a more rabid Republicanism. I can still recall how, at the height of his fulminations against the British, from 'Lizzie' (Elizabeth I) or Cromwell to Lloyd George and beyond, he would crown his argument in these uncompromising terms, and with a terrible emphasis: 'Time and time again, throughout our history, it has been clear that there is only one way to deal with the British. The only way, as our sad and sorry history has time after time proved, and the record is there for all to see – the only way is' (pause) 'the gun!' And this climactic phrase would be repeated like a deadly mantra, both in that lesson and in subsequent ones.

There can be little doubt that whether or not we are to see this history teacher as a recruiting sergeant for the IRA (who ran an abortive but nonetheless destructive and bloody campaign in the 1950s), he succeeded in urging some of my contemporaries into a more militant political position than they would otherwise have held. One contemporary or near-contemporary (he was not in my class) blew himself to pieces while priming a bomb just across the border from Newry on the way to Dundalk. It would be unfair to lay the blame for his death at the door of the Brother of whom I speak; the boy in question came from a family with a hardline Republican attitude. But, looking back, I am appalled at the naked fervour of the Republican rhetoric to which that Christian Brother subjected an impressionable group of teenagers in his charge. It remains, for me, one of the most glaring instances of pedagogic irresponsibility.

That Brother was, of course, exceptional in the degree of his political militancy, and few of the other members of the order would go that far. Equally, it would be a distortion to imply that they were all a gang of sadists, who got their 'kicks' from beating and humiliating the young boys who were at their mercy in the classroom. Many of them were not only splendid and dedicated teachers, but were both conscientious and humane. Nevertheless, I shall until the end of my days retain the memory of scenes of brutality which made me shudder, and still shock me in the recall.

The major problem for many of the Brothers was that they did not have a true vocation for the role that they were intended to play. For a number of them, it was not only that they had no commitment to the demanding and exhausting job of educating boys, many of whom had no wish to be educated. That made things tough enough for them, and they struggled both with the subject they were expected to have mas-tered (Latin or maths or whatever) and with the recalcitrant youths who gazed up at them (often with blank faces) from serried rows of desks. But even tougher for some of them was the fact that they had no sense of vocation to the entire lifestyle foisted upon them.

They were celibate, and lived in an all-male community according to the strictest vow of poverty; they had neither worldly possessions nor even (and here was the additional rub) the kind of respectability that in Ireland and elsewhere accompanies (or used to accompany) the title of 'Father'. For they were clearly not priests; they did not say mass, hear confessions, or preach to a submissive congregation from the pulpit or the altar. It might be said that they had all the disadvantages of being priests (celibacy, the exclusion from the warmth of family life), but without the attendant compensations (spiritual and social prestige). One would need to enter into that kind of commitment entirely of one's own volition, and with the open eyes of maturity, to understand well in advance the kind of lifelong sacrifices involved. But while many of them did enter on those terms, there were others who, carried away by adolescent enthusiasm, gave a premature commitment; while of others it was darkly muttered that they were Christian Brothers only because their families had insisted on it. In one case, the rumour was that one of the Brothers who taught in our school – a man who looked like a follower of Dionysus condemned to wear the incongruous black of the order – had been obliged to join up because he had been adopted, and the 'deal' had been that the adoption would proceed only on the understanding that he would end up as a Brother.

In fairness, then, one should distinguish between those members of the order who were contented with their vocation – usually dedicated and civilised – and those who, deeply frustrated by the position they found themselves in, took a sadistic delight in venting their frustrations on their pupils. It was not so long ago that the Head of the Christian Brothers in Ireland felt obliged to issue a public apology to all those pupils who had over the years been physically or sexually abused by the order. I am happy to report that (in spite of the recent proliferation of evidence of sexual scandals involving Catholic priests and other celibate orders, many of these going back a number of years), I had absolutely no experience of sexual abuse, and have little or no reason to believe that any of us were subjected to such treatment. Yet physical abuse there certainly was; and one example in particular (involving again, as it happens, the Brother from Cavan), I feel obliged to put on the record. It is painful for me to have to relive it (even though, mercifully, I was not the victim); but it may also be vaguely therapeutic.

A student of catastrophe theory would find rich pickings in the complex of circumstances which eventuated in this particular explosion of violence, for events conspired to produce an almost inevitable devastation. First, because the school had set aside certain assigned teaching periods for the inculcation of Religious Knowledge, the time lost had to be made up by bringing us (at that time thirteen- and fourteen-year-olds) into school on a Saturday morning. Both the teacher and ourselves had the feeling that there were better ways to spend a Saturday, and it may be that the restlessness and disaffection commonly present in boys of that age were further exacerbated by the sense that it was in the first instance unjust to deprive us of a portion of our weekend.

Add to this circumstance the fact that the subject to be taught, over two consecutive periods in the mid-morning and without a break, was trigonometry, and that this was, moreover, our first brush with what was a new and difficult branch of mathematics, and the possibility of catastrophe deepens. Then note the final fatal ingredient: not only was our Cavan teacher a man perpetually on a short fuse, but at this period in his life he was suffering from acute sinusitis. So the outburst was, in a sense, predictable. Yet, when it did come, nothing could have prepared us for the shock of it.

The victim was Niall Kelly, a most likeable youth, without malice, but utterly devoid, also, of anything approaching academic ability. Niall was usually astute enough to keep out of big trouble; but if he did get into hot water, he usually took his punishment (perhaps a few 'biffs' from the leather strap on his open palms) with an amiable stoicism, remaining unruffled by what was a recurrent event. Perhaps it was this very imperviousness that drew down on his head the full wrath of our frustrated trigonometry teacher, himself the victim of his painful sinuses and resolved to create a fellow-victim.

The sequence began innocently enough. It was clear to most of us that the teacher was in a worse mood than usual; and when we failed to answer to his satisfaction the questions he put to the class, he decided to pick on Niall. At first Niall was allowed to answer from his seat at the desk; but since his answers continued to be wide of the mark, and the anger and frustration of the Brother grew, he was ordered to stand out in front of the blackboard. It was then that the sustained inquisition began.

The teacher draws a triangle on the board, and marks one of the angles on it. Then the first question.

'This is a triangle. This is the angle in question. How do we get the sine of that angle?'

Silence from Niall: he has no idea. A slap to the back of his head from the hand of the teacher. We begin to feel anxious.

'I am asking you again. How do we get the sine? What is the procedure?'

Niall mumbles.

'Speak up!' Another slap to the head.

Niall clears his throat. 'We get …we get the length of one side and …'

'Yes? We're all waiting.'

'The length of one side and the length of another, and add the two.'

'No, we do *not*!' Another slap.

One or two boys in the front rows are shooting up their hands. They know the answer, and expect that they will be invited to give it. But the obsessive Christian Brother is determined to keep the victim in his sights:

'Sit down! Let Kelly answer.'

Niall is looking lost, sheepish. He has nothing to say. Another slap. The next question is delivered with an exaggerated emphasis on the individual words.

'How – do – we – obtain – the – sine – of – the – angle?'

Niall is slow to reply. The situation is increasingly ominous.

'I don't know, sir.'

Another teacher (perhaps, even, this same teacher on a different day) might have commended Niall for his honesty. But on this occasion the answer, given, it must be said, with Niall's general air of insouciance and imperturbability, serves only to stoke further the fires of the teacher's wrath. Two or three boys titter, perhaps out of nervousness. That is the last straw.

'So, we don't know and we don't care, is that it? *Is that it?*'

The final words are accompanied with a lunge at Niall and a ringing slap on his ear. What stuns us is not just the viciousness of the slap but the sudden realisation that Niall is no longer unperturbed. He is looking down the barrel of a shotgun, and the recognition of his plight is beginning to dawn on him.

It is still, at this distance, painful to report that the systematic interrogation and beating of Niall went on for a whole hour or more; while the rest of us, in an unholy silence broken only by the slaps and thumps and, eventually, the sobs of Niall as he collapsed into a shivering human mess, looked mutely on. I suspect that a deep and subtle shame, even if we did not at the time name it as such, began to pervade the entire class. There was first of all the obscenity of seeing, of all people, Niall, he who had borne so much punishment before this without the least compromise to his innate strength and dignity, stripped naked of those attributes for which he was most admired. This was no longer Niall, but an unrecognisably pathetic and broken creature, reduced to snivelling inarticulacy. And there followed on from this a sense of guilt, tinged by frustrated rage, that not one of us had the authority to intervene and end the display of savagery that had unfolded before us.

Wherever you now find yourself, Niall, I am moved, even at this late date, to plead for your forgiveness. For, it might be argued, all of us collectively owe you that belated apology. Forgive us our weakness, our inadequate reaction, our collective lack of self-assertion. Even now I do not know if Niall Kelly recovered from that awful mauling; though when I see him in my mind's eye, I think of him, still, as the living embodiment of that *Mad* magazine portrait of Alfred E. Neuman (a copy of which my father hung up at the back of our bar), under which is written: 'What, me worry?'

*

I was fortunate at school in that I was usually able to produce a good or at least acceptable performance in most of the subjects we were taught. There were, though, some exceptions. I never did get the hang of science, and more or less gave it up in despair after I had tried and failed repeatedly to understand the difference between density and specific gravity (I am willing at this stage to believe that the failure was in part at least attributable to poor teaching). I struggled, too, with both geography and geometry. Perhaps my problems with geometry arose from a very limited capacity for abstract analysis. The truth is that I was always more attracted to the immediacy of the concrete, the vivid image or symbol, the powerful description or evocation of person, landscape or event.

It is that, I now think, which accounts for the fact that one of my favourite parables was that of the Sower and the Seed, as recounted in the Gospel of St Luke which we read as part of our second-year course in Religious Knowledge. I was only twelve years of age, but I responded instinctively to the neat structure of the narrative. Four brief and precise images are given, in three of which the seed fails to prosper, followed by one in which it yields fruit 'a hundredfold'. Then comes the equally precise explanation as to what each allegorical image (still kept vividly before us) means: the seed is the word of God, the rock where it fails to take root stands for those whose reception of the word of God is too shallow to last, the thorns which stifle the growth of the seed are 'the cares and riches and pleasures of life', and so on. That intuitive sense of the lovely correlation between the image and the meaning of the allegory (between, as I was later to learn, 'vehicle' and 'tenor') was one of my earliest experiences of literary-critical perception. I enjoyed learning that parable off by heart and reproducing it in the examination.

The more a subject approached the conditions of abstract summation, the less likely I was to care for it. Thus, although I did manage to do reasonably well in history, I was thoroughly bored by it, especially as it was conveyed in the pages of the set textbooks (one on Britain, the other on Europe) by G. W. Southgate. He seemed to allow not at all for the force of human personality or for the unforeseeable event or intervention, but gave you history as the achieved record of something that was fully explicable in a series of dry facts. It is my recollection that interpretation was minimal, and this catalogue of salient historical happenings was unenlivened by anything as risky as speculation. To make matters worse, he added as an appendix to this deadly anatomisation an even more skeletal summary consisting of bare dates and the brief records of the main events. This, naturally enough from the teacher's point of view, was what we were expected to commit to memory. I rapidly reached the point where I could not give a tuppenny curse about the contribution of the spinning jenny to the progress of the Industrial Revolution; I could not care less when Robespierre came to power during the French Revolution, nor whether a Girondin was more or less moderate than a Jacobin.

I now know, thanks in part to television documentaries and biographies of the politically powerful, that there is much more to history than the dull diet of facts fed to us by Southgate. Yet I still retain a sense that history (or indeed politics) is simply not as interesting for me as it is for many others. If, as Aristotle suggests and Sir Philip Sidney confirms, literature's first cousins are history and philosophy, then my instinctive preference is for the speculative freedom of the latter; and I am, more-over, far more fascinated by myth than by history.

In my penultimate year at school, I indulged my imaginative freedom and escaped from the intolerable statistical factuality of Southgate whenever and wherever I could. We were fortunate to have for our study of Latin a little anthology filled with short extracts from Ovid, Virgil and Horace as well as from Latin prose, many of which were as vivid as they were brief. One excerpt from Ovid dealt with the consequences of the flood sent by Zeus and survived by Deucalion. How much more appeal-ing than all the facts of history were those few lines of poetry, and how much more did they offer to the imagination! Ovid describes how a soli-tary bird flies back and forth across the wholly submerged surface of the earth, looking in vain for even one station on which it might perch; until, exhausted, it falls inexorably into the waters:

> *Quaesitisque diu terris, ubi sistere possit*
> *In mare lassatis volucris vaga decidit alis.*

('And having for a long time searched for land on which he might rest, the wandering bird falls, with weary wings, into the sea.')

I found that succinct image full of inexhaustible implication, and it tired my own imagination as much as it tired the wings of the unfortu-nate bird when I attempted to comprehend the immensity of that earth-concealing deluge. Although I did not know it at the time, this was my first encounter with that aesthetic category, found in literature but also in the pictorial and plastic arts, known as the sublime. The effect arises when the mind confronts an immensity (perhaps the sea or the immea-surable Alpine ranges) which it cannot assimilate or wholly come to terms with. In the Romantic version of the encounter with the sublime, the imagination loses its grip upon the empirical world that is normally there to 'anchor' it to reality, soars beyond that usual reality, and, in Wordsworth's phrase, 'feeds upon infinity' – a dizzying but exhilarating experience. I was always instinctively, it seems, on the side of imagina-tion over boring old reality; and what I was avid for was the vicarious intensity the literary text could provide.

*

One of my earliest enthusiasms in literature was for Shelley's lyric, 'To Night', which begins, compellingly, 'Swiftly walk o'er the western wave,/ Spirit of Night!...'. At the age of fifteen, when I was at the beginning of the senior cycle, I submitted an essay on the poem to a gifted and dedicated teacher of English (a Christian Brother from Kilkenny). The script was returned to me with a number of positive comments, and larded with a wealth of approving ticks. It was, for me, something of a breakthrough; for not only had I myself been deeply stirred by a poem, but I had managed to express my strong feelings within the formal discipline of the school essay.

I fear, in retrospect, that in my adolescent response to Shelley's lyric I may have been unwittingly guilty of that fallacious estimate which Matthew Arnold calls the 'personal' (that is, overvaluing a work because 'our personal affinities, likings, and circumstances...make us attach more importance to it as poetry than in itself it really possesses'). It was undoubtedly the case that I was reacting not only to the sweeping alliteration of those opening lines, but also, in my teenage condition (my 'personal circumstances' at the time), to the erotic stimulus of such lines as 'Blind with your hair the eyes of day:/ Kiss her until she be wearied out...'. The fact that I can still, after four decades, quote these lines from memory is suspicious (for I am not a great memoriser of verse); and, if I am honest, I have to acknowledge also how disturbed I was about the same time by Robert Browning's 'Porphyria's Lover':

> She put my arm about her waist,
> And made her smooth white shoulder bare,
> And all her yellow hair displaced,
> And, stooping, made my cheek lie there ...

The supreme challenge in this regard, however, was provided by the sudden appearance in the same school year of the first female teacher in our classroom. She was married, but young; also, God between us and all harm, blonde. I seem to remember sitting in a state of delightful awkwardness as she bent down over me to correct what I had been writing (in French: she was replacing our usual French teacher for a year). The thought that her body was so close, and might even fleetingly touch mine, was a source of fearful fascination.

The following year my commitment to English literature was more or less definitively sealed, and my fate decided, when we studied Shakespeare's *King Lear.* I had some years earlier enjoyed *Julius Caesar,* but only up to a point: I thought that Antony's speeches to the mob after he has carried out the body of the dead Caesar were extremely clever, and I hugely enjoyed the black-and-white movie (Marlon Brando as Antony) we were encouraged to go and see. But perhaps my imagination was more readily drawn to the storm scene in Act One, Scene Three, 'when the cross blue lightning seemed to open/ The breast of heaven'; or else to the tense and emotionally charged exchanges between Brutus and Cassius in Act Four, when both men indulge their 'rash choler' and magnificently quarrel. If this was the kind of 'strong meat' on which my imagination wished to batten, I found it to the *n*th degree in *King Lear,* and I savoured not only the cataclysm of the storm, but the emotional intensities of a great family quarrel on a scale that matched the wildness of the elements.

In my final year at school I took three subjects (English, French and Latin) at Advanced Level, in what was known as the Senior Certificate (which operated not in the UK generally, but in Northern Ireland only). Given that in many ways my love of Latin was the only serious competitor with my passion for English literature, I can't help wondering whether I would have studied Latin at university instead of English if I had been allowed to (in those more rigorous days, you could study Latin at third level only if you took Greek along with it, and our school did not teach the subject at all). One obvious appeal of Latin, for me, was that, unlike French, you never had to speak it: I have always been a very middling kind of linguist, and even though I make a point of mastering the grammar and the rules of expression, am rarely fluent. In the case of Latin, I was in addition attracted to its poised and self-assured completeness of statement. I learned to appreciate the rhythmic movement of the Ciceronian period, the way the syntax created pauses and suspensions before the sentence reached a full and definitive closure. Like many others, especially those involved in education, I greatly lament the disappearance of Latin from the school curriculum; it was always one of the best introductions to sentence structure and grammar generally. Is it, one wonders, too late to restore it even now?

*

I was just on my way down the stairs in the house in Newry when a premonition overcame me like Macbeth's 'summer cloud', 'begetting', though, not 'wonder', but a chill sense of unease. I normally do not believe in such preternatural signs and portents, but on this occasion I was proved right. What I dreaded was that the priest who for some weeks had been 'head-hunting' me for the priesthood was about to turn up, once more, on our doorstep. I sensed that he was imminent, as if his will were reaching out at a distance to master my own. Sure enough, I had barely time to interpret my own bleak feelings to myself when the doorbell rang, the inner connecting door to our hall was opened, and there he was, ushered into the house and waiting for me at the foot of the stairs.

I had brought this trouble on myself by my timidity, my lack of decisiveness, my trying to 'have it both ways'. This priest was one of a number of vocation-hunters who visited the school when we were in our mid- or late teens and one or two years away from leaving. We were subjected to cajolements, warnings, and expert rhetorical appeal by these visitants, to whom the senior class or classes were usually given over for a substantial period of twenty or thirty minutes. At the end of the harangue, the procedure then was that the priest gave to each of us in the class a small form, about the size of a prayer-card, which one might insert in one's missal, and perhaps carrying on one side a picture of the Sacred Heart or of Mary Immaculate or a saint who had a special connection with the order in question. You were asked to fill in this form in full confidentiality, the key question which you had there and then to answer being: 'Do you think you have a vocation to the priesthood?' I suspect that some readers will smile at the notion of sacerdotal talent-spotting of this kind, seeing the visiting priest as a 'scout' on the lookout for spiritual promise, but I can assure you that for most of us it was no laughing matter. We were all Catholics of a traditional stamp, in whom had been implanted from a very early age the notion that, in the words of the catechism, our entire duty on earth was 'to know, love and serve God' to the best of our ability; and it had been thoroughly impressed upon us that the highest service we could possibly render our Creator was to devote our lives to the priesthood. We were, moreover, adolescent, idealistic and vulnerable, willing to seize the Great Opportunity for Salvation; or else, on the down side, deeply fearful that, in making the 'wrong' choice and refusing to serve God, we would forever after wander disconsolate through a pointless life, and forfeit, in addition, any chance of eternal happiness.

It is, as usual, James Joyce who captures much of the drama in this representative Irish male Catholic experience, when he has Stephen Dedalus in *A Portrait of the Artist as a Young Man* deliberately choose to turn his back on the Catholic priesthood and opt, instead, for the priesthood of the imagination, the role of artist who engages with the profane or secular world. But Joyce saw the choice in terms very different from those in which it presented itself to me. What Stephen has to resist in the blandishments of the director of vocations is the promise of power and prestige in becoming *Stephen Dedalus S. J.*, a Jesuit priest who would have access to special rituals and would be dramatically invested with the ability to forgive sin. The priesthood never presented itself to me under those positive aspects. It was more a call to absolute self-sacrifice, the death of my sexual life, the banishment from the comfort and security of family home, the abandonment of everything I regarded as normal. It was a plunge into the infrahuman sea of the unknown.

I had usually managed to resist the appeals of the various priestly visitors, and was subsequently able to square my decision with a sometimes hyperactive conscience. But on this occasion I must have been affected by the 'hard sell' of the vocation-hunter. Was I prepared to give up a life of material ease and go abroad (I forget where) and *save souls for Christ?* He impressed upon the class the dire need to bring salvation to a benighted people, and how pitifully few there were, however many might claim to be true Christians, to undertake this essential work. Yes, indeed, the harvest was great, but the labourers few! Was there one of us, or more than one, who could hear within us the call of the Lord – or the call of conscience – inviting us to give our lives for Christ? If that were the case, could we turn away from Him who had given His very life for our sakes? Could we deny Him in return the gift of our own much more imperfect life? And if we were to choose a life of ease and self-indulgence, for the duration of our earthly span – for the brief period of our mortal existence, which seems so long to us, but in comparison with eternity is but the blink of an eye – if, he said, we were to turn away from Christ and reject the appeal of those eyes that had borne so much pain and suffering for our sake – how then in the eternity of our afterlife could we hope to meet His accusing gaze, the gaze of Him before whom the angels, purer by far in their condition than we could ever hope to be, trembled and veiled their eyes!

I was deeply troubled. I did not want to abandon the comforts of my earthly existence at home with my parents and brothers and sisters. To leave forever the comfort of the hearth – it was unthinkable. But how could I act like an ungrateful wretch and ignore the appeal of my Saviour? Did I not at that very moment feel a voice in my conscience rise up against me in the clear tones of accusation? And out of this conflict came the indecisiveness I have spoken of, my attempt to have it both ways. In brief, I kept my options open; and when the little forms with the leading question were distributed, I wrote neither yea nor nay, but a timid 'Perhaps'. It was to prove a costly exercise in hesitancy; for the vocation-hunter, once given his opening, pursued me assiduously for weeks thereafter.

So there, at the foot of the stairs, he awaits me, smiling encouragingly upwards. I am by this stage familiar with the routine. We proceed to his little car (a small Austin or Ford), parked around the corner in The Mall, having first notified my mother of our departure, and I sit into the front passenger seat beside him. We drive to the outskirts of the town, we find a quiet spot, he pulls over and parks, and we engage in earnest colloquy. All the way out on our drive, I have had to recognise that this is it, this is the moment of decision one way or the other. I decide that I cannot, realistically, leave my home; I am after all fifteen years of age, and could not, psychologically, cope with it. But I must steel my resolve, for I know from experience how determined he is not to lose me, how difficult he will be to shake off.

After a brief exchange of pleasantries, he comes to the point with what seems like surprising directness.

'Well, have you decided whether or not you can devote your life to Christ?'

He is looking at me, I know, while I sit with head bowed and try to find the courage to articulate my refusal. The silence is beginning to drag.

'I'm sorry, Father,' I eventually hear myself say. 'I don't think… I just can't go through with it.'

'And why is that?'

'I can't bear the thought of, you know, leaving home.'

'Ah, yes! That is a major sacrifice!' He pauses, but I know he has more to say, and is about to add some qualification.

'I well remember,' he resumes, 'the pain of leaving my own family. But since I knew that Christ was calling me, I had, at the end of the day, no hesitation. Oh yes, I still felt the pain of it! But what was my pain to the pain of Him who died on the cross? And how little was my sacrifice compared to His!'

I could think of nothing to say.

'Is it,' he urged upon me, 'is it perhaps the case that you are thinking of your own satisfaction only? The devil is cunning; he can turn our selfish acts inside out and make them *look* like something else. Oh yes, your attachment to your family does you credit. But, after all, that attachment cannot last forever. Your brothers and sisters will go on to lead their own separate lives. And' (here he caught my eye) 'neither your mother nor your father will be there forever. They are one generation, you are another.'

A lump began to form in my throat, and a vague melancholy threatened to swim through me. But I had to be strong.

'I accept all that, Father. But I… I just can't make the break.'

Another pregnant silence.

'Is this then your final word, Brian? Will you refuse the call?'

'I'm sorry, Father,' I mumble. 'I'm sorry.'

He takes his last shot at it.

'What if the devil, at some future time we cannot quite foresee, what if the devil, who is always busy to seize the souls that rightfully belong to Christ – what if that devil should place before you a fair and tempting woman, to lead you astray? Lead you perhaps to perdition?'

Even in my deeply affected state, this, it struck me with some clarity, was too much. It did not cross my mind to wonder if he himself was not heterosexual (though there had always been, I recognised, an uncomfortable degree of intimacy in our cosy *tête-à-têtes*). Looking back, I am more inclined to interpret his remark as a coldly calculated rhetorical appeal, a politic (I am tempted to add 'Machiavellian') attempt at manipulation. But deep within me I knew in any case that his attitude to women was no necessary part of Church teaching. For the Church could hardly endorse the attitude towards women implied in his comment, and at the same time recognise matrimony as a sacrament, or commemorate the many saintly women who shine like beacons throughout its history. And had I myself not an example of such a woman (a great loyalty arose in me to claim) in my own mother, mortal and imperfect though she was?

He had clearly overplayed his hand; and I began to feel something like relief. Like a Henry James character who has successfully negotiated the snares and pitfalls of a loaded conversation, on which his fate depends, I had come through the forest of my trial and emerged in open country on the farther side. I was, as the saying is, and in more senses than one, 'in the clear'. My reply to his proffered image of the female temptress was mostly a shrug, and I think I murmured something like: 'I hope I will always be a Catholic. Even if I'm not a priest.'

We both knew then that it was over. I had only now to suffer his presence (which I began to fear, rightly or wrongly, was a resentful one) on the journey back – a return journey that seemed longer than the outward trip. I could hardly wait to get out of the car, and longed to draw a line under the entire episode. We duly arrived outside the familiar 'Buffet Bar'; he gave me a perfunctory shake of the hand; and his farewell remark was a cliché rather than the loaded statement it might have been.

'God bless, Brian. I shall remember you in my prayers.'

'Thank you, Father.'

His head is turned away, and he is putting the car into gear. The car pulls away; turns the corner; is gone. I am like the Ancient Mariner when the heavy guilt-laden albatross falls from his neck and sinks beneath the sea. I am free and normal, and breathe the air of liberation. I enter my home with a light step, though still earnestly replaying in my mind the exchanges in which I have just participated.

*

In my final year at primary school I was under the care of one of my favourite teachers, a Christian Brother nicknamed 'Tiny'; not, in his case, ironically because he was huge and tall, but for the obvious reason that he was about five feet in height. He could just as easily have been known as 'Baldy', for he had not a hair on his head. It was rumoured that he came, an only child, from a wealthy background; which perhaps accounted for his gold-rimmed spectacles (a gift from his family that did not compromise his own vow of poverty) and his unusually cultured habits. One of these was playing chess by post, and the games would progress with a slowness of exchange that seemed to suit his placid and patient nature. If he were playing long-distance nowadays, he would doubtless do so by e-mail.

This was an exceptionally happy time for me, and one from which I bore away a lasting insight into my future course. Aged only nine or ten, I had begun to confirm my earlier academic promise (if such a phrase is not too portentous to apply to one so young). I felt able to handle with some assurance the intelligence tests that formed so large a portion of the notorious eleven-plus examination we would face at the end of primary school before proceeding to secondary. Moreover, 'Tiny' provided a context of supportive stability inasmuch as he was a constant, if unobtrusive, source of quiet encouragement and interest. I remember even at this late date some of his more stimulating pronouncements.

One day, for instance, speaking in his habitually precise manner, he confronted us with a major problem of a theological kind. The opening proposition was: in heaven the blessed are all completely happy, yet some are more happy than others. How could this be so? Was this not a contradiction? But imagine, he said, that every soul is a vessel or receptacle – a jug or a bucket, say – each of a different size. Each is filled to the brim with water. Now, when that happens, it is clear that every jug or pitcher holds all the water it possibly can; yet at the same time some pitchers hold more, and some less. So it was with human souls. All in heaven would receive their fill of joy; but some would 'hold' more joy than others.

I was deeply impressed; and looking back would now say that rarely was analogy so instructively employed. I was not to know that the illustration was not his own, but drawn from the broad tradition of Catholic lore. It remains true, though, that 'Tiny' was always ready to challenge our capacity for thought, and he ranged widely in his instructive investigations. There is one pronouncement of his in particular which entered permanently into my reckoning. Seated as was his wont behind his desk at the top of the room, in his placid celibate self-sufficiency, he told us with his usual clarity that, although he and the other Brothers were not married, yet the choice of marriage was still open to us, and marriage was a worthy vocation. Were it not for marriage, and our mothers and fathers, sure none of us would be here! But (and here his voice took on a more serious note), we should all remember this: 'Once you decide to get married, you are married for the rest of your life.'

In the solemn pause that followed, I took in something of the force of his remark. Had the reality of it not been evident in my own family experience up to that point? Even though we sometimes heard them quarrel, though never violently, in their bedroom at night, were not my mother and father clearly committed to each other for the duration of their lives? Yet when the matter was placed squarely before you, it seemed a huge choice for any individual to make. So there it was, set forth in the clearest terms: marriage was indeed a 'vocation', but it was one entailing an awesome responsibility, especially as entertained by the thoughtful little ten-year-old who eagerly took it all in.

CHAPTER EIGHT

Sport, Politics and the 'Other Side'

At the Christian Brothers' school in Newry (known as 'The Abbey') it was regarded as an essential contribution to our ethnic purity that we should play (and take an interest in) only Gaelic games. Since, unlike the northern part of the county, south Down is not in any sense notable for its hurling tradition, this concentration on Gaelic games meant that in practice we played only Gaelic football; and were, in fact, obliged to play it during the weekly 'games period' on a mid-week afternoon. I had considerable difficulty with this, not just because I was far from being a born athlete or even naturally robust, but because, from the age of nine or ten (that is, before I began to attend secondary school), I had to wear glasses for a fairly severe case of shortsightedness. When I removed my glasses (as I had to, given their fragility) and took to the field, it was as much as I could manage to make out which of the other boys were on my team and which on the other. As for seeing the ball, well, that was a matter of chance; if it came to me slowly, I could just about respond to its arrival. If it came at speed, the more normal occurrence, I had little time to adjust to a strange object emerging from the general blur. I have a good deal of fellow-feeling for young Stephen Dedalus who, in the opening chapter of *A Portrait of an Artist as a Young Man*, feels himself 'small and weak amid the throng of players' on the football field – though in his case, since the school in question is the Jesuit college at Clongowes, the game is rugby.

The inevitable consequence of my lack of expertise was that I was excluded from the main field of play and consigned to 'Cripples' Acre'. This was the top corner of the field where those who were not sufficiently athletic to play the game properly were more or less left to their own pathetic devices. The name 'Cripples' Acre' had been coined by one of the more waggish non-athletes, and at times we threw the term around with a kind of defiant bravado; but in fact the experience of playing there was subtly demoralising, since we had no supervision and ended up, out of sheer boredom, indulging in all kinds of tomfoolery. To begin with, there would be a half-hearted attempt to set up two opposing teams; but in due course all discipline would collapse, and we would end up having pointless mud-fights. The evening would begin to descend and the air grow chilly; and I would look longingly down across the field, hoping for a quick and merciful release from the sheer futility of the entire exercise.

Once or twice I decided to defy the authorities, and refused to participate in sports on the appointed day. In that case, you were obliged to stay in the classroom and take extra classes, as a punishment for your non-cooperation. At times this seemed to me the better course; although on one occasion I was further penalised in a way which I finally determined to oppose. What happened was that the teacher (not a Christian Brother on this occasion) who was supervising the extra work of the non-athletes decided to add a further punishment by insisting that we do extra homework arising from the subject we had been doing during the games-period. On my return home, I took a conscious decision not to do this extra work, since I was utterly convinced that the further penalty had been imposed against all known rules of justice. It was a rare example of defiance in the school on the part of one who had up to that point an unblemished record; and I paid (as I expected to pay) the penalty. When I failed to present the extra homework the following day, I was asked to explain myself. With a voice that faltered but remained firm, I stated that I felt unable to do the homework because it was unjust to ask me to do it.

I was promptly given 'six of the best' – three hard slaps with a leather strap on the palm of each hand. I made my way back to my seat fom the front of the class where the scene of my ignominy had occurred, determined not to allow the tears welling up to spill over and run down my cheeks. I sensed from the other boys a vague wave of sympathy, as if they, too, felt that the proceeding had been unjust, and this helped to sustain me; though far more powerful in helping me through the ordeal was my unshakeable inner conviction that Right was on my side. I have never regretted making that small stand for justice, and only wish that on other occasions I had been able to show the same degree of commitment as that stubborn twelve-year-old.

Experiences of this kind might have been enough to put me off Gaelic football for life; in fact the truth is quite the opposite. Although I recognised that I would never play the game at any meaningful level, yet I was caught up in the football games between ourselves and the other competing schools. Our greatest rivalry was with St Colman's, the other boys' secondary school in Newry; and it was a matter of honour to cheer yourself hoarse when our team played theirs. The fact that it was they who won most of these encounters made the duty to support your own school all the keener; so that you embraced your fate in a spirit of heroic martyrdom, savouring within yourself the bittersweet delights of loyalty to a lost cause. 'Though all others should desert them,' you might inwardly feel with adolescent fervour, 'I vow to my school and team the utmost allegiance!'

Sometimes the impossible did happen: we would beat St Colman's. Then the joy was all the sweeter for being so rare! And it was as well that we did record such a victory from time to time, for even the staunchest loyalty requires periodic vindication. Moreover, we were able to record some significant success with our senior school team, and I am grateful for the fact that such success occurred early on in my secondary school years, so that I was young enough to be suitably (and indelibly) impressed. In 1954 we became the first Christian Brothers' school to win the MacRory Cup, the Gaelic football competition which involves all the senior teams of the secondary schools in Ulster (that is, the six counties, plus Cavan, Donegal and Monaghan).

It was in the course of that campaign that I first became aware of the existence of one Seamus Mallon, who was to become such an outstanding political representative for the SDLP; at that time, though, he was not so prominently in the limelight, being a sub for the school football team. My abiding memory is of a figure in the school team-jersey (red, black and amber, a combination, as I was given to believe, of the colours of Down and Armagh), toiling along in the wake of his jogging team-mates as they ran in single file around the field prior to the training-session. It may have been that even then Seamus was a heavy smoker, as (I gather) he has since remained to this day.

It was also in connection with this MacRory campaign of 1954 that the school devised its first (and, to the best of my knowledge, only) school song, the words being set to 'Marching through Georgia':

> Here's the good old Abbey boys all out to win the cup;
> The forwards do the scoring and the backs they follow up;
> We'll never give up cheering, lads, until the time is up,
> As we go forward to vic-to-ry!

(Perhaps it sounded better when set to music.)

In spite of that signal triumph in the MacRory Cup, and indeed in the Ulster schools' intermediate and junior championships, we were always to regard ourselves as, if not quite underdogs, then certainly not favourites either. And over the years (though it galls me to admit it) our rivals, St Colman's, probably had the more consistent record. But that rivalry was as nothing compared to the rivalry between the two neigh-bouring counties, Down and Armagh, at the level of national competi-tion. Newry, according to the official line of demarcation at that time, straddled both counties; thus divided, it allowed likewise for divided allegiances. For reasons which seem to me, on the face of it, irrational, I and most of my friends became Down supporters. And the reason such loyalty to Down seemed so irrational at that time is this: not only had Armagh shown great prowess in 1953 in reaching the All-Ireland final (much to my father's delight, for he was Armagh-born), but to all intents and purposes Down, on the evidence of all previous perfor-mance, were absolute no-hopers. As well imagine that Fermanagh, Carlow, Westmeath or Leitrim could win an All-Ireland as (God help us) Down! Yet we stuck to our guns, perhaps because we had grown used to supporting the underdog in rooting for our school team against colleges with a much higher pedigree and tradition.

Armagh (and it is one of the most memorable chapters in the history of Gaelic football) were fated to fall at the last hurdle when they were beaten by Kerry in the All-Ireland decider. My father had taken a keen interest throughout their progress to the final, and even took me to Croke Park in Dublin to see the semi-final when Armagh beat Roscommon. All I remember is rising on tippy-toes and trying in vain to see over the mass of adults standing in front of me, and catching a fleeting glimpse of the ball only when it was punted into the air – while bursts of noisy excitement came and went like mild tempests around me.

Once this hurdle had been cleared by Armagh, my father probably relished the prospect of his native county defeating Kerry in the final for a number of reasons, some personal. Kerry had (and still have) the finest record of all the counties in All-Ireland football, so to outplay them would indeed set the seal on a great achievement. Moreover, when he had travelled out to America on the *Queen Elizabeth* in 1947, my father had met the Kerry team of that year on the voyage: they were on their way to play Cavan in the All-Ireland final which, following representations from an Irish-American lobby, was memorably staged, for 1947 only, in the Polo Grounds in New York. For reasons which were never fully clear to me, he had not warmed to the Kerry players; some of them at least struck him as big-headed, and one in particular was dismissed by him as a 'blow'. It might have been an additional source of satisfaction to him to see his native county, up to then unrecognised in the annals of Gaelic football, take the 'Kingdom' down a peg or two. Sadly for him, it was not to be.

The key incident has entered the folklore of the game. At a crucial point in the second half, Armagh were awarded a penalty. Up stepped Bill McCorry (the name is indelibly etched on my memory) to take it. The ball is placed, he runs up, he strikes – he misses! And that was the turning point in the game, the Aristotelian *peripeteia*. Kerry recovered their composure, settled themselves, and went on to win. Armagh's chance had come and gone; and, to this day, they have not won an All-Ireland.

It remained the case, though, in spite of that failure, that in the mid-fifties Armagh were regarded as a force to be reckoned with, whereas Down – you must be joking! And yet it was indeed 'no-hopers' Down who were to triumph – eventually, it must be said – where gifted Armagh had so tragically failed. I still remember vividly one of the earliest tokens of Down's ultimate success; and there is a photograph in the family album in Newry which records it. What the photo shows is a group of teenagers, myself included, protected from the elements by gaberdine raincoats, standing along the sidelines in 'The Marshes' (so the playing-venue was called) in Newry. As the photograph suggests, it was a foul day; but the result of the game that Sunday mightily raised our spirits. In those wet and windy conditions, Down, after a seesaw struggle where the result remained in doubt up to the end, finally triumphed; and what made the victory especially sweet was that our opponents on that day were none other than our great rivals, Armagh, who had but four or five years previously taken on the might of Kerry. Down, formerly the 'poor relations', were moving up the ladder of success.

There were to be one or two false dawns, but at last, in 1960, Down reached the All-Ireland football final. The whole county seemed to be in the throes of football fever; and as the countdown to the decider began over the last week, the sports pages of the newspapers were scanned and devoured with a fervour never previously known. There were at least three factors which added to the interest. First, Down's opponents were, as they had been Armagh's some seven years previously, the team with the proudest tradition in the game: Kerry. Second, there was a real possibility that Down would achieve what no northern county under British rule had hitherto achieved; for up to that point none of the 'occupied six' (as in those unregenerate and politically careless days we termed them) had won an All-Ireland title (only Armagh had come close). And finally, there were rumours that even Protestants in the county (who normally would dismiss Gaelic football as a game for 'Fenians') were taking a huge interest and getting behind the team – even to the point (so it was claimed) that some were prepared to travel on the Sunday to Croke Park and attend in person. They were more than welcome, as far as we were concerned; they were Downmen (and women) like the rest of us.

On the day of the football final, our own fervour took the form of that absolute but usually innocent devotion to the team of one's choice; and, at least for this one day, our commitment to the 'Mourne men' (as the sportswriters had dubbed the Down team) was total. Partisan we decidedly were, but sectarian only in our devotion to that secular cause. We rose that Sunday at an ungodly hour, and took a train (a 'special' laid on for the day) early in the morning. We were nineteen or twenty years of age, and few of us had been to Dublin before; so once there, and with time on our hands, we decided to stroll around the city in the late forenoon to see the sights. At one point we found ourselves on St Stephen's Green, just opposite the Shelbourne Hotel, when we saw a figure approach us (the streets were almost empty) from the hotel itself. He struck us as vaguely familiar, but it was only when he came close and hailed us that we recognised him.

'Would you have a penny for two ha'pennies, lads? For a phone call.'

We duly obliged, and by this time had realised that the man asking the favour was none other than Brendan Behan. He was wearing a jacket, but no tie; and the one detail of his appearance that I most vividly retain in my memory was the presence just under his nose of a tuft of unshaven hair. I was subsequently to wonder if this was an area of his face too dangerously close to his nose to be exposed to the ravages of a razor (especially if, I somewhat unkindly speculated, he was suffering from the DTs after a skinful the night before). He quickly made it clear, in any case, where his sympathies lay.

'You're down for the match, lads?'

(An obvious deduction, given that we were festooned in red and black rosettes and other favours in the Down colours.)

'Well,' he continued, wishing us well in classic style, 'I hope you beat the shite out of those Kerry bastards!'

None of us entertained any vindictive feelings towards the Kerrymen, and we were quite taken aback (though also amused) by the strength of Behan's antipathy towards the other team. It was not until later that I came to appreciate the extent of the rivalry between Dublin and Kerry in Gaelic football; and clearly it was as a 'Dub' that Behan was expressing his preference (it was certainly not, in spite of the memorable vigour of the utterance, as a literary master).

Nonetheless, we took it as a good omen that we had not only

encountered the famous Brendan but had received his 'blessing' (if that is what it was) on our cause. He was subsequently to demonstrate this support for our northern team in an entirely different and somewhat incongruous context. Not long afterwards, he was on a visit to New York, and disembarked from the plane at the airport wearing a rosette on which was written 'Up Down'. He was well enough known to attract the media, and succeeded in puzzling the assembled American reporters, who may have assumed that he was making a rather banal comment of an aeronautical nature.

By that time, the rosette he was wearing was an endorsement of a victorious team. Down – the no-hopers without any footballing tradition – not only defeated the 'Kingdom', who had the highest tally of victories in the competition, but did so by a record margin, 2-10 (or 16) to 0-8. The crucial battle was fought at midfield, where it was expected that the great Mick O'Connell of Kerry would control the play. But Down had worked out their winning tactics and, in the shape of midfielder Jarlath Carey, played a spoiling game in that sector of the field. O'Connell failed to produce on the day his normal aristocratic fluency, and Kerry lost their potential dominance in that vital area. Once the brilliant Down forwards (among them Sean O'Neill from Newry, whom we had known at school and at Queen's University) received a steady supply of the ball, then Down were on their way. We became the first Northern Irish team to win the Sam Maguire Cup; and that game, played before a capacity crowd of almost 88,000, remains for me one of the greatest of all sporting memories. It ranks alongside the two Wimbledon singles finals between Borg and McEnroe in the early eighties, or Ireland's qualification for the quarter-finals of the World Cup in Italy in 1990, when they won that unforgettable penalty shoot-out against Romania.

*

If you were a Catholic growing up in Northern Ireland in the fifties and sixties, it was assumed not only that you would rarely have the opportunity to socialise with Protestants (who after all attended different schools), but equally that you would never under any circumstances reveal sympathies which might even vaguely be interpreted as British. This is not to say that Catholics and Protestants did not mix; it was very much the case, for example, that in the local Musical Society and in the Newpoint Players (the amateur drama group which derived its name from the first and last syllables respectively of Newry and Warrenpoint) both sides worked happily together to produce work of often remarkable quality. But 'they' remained different; 'they' had names like Ronnie, Stanley or Sammy, while 'we' proclaimed our Irish identity with names like Sean, Seamus or Colm. (Just for the record, 'Brian' makes the grade, since it was the name of one of the most famous high-kings in Irish history, Brian Boru; he defeated the Danes at the battle of Clontarf in 1014.)

I often heard my sister Harriet (who was and remained deeply Catholic, but was otherwise never in any way sectarian) speak of such-and-such as a 'very nice fellow', only to lament in conclusion: 'It's a pity he's a Protestant!' Perhaps her regret as to the man's religion had to do with the possibility that, had he not been from the 'other side', she would have been able to go out with him; since 'mixed' marriages were a non-starter, however, there was no question of her responding to such a male's charms. I think it only fair to the facts to stress that there was little real bitterness (of an overt kind, at any rate) in this constant recognition of the gulf between 'them' and 'us'; though any sociologist or political analyst would probably argue that, once such difference is instituted in a society, the potential for conflict remains very real. Yet we knew nothing in the fifties or early sixties of the sectarian viciousness that was to overtake the province later – a growing bitterness which, according to many who lived through that formative period of the sixties, owes less (originally at least) to IRA intransigence than to the sectarian feeling fomented by Ian Paisley. I have heard residents from towns in the vicinity of Newry comment on the rapid deterioration in community relations once Paisley had appeared as itinerant preacher in the town, and ranted from the back of his lorry. It is impossible for me to be objective in any attempted evaluation of Paisley; in fairness to him, perhaps one could argue that he was merely bringing to the surface the tensions endemic in that society.

There was even less leeway in the matter of British sympathies; and it is perhaps significant that, having just mentioned the contribution of the Reverend Paisley to the deterioration in relations between the two sides, I should now find anti-British prejudice so richly exemplified by a clergyman from the Catholic side, a local priest whom I shall call Father Curtis. He was a good friend of the family, and I have the happiest memories of his visits to our house, when the good china would be produced and my mother would give him 'the treatment' in the form of an elaborate high tea. You knew that it was a special occasion, not just because the best cutlery was on display, but because, most telling detail of all, the butter was set out in specially rolled 'butter-pats' on a silver dish. Fr Curtis was in his own right an intelligent and witty man, and rose in due course to the rank of Monsignor. I am grateful to him because, among other things, he introduced my brother Art and myself to the delights of the crossword. In truth, I think I relished the opportunity to show off my knowledge by managing to find the answer, at his prompting, to a difficult clue (though once he enjoyed my mortification when, at the age of about eleven, I correctly worked out the answer 'nude', and found myself, to his amusement, covered in uncontrollable blushes).

Fr Curtis was not, however, a favourite with everyone, and this must be put down to the fact that his wit was often of a rather caustic nature. Some of his *bons mots* had a neutral appeal, and were worth hearing. So, for example, speaking of relations between the sexes (and secure in his own celibacy), he would produce his epigrammatic summary: 'The desirable are not obtainable, and the obtainable are not desirable.' But he mortally offended both my sisters (and I question if even to this day they have found it in their hearts to forgive him) by resorting to an epigram which had more syntactic balance than evaluative justice. On more than one occasion, referring to my sisters, he would say, with obvious satisfaction at his own judiciousness, 'A has the looks, and B has the personality.' The upshot of this was highly predictable, and might have been foreseen by a man who had a little less concern for his own cleverness and a little more knowledge of young women (both sisters were in their late teens or early twenties at the time). Sister A retired to her room reflecting that she had no personality (quite untrue), and sister B was instantly undermined by the fear that she had no physical attractions (equally false).

Fr Curtis, however, was kind and generous to my brothers and myself, and would from time to time take us out on day-trips, driving us in his car most commonly to Dundalk (thirteen miles away, across the border) or, less frequently, to Belfast (perhaps a visit to the zoo). It was on one such trip to Belfast that we were left in no doubt as to his extreme Nationalist sympathies. We went to a performance of Chipperfield's Circus in the King's Hall, a huge treat for boys of our age. All went smoothly until the show had ended. As was far too often the custom in Northern Ireland at the time, the performance had to end with a rendition of the British national anthem. Automatically (if not dutifully) we struggled to our feet, only to realise that our priestly companion had not only remained in his seat, but was clearly indicating to us by both voice and gesture that we should on no account stand up.

'Sit down! Sit where you are!' he insisted, and that in no subdued whisper but in a voice loud enough to carry. The advice was accompanied by restraining efforts of his hands on whichever one of us was within reach. Sheepishly, we did as we were told, though my own clear recollection is that throughout the playing of the anthem I felt distinctly insecure, even to the point of expecting that I would receive, any minute, a slap on the head from some unknown and irate Loyalist behind me. My neck tingled: my fear grew that, somewhere rearward, a swift and unforeseeable retribution was imminent. But on that occasion we got away with it. On the way home in Fr Curtis's car, I imagine that the three of us exchanged looks, and wondered if he had not gone too far. But he was a tough countryman from a farming background, and was of a generation which saw no reason to compromise. From our point of view we had a dim recognition of intransigence (though at the time I did not know the meaning of the word), along with an obscure feeling that Fr Curtis's was perhaps not the ideal attitude to adopt.

*

I like to think that, as I matured, I increasingly developed an attitude of critical detachment towards incidents like the one I have just recounted. For the society in which I grew up presented more than one instance where you felt called upon to make the 'right' evaluation; and whatever innate tendencies I did or did not possess, the role of critic, in which you strove to 'see the object as in itself it really is', was one that was repeatedly called into play. Probably, though, for one growing up in Northern Ireland that formula assumed a greater urgency than Matthew Arnold could have foreseen. In the matter of my own development, the greatest challenge to clarification occurred in the mid-fifties, when I was about fourteen.

I refer here to the abortive IRA campaign of that time. I should make it clear at the outset that I at no time 'welcomed' such a development; but there were moments nonetheless in which it was possible to drift into a dangerously uncritical attitude, so that you might begin to think something like, 'This will show the British!' or 'We have some fight left in us yet!' I ask the indulgent reader to remember at this point my immaturity, as well as the constant inculcation at school of extreme Nationalist or even Republican views. But I was rapidly enough to come to my moment of clarification.

The crucial episode was one widely reported in the news. An off-duty RUC man had gone across the border to the Republic to meet his girl-friend. The IRA gunned him down without mercy; and this, for me, was a turning point. I could have absolutely nothing to do with a campaign which took the life of a man who, policeman or not, had been engaged in the entirely innocent activity of seeing the woman he loved. Further, though, I had to ask myself if such a killing would have been defensible had the policeman been on duty on the Northern side of the border. On reflection, it appeared to me the merest casuistry to distinguish between a man out of uniform and the same human being in uniform. I recoiled from the possibility of any such death; I could on no account be reconciled to it.

An additional consequence was that I had to confront and analyse the hitherto largely unexamined notion of a 'united Ireland'. To define yourself as 'Nationalist' was *de facto* to endorse some such ambition. It was about this time that I began to feel that if the establishment of a united Ireland entailed force and coercion, then it could not be acceptable on those terms. Gradually I began to move towards the position that I have held ever since: that before there can be a united Ireland, there must first be a united Northern Ireland. As John Hume has repeatedly said, the division is not territorial, but in the minds and hearts of those who oppose each other. If Unionists and Nationalists could work side by side with respect for each other's traditions, and Nationalists could stop talking glibly about 'a united Ireland', some real progress might become possible. It is, then, a positive step in the right direction that the Republic should have accepted, with remarkably little fuss, the need to revise Articles Two and Three of the Irish Constitution, which define the national territory as 'the whole island of Ireland' – including, of course, Northern Ireland – and seek to uphold the right of the Irish Government to exercise jurisdiction over that national territory. The way has thereby been opened for whatever reciprocal gesture or gestures the Unionists might decide to make.

I have never since felt obliged to change my mind with regard to the use of violence to attain political ends. Each human life is infinitely precious – a truism, I know, but one which we must try to hold onto, whether the atrocities we contemplate are those of Belsen in the past or elsewhere around the globe in our painful present. To massacre thousands is mathematically a greater evil than to murder one; but in truth we are misled by a false mathematics if we forget that we are dealing in multiples of infinity, and that the slaughter of one is in itself an infinite evil. It is for reasons such as this that I have such a high regard for a novel which was shortlisted for the Booker Prize in 1981.

The book is *The White Hotel* by D. M. Thomas. In the opening pages we are introduced at length and in great detail to the fantasy-life of the female protagonist, including her sexual fantasies; by the end of the novel we are witnesses as the same woman is, along with countless others, herded to an ignominious death by Nazi soldiers. The cumulative effect is stunning: the external perspective on innumerable bodies in a mass grave, from which we might turn away as from a spectacle so overpowering that we cannot hope to assimilate it, is offset by the previously established insight into the infinite riches in the female protagonist's mental life. What we find ourselves involved in is not some mind-numbing body-count, which allows no play to our emotions, but the feelingful acknowledgment that this unique woman, with whom we have been encouraged so intensely to empathise, has now been destroyed, along with thousands of human beings just as unique as her.

I have a special reason to be grateful to that novel, for, when I first went up to Queen's University in Belfast, I found myself confronted by a challenge I could not cope with, in the form of an open display of photo-books detailing in the most realistic way the atrocities of the Nazi concentration camps. I eventually forbade myself to look at them, because I could not pay them an adequate tribute. They required an immensity of emotional response, and not the limited feeling of which I was capable. I felt that to surrender to a genuinely commensurate emotional response would usher me into the realm of the unspeakable; but, in withholding such a response, I feared I would become a mere voyeur, spectating the obscene suffering of others in a mode of enforced detachment. It was Thomas's novel which, to some extent, permitted me to come to terms with that horror.

Only once have I wavered in my total dissociation from the Republican movement, and that was at the time of the hunger-strike which claimed the lives of Bobby Sands and nine others. It is difficult for me to put into words how I felt at the time; I was buffeted by feelings which astonished me by their strength, and which eluded all efforts to bring them to the bar of reason. What exasperated me most was the hard and unyielding attitude of Margaret Thatcher (whom I always, on other grounds and from the very beginning, detested: she has always appeared to me a thoroughly divisive personality, one who positively thrives on division). Faced with a choice between official intransigence represented by her, one of the leaders of Western democracy, and the intransigence of Bobby Sands, undertaken as a last resort under painful conditions, I felt that I must betray myself either way. But Sands was Irish (even if not my kind of Irish) and Thatcher was British (and how); Sands was dying, and was in a sense a victim of her inflexible stance. I was to remain throughout the hunger strikes uneasy with any nascent sympathy towards him, but Thatcher was beyond the reach of any sympathy.

Here I should attempt to generalise from my experience at that time. And, first of all, I doubt if anyone can understand the collective psychology of Northern Nationalism unless they recognise the potential continuity of feeling (and the slipperiness of such feeling) across the 'green' spectrum. I should make it clear at this point that I am *not* talking about any 'pan-Nationalist front', that is to say, a deliberate political alignment. I am referring rather to a spectrum of feeling that lies below the level of consciousness, and which is fluid and unstable. Thus, at the period of which I am speaking, I had no *conscious* acceptance of the hunger-strike campaign (rather, in fact, the opposite); but it was quite possible for extreme Nationalist feelings to gain, momentarily, the upper hand, and put reason to flight.

I am conscious here that, as far as any Unionist readers are concerned, I may appear to be endorsing their dismissive view that all taigs are the same, or that if you scratch a taig you'll find a Republican. But such a reading would be a gross oversimplification, of the kind I am trying to avoid. A Nationalist begins in good faith by taking up a defensible Nationalist position, but may, before he is fully aware of what is happening, find himself slipping into positions which at the outset he would not have countenanced. The pale end of the green spectrum is in fact (not in theory) poles apart from its dark green counterpart; but the spectrum itself is, almost across its entire length, prone to invasive flux. So according to the degree of political heat generated at any given moment, the spectrum (see it, if you will, as a long receptacle filled with water) permits of the occasional 'flooding' of dark green towards its comparatively 'clear' or pale green sector.

Yet my reaction to the death of Bobby Sands is a unique example of loss of detachment on my part. The additional and complicating truth may be, though, that such detachment was bought at a price. Unable to identify with a Unionist state, nor could I accept what in my view was an extreme or even rabid Nationalism. The consequence was that I ran the risk of falling into a political limbo – a tendency further encouraged by the apparently unalterable stalemate of Northern Irish politics. Where there was little or no prospect of political change, why waste one's energy on politics at all? I seem, too, to have been a mere spectator of events in which others played a risky part. One memory I have is of a mass rally by Nationalists just fifty yards away from our house, in Margaret Square, one Sunday in the mid-fifties. The RUC mounted a baton-charge, and my memory is of confused noises, and indecipherable figures fleeing past the frosted panes of our sitting-room. I was secure in that domestic interior, not exposed to the raw actuality on the streets outside.

To this day I feel that I bear the marks of that early experience, and I have a bad conscience with regard to my critical writing and my teaching, in that I have an insufficiently sustained awareness of the political implications of literature. It requires a conscious effort on my part to acknowledge the politics of the text, and when I do so, I perhaps carry less conviction than when thinking or writing in a different mode. Possibly, though, this shortcoming is not entirely attributable to a Northern Irish background. I seem to recall a statement somewhere in Marx to the effect that those whose origins are in the lower middle class (as mine, I think, were) never know whether they are for or against the status quo. In other words, those whose class origins are of that kind tend to absent themselves from political struggle.

I was to hear from the lips of a good friend in my Oxford days, Adjit from Sri Lanka (then Ceylon), a memorable assessment of my lack of socio-political commitment. Like all those with whom I consorted at that time, Adjit was a devoted political leftist (the left, it seemed, was the only part of the political spectrum kind enough to accommodate me in that phase of my existence). We were drinking our beer in the Turl Tavern, and talking freely on various subjects. He made sure, after a pause in the conversation, that he had my full attention, before delivering a summary judgment.

'The trouble with you, Brian,' he said with some deliberation, 'is that you cannot make up your mind whether you are a bourgeois or a bohemian.'

I dare say that, by this time, the bourgeois is in the ascendant, though I retain the hope that the bohemian is still somehow alive and well, and capable of declaring his reality should the need arise.

*

A Monday morning early in May, and the classroom is buzzing with conversation as we relish the last moments of freedom before the mid-morning break is over. The statue of the Virgin is in its usual place on the little wooden stand up on the wall, and, since this is May (the month of Mary), there is a small container of flowers before it. Next we are to have 'Boss', the principal of the school, who teaches us, in this our fourth year (I am fifteen), Religious Knowledge and Irish. The door opens; a sudden silence falls. 'Boss' is not a Christian Brother to be messed with. He is not just authoritarian; he is authority itself. He is the superego uncompromisingly embodied in the burly form of a grey-haired Kerry-man with a strikingly florid face.

'Boss' has some disconcerting habits, and I have at least once before experienced the weight of his displeasure. On that occasion I heard his footsteps approach from behind (the door into the classroom was to the rear), sensed him pausing briefly behind me, and listened to his deep and dramatic inhalation, before he enunciated in his firm voice: 'Still smoking the cigarettes, Cosgrove, I see.' Which at the time I was; although I was not allowed to smoke publicly, at home my mother tended to turn a blind eye. I had allowed myself to be nabbed because I had forgotten to remove the nicotine stains on thumb and forefinger by rubbing them along a rough wall on my way to school. Today, though, his displeasure is to have a different object.

The footsteps approach from the rear. 'Boss' has suddenly stopped, and stopped immediately behind me. The pause is longer than before. The deeply taken breath. I am for it. But for what?

'One week to the Religious Knowledge exam – and what was Cosgrove doing?'

I have no doubt that, given time, the fifteen- and sixteen-year-olds all around me could have imagined something sufficiently blasphemous, or at least heinous. I am myself at a loss to know what he is getting at. I have just time to begin to feel ashamed and confused when the voice behind me comes out with it: 'Playing English cricket!'

I had indeed been playing cricket, the previous Saturday, in a field appropriately known as 'The Meadow', just outside Newry. Alongside the field ran the railway to Dublin; and, unknown to me at that time, the 'Boss' had been travelling on the Dublin train and had spotted me at my irreligious and unIrish frolics. For that is what makes the story so revealing and so representative: in playing cricket, I had contaminated myself with Englishness, but equally, as the reference to the Religious Knowledge exam made clear, I had compromised my Catholicism as well. As far as the 'Boss' (and others like him) were concerned, you had to subscribe to the full ethnic membership or be excluded from it entirely. To be Irish was to be Catholic, and to be Catholic was to be Irish: if you compromised one of those two terms, then you automatically placed the other in jeopardy. Conversely, and even more simply, to be British in Northern Ireland was to be non-Catholic (or it was, at the very least, enough to call your Catholicism in question).

I cannot remember how my classmates received the news that I was, as far as sport was concerned, outside the cultural pale; but I do not recall any adverse reaction on their part. It may have occurred to some of them that since I was a duffer at a 'real' game like Gaelic football, it was only to be expected that I should find some alternative outlet for whatever dubious athletic abilities I might be supposed to possess. And in truth this was indeed one of my reasons for playing cricket; for the fact that I wore spectacles was not at all as insuperable an object to participation in cricket as it was in football. True, the glasses could be a major source of danger when you were batting (because the hard ball flew unpredictably from a bumpy pitch), but my prowess lay, I felt, in bowling, and the spectacles were no hindrance to that. I was, in fact, a fast bowler; and, partly because of the identity of Christian names, took as my model Brian Statham of Lancashire. Naturally I respected Freddy Trueman, but my own temperament led me to a preference for the steady performer, disciplined and accurate, such as Statham was.

But perhaps 'Boss', however extreme his reaction may have been, was right to point up the anomaly of my devotion to cricket. How was it that someone like myself, from an explicitly Nationalist background, came to have such an intense interest in that most archetypally English game in the first place – a game, moreover, which is so intimately linked to the history and culture of the British Empire? To this day I have no certain answer, but suspect that an interest in reading had a lot to do with it. Here I am referring not primarily to those English public-school stories mentioned previously, but rather to the numerous well written books on cricket which we discovered in the local library. It is generally acknowledged that, of all sports, cricket has produced the finest body of literature (whether the writer be the English Neville Cardus or the West Indian C. L. R. James). Be that as it may, we raided the local library and read everything on cricket we could get our hands on, going back as far as Sir Pelham ('Plum') Warner and D. R. Jardine and the infamous 'Bodyline' tour of Australia in 1932–33. Later, I was to purchase Keith Miller's *Cricket Crossfire*, and read other more up-to-date works; by then the reading habit was well established, and I had become better versed in the lore of cricket than in that of any other sport. Such an acquisition of the lore of the game is, it seems to me, as much a tribute to the quality of the writing about it as to the sport itself.

I sometimes wonder, a little uneasily, if the ghosts of my forefathers are continually looking askance on my passion for an 'alien' sport; or even if, when I eventually cross the River Styx, their shades will congregate accusingly around me, for the purposes of stern denunciation. I have my defence in part prepared; for I can argue in the first instance that by playing cricket I got to know the 'other side', and in both Newry and Warrenpoint met and played with Protestants with whom I had otherwise nothing in common. Was this not, I might urge, a legitimate extension of my father's ecumenical way of running his public house?

Then I might further argue that many famous Irish literary figures have indulged a passion for cricket, most notably Samual Beckett, who, all-round sportsman as he was, displayed his talents on the cricket field, and features in *Wisden Cricketers' Almanack* in 1926 and 1927. And no less a figure than James Joyce got to know the Englishman Frank Budgen (who has left one of the most valuable memoirs of Joyce, providing insights otherwise unavailable) only when, in Zurich, they came together out of a common interest in the English county cricket scores.

Yet I can see those shades shaking their unconvinced heads, and imagine myself faltering in my attempted self-defence. For in the first place my decision to play cricket was made without any conscious ecumenical intention; and, in the second place, when I started playing, I knew nothing of Joyce's or Beckett's interest in the game. Moreover, in the early years of my interest, I was (may the shades of the forefathers forgive me!) an enthusiastic supporter of England. This is a further anomaly in its own right, since in other competitive encounters, whether in soccer or rugby (or, for that matter, tiddlywinks), I would never have thought of rooting for England. I still bear the pain of that appalling moment in the soccer game in Dublin in 1957 (Sunday, May 19) when, two minutes into injury time, Atyeo of England scored the equalising goal against Ireland which cancelled out Ringstead's goal scored in the third minute, thereby closing the door on all possibility of our qualification for the 1958 World Cup. Equally, I was hugely delighted when, not long afterwards (in 1958) Northern Ireland afforded some compensation by defeating England at Wembley, 3-2, thanks in large part to an astonishing display of goalkeeping by Harry Gregg. And in rugby I fervently rejoiced (and still rejoice) when (or if?) we put one over on the English, from the days of Kyle and O'Meara to Mike Gibson and beyond.

But in cricket, curiously, I identified (at the outset) with England, whoever their opponents might be, and particularly when they played Australia for the Ashes. As a fast bowler, as I have said, I modelled myself (or tried to) on Statham; but Hutton, Compton, Graveney, Godfrey Evans, Laker, Lock, Trueman, Tyson, and others were all my heroes. I can still recall how shocked I was when in one brief spell in a morning session during the Ashes series of 1953 Ray Lindwall removed Hutton for a duck; and the whole cosmic order seemed to be shaken when shortly afterwards Lindwall did exactly the same thing to Compton. Was nothing to be trusted under the visiting moon? That one such hero should prove to have feet of clay was disturbing; but that both should so signally fail on the same occcasion seemed portentous, as if some catastrophe were imminent.

One difference between soccer or rugby and cricket is that Ireland does not seriously compete against England in cricket, whereas in the other field sports we do. So in a sense my loyalties in cricket were 'up for grabs' in a way in which they never could be in soccer or rugby. Nowadays I have swung round full circle and support whichever team is playing against England; and I avidly scan the list of Australian players, for example, to find an Irish-sounding name. Perhaps it is one way for me to silence the accusing whispers of my ghostly forebears; and, just as my father could listen to the King's speech on Christmas Day only if he was also able to dismiss the British monarch as 'stuttering George', so I can indulge my interest in such an archetypally English sport only when I can declare my Irish credentials by looking for Albion's downfall.

Yet for the true devotee, an interest in cricket transcends any such narrow partisanship. I can as readily admire Michael Atherton of England slowly and heroically, against the odds, accumulating a century against hostile bowling on an uncertain surface, as Tendulkar of India moving in one sweet stroke from 194 to 200 by taking one-two-three steps like a dancer down the pitch, and lofting a six with that deceptive ease which comes from perfect timing and coordination. I am as entranced now by the wiles of the Australian leg-spinner Shane Warne as I once was by the canny variations in flight, pace and spin of the astonishing English off-spinner Jim Laker. And if I am trying to convince my sceptical friends of the fascination of cricket, I shall recall (as seen by me on television) a little sequence of events during the 1956 series in England when Laker was bowling to the gifted Australian batsman Neil Harvey.

Laker bowls; Harvey plays a careful forward defensive stroke, smothering the ball.

Laker bowls; Harvey plays the same stroke, with the same result.

Laker bowls; Harvey plays the same stroke – and misses.

That, however, is but the smallest cameo of the unending duel that goes on between not just batsman A and bowler C, but batsman A and bowlers D, E and F (all different), and also between that batsman's partner, the very different player, B, who also faces the combination of bowlers just listed. And when one of those batsmen is dismissed, another very distinctive player takes his place, and so on down to batsman number eleven. The drift here into mathematical combinations is one indication of the intellectual appeal of cricket; and, if, as some aestheticians would argue, music is close to mathematics, then we might also speak of cricket as an endless series of variations on a theme.

All this variation occurs within the strictest and most ritualised procedure (the immediate outward sign of which is the large vocabulary of precise technical terms for field placings and so on, which is often in itself enough to turn off those who are trying to fathom the game). But once you grant the ritual, take it as a given to the point where it becomes, if not invisible, then at least a part of the background rather than the foreground, you are free to concentrate on the highly aggressive contest unfolding before you. It is not just that a fast bowler may be defined (with apologies to Jonathan Swift) as a Yahoo, in cold blood and with malice aforethought hurling a compact missile as fast as he possibly can (the ball reaching speeds of over ninety miles an hour) at one of his own species who has never offended him; but that the individual batsman is continually engaged in a *psychological* battle which takes many changing forms (the shifts in field placings all around him, the replacement of a fast bowler by a slow, the variations in the repertoire of the individual bowler). It is for reasons such as these that C. L. R. James rightly claims that the 'interplay' between batsman and bowler is 'as subtle as that of men playing bridge or poker'.

Cricket may have been invented by the 'Brits', and may appear to be a game for the phlegmatic; but it's still capable of providing some epic contests. 'Boss' never knew what he was missing.

*

In the late spring of 1956 we had two welcome visitors to our home in Newry. They had come all the way from Australia and were 'doing' not just Ireland or the British Isles but Europe. One was a second cousin (up to that point I had not been aware that we had any relatives 'down under') called Mary Perkins, but known as 'Polly'; her travelling companion was a Mary O'Sullivan, also of Irish extraction.

What made them particularly welcome as far as I was concerned was that they came bearing a gift of a very special kind. They had travelled from the Antipodes on the same ship as the Australian cricket team on its way to England (under the captaincy of Ian Johnson) for the Ashes series of 1956; and I had learned of this happy accident in advance. Since they were friendly with the great Queensland all-rounder Ron Archer, I had asked if they could obtain for me the autographs of the Australian cricketers; and these they duly presented to me on their arrival. It was just about the most charismatic sporting memento I ever possessed, for even at that time the names were legendary – Ray Lindwall, Keith Miller, Neil Harvey, and so on. Given, too, that 1956 was the series in which Jim Laker of England was to set a world record by taking nineteen wickets in one match (including all ten in one innings), the memento was to acquire an even more lustrous aura.

Moreover, since the visitors were personally acquainted with Archer (or as they had it, in their Queensland accents, 'Aytcha'), they provided a further link with the sporting heroes who up until then had been seen only far off in the epic distance. So I was able to sit chatting with the two girls in our upstairs 'drawing-room', trying to extract from them anecdotes that would bring Ron Archer to life before my very eyes (so to speak), and warming my imagination in the glow of their proximity to one of the cricket 'greats'. But it was on this occasion also that I was to receive in the course of our casual exchanges a severe reminder of my own unthinking sectarianism; and it was, if a well learnt lesson, a painful one too.

I should first explain that I had been in the habit of reading the Catholic weekly newspaper *The Universe*, and in particular (a fact highly pertinent to the present anecdote) its own special sporting section. Indeed, in my mid-teens I was a fervent member of the local praesidium of the Catholic youth group known as the Legion of Mary, and the main part of my duties was the delivery every Saturday of Catholic newspapers to subscribers who lived in the town. So, in all weathers, off I would go with my bundles of *The Catholic Herald*, *The Irish Catholic*, *The Standard* and *The Universe*, spreading the word of God (in my own humble way, of course) throughout the assigned district; consoling the elderly with their weekly Catholic reading-fodder, and providing for the thoughtless young from whose radios blared the latest Elvis Presley some inkling at least of those other realities which they seemed to be in danger of forgetting. It was in this way that (young Catholic prig that I was) I became acquainted with *The Universe.*

What was special about that newspaper's sporting column was this: that while it was liberally catholic in its concern with every sport under the sun, it was also narrowly Catholic in its attention to the sporting performers. In other words, it referred in its reports only to the achievements of those who were known to be Catholics. Thus, the West Indian cricketer Roy Marshall, playing for Hampshire, was frequently mentioned, along with Matt Busby, say, the manager of Manchester United, or perhaps an Irish jockey who was making his name on the English horse-racing circuit. It was from reading this sporting section that I acquired, I believe, the notion that while one should applaud sporting achievement in general, one should be particularly gratified in knowing that the achievement was that of a co-religionist. And it was this inexcusable bias which betrayed me into my major *faux pas.*

We had been discussing the career and performance at both state and national level of Ron Archer, when it crossed my mind as a natural assumption that since my companions were Catholic (as well as being of Irish origin), they could hardly be so friendly with him unless he were Catholic too. There grew within me an urgent need to clarify the matter; so that, in a suitable lull in our fluent exchanges, I heard myself ask the pointed question: 'And is Ron Archer a Catholic?'

It was one of those moments when, in the split second after you have spoken, it hits you that you have said the wrong thing. There was a short but highly fraught silence; until Polly turned to me with a strange look on her face. At this stage my own face was beginning to go up in flames.

'No,' she said. 'But what has that got to do with it?'

I floundered: just curious, you know... just thought that since you are both Catholic maybe he was too... that kind of thing. But I was conscious now that both my female companions were unable fully to conceal the kind of critical gaze which might be said to reveal an emergent anthropological interest. I was sufficiently self-possessed to recognise, through momentary identification with their perspective, that I was offering to their regard a specimen of sectarian narrowness which was alien to their own culture. I could not wait to excuse myself and get out of the room; but the pain I bore away with me was an educative one. I was to reflect that I had betrayed in their eyes a bigoted concern with the religion of another which was, in addition, utterly misplaced and nothing to the point. How could I have become so shamefully myopic in my views? Clearly I had much to learn; but I resolved to somehow get it right (or try to). Just over two years later, I was on my way to Queen's University in Belfast, where I would be further challenged to enlarge my point of view.

CHAPTER NINE

Queen's University

Queen's University in the late fifties and early sixties was, in various ways, an exciting place to be; and there were a number of contemporaries who were later to achieve a measure of fame. Among these were Phil Coulter (who was marked out early on as a musician to watch out for) and Austin Currie, who in due course was to become a prominent member of the Nationalist grouping, the SDLP (Social Democratic and Labour Party). In the year ahead of me in the English Department were the two 'Shamies', Heaney and Deane; a couple of years behind me came the playwright-to-be, Stewart Parker (one non-Nationalist, at least, for whom I was to feel a high regard).

Many of us of Nationalist origin felt that we were breaking new ground; for up until that time it had been more usual for Catholics to proceed, not to the secular or 'heathen' context of Queen's, but to the safer orthodoxy of the teacher training college in Belfast, St Joseph's (Trench House). Indeed, I recall how at that time the principal of my school – a delightful man named Mullins, a Christian Brother with a rare sense of humour – expressed surprise at the insistence of a number of us that we would indeed go to university in Belfast. We had just received our exam results, and it was clear that the scholarships were available. But would we not be better off, he wanted to know, going to St Joseph's? We were, however, adamant; we would aim for the higher institution.

One reason why Queen's was a good place to be at that time (though we had no way of knowing this until we went there) was that a number of bright young British academics, who were later to take up chairs and establish major reputations in England and elsewhere, were in the process of starting their careers in Belfast. I recall with gratitude my assignment in my first year to a 'moral tutor' (as they were then called) who took his duties seriously enough to set me essay topics, correct the essays in a detailed way and discuss my arguments with me. The 'moral tutor' system was loosely structured, and it involved assigning each first-year student to an academic whom you normally would not otherwise meet (as teaching tutor in one of your three subjects, for example). You could be lucky or unlucky in what you got. Some moral tutors, for instance, would meet with you once and simply tell you to let them know if you had any problems. You never saw them again.

But my moral tutor was a bright young man in the French Department who later (having written books on Camus and Sartre) took up a chair in the English Midlands. He knew that I was studying English, and wanted to enlarge my sense of modern culture. I still remember the two essays he set, both on twentieth-century English fiction, a kind of writing that I would not have encountered in my first-year English syllabus (which was largely concerned with Renaissance literature). One essay involved a comparison and contrast between the different visions of the future in Aldous Huxley's *Brave New World* and Orwell's *Nineteen Eighty-Four*; and while such a topic is run-of-the-mill fare on English Leaving Certificate examination papers nowadays, it was a different matter forty years ago for a seventeen-year-old just out of a provincial school run by the Christian Brothers. In our final year at that school, we had studied in English classes not one text from the twentieth century, because our teacher (an elderly Christian Brother) had, given a choice of two kinds of syllabus, conservatively opted for the one that was pre-modern (I can best convey his squeamishness by recalling that he did not wish to teach *The Waste Land*, on the grounds that its sexual references made it 'immoral'!).

It is from that background that I came to the novels mentioned, both of them (and Huxley's in particular) explicit with regard to sexual matters, and both of them set in worlds pointedly secular. The second essay set by my moral tutor was on William Golding's *The Lord of the Flies*, now, of course, safely enshrined as a modern 'classic', but at that time only four years in the world (having been published in 1954). I was bowled over by the intensity of the writing; and it was the first time I was to be made vividly aware that significant 'literature' was not just something safely removed in the past, but something that emerged from and engaged with contemporary culture. My moral tutor treated my arguments with scrupulous fairness; while it was clear that he was my intellectual superior (and was far better read than I was), it was equally clear that I was being admitted to the academic community on terms of strict justice, and that I would be assessed purely on the merits of my intellectual performance. Here, then, was an open field of activity, where all you had to do was perform consistently and try to do your best.

Like many of the young academics at Queen's at that time, my moral tutor was cool and urbane in a way that seemed typically English, given to procedures that would be characterised as deftly analytical, and unashamedly agnostic in his beliefs. In retrospect, I question whether some of these young academics were really as aggressively agnostic as they sometimes appeared to be. One or two, at least, may have decided that the best way to deal with a mixed class containing both Catholics and Protestants (each side in its own way as fundamentalist or literalist as the other) was to stand apart from Christianity. Moreover, to a young academic teacher it may well have seemed the best path, from the point of view of a liberal education, to challenge all dogmatic views of a Christian kind, and perhaps drag us away from such false securities (kicking and screaming as some of us doubtless were) into the problematic mid-twentieth century. Such teachers in a sense transcended the sectarian space in which most of us were confined, and probably hoped to encourage in us, their charges, a similar liberating transcendence.

Some of my Nationalist contemporaries had difficulties with the fact that almost all our teachers were British (Scottish and Welsh as well as English); there was, for instance, only one Irish-born lecturer in the English Department at that time. What this may seem to point to is a classic colonial situation, in which the native population are subjected not just to the alien discipline of 'English' literature, but to the equally alien ethos of the coloniser, as embodied in British-born instructors. In practice, I do not feel that this was the case; partly because 'English' literature also included American writing and poetry and prose written by Irishmen such as Yeats and Joyce. As well as that, the young academics

who taught us were mostly of a liberal or even left-wing bent, and intel-
ligently alert to the divided nature of the society and to possible injustices within it; and usually willing to learn during their sojourn in
'Ulster'. Even where they were neither young nor liberal (as in the case of
a man of whom I became extremely fond, Matthew P. MacDiarmid, a
Scottish Protestant who had fought with the British forces in World War
II), they educated us by challenging repeatedly some of our most
cherished notions, whether religious or political. It was usually the case
that where you disagreed, you had the right (subject to certain conven-
tional procedures, many of which strike me now as extremely old-
fashioned in their formal politeness) of reply.

Sometimes, though, a national or provincial resentment against these
strangers with unIrish accents would boil over in a peculiar way. The
best example I can recall concerns the young French lecturer who was to
prove, for me, such a fine moral tutor. Brisk, articulate and businesslike,
he gave a series of lectures (well worth hearing) on seventeenth-century
French literature to the large first-year class, consisting of some one
hundred and fifty students. It took place in one of the bigger, tiered lecture theatres, in the back rows of which lolled the 'hard men' who might
be giving less attention to the lecture than to the newspaper and their
attempt to divine the winner of the 3.30 at Redcar. On one occasion the
young lecturer arrived in a rather snappish mood, and that was to prove
his undoing.

He passed some witty remark which, for whatever reason, none of us
in the massed tiers picked up. Another lecturer might have been content
to cut his losses and let sleeping dogs lie – but not this one. He instantly
decided to expose our lack of perception.

'Oh you *are* a stupid lot,' he announced in those English tones which
to all Ulstermen (from both sides of the divide) are synonymous with
arrogance. 'I've just made a joke and you failed to notice. I'll make it easy
for you. Next time I make a joke, I shall produce my handkerchief so that
you'll know when to laugh.'

By now the hard men at the back were beginning to attend to the proceedings with an unusual degree of interest. The sense was that they
were biding their time, and that, if an opportunity presented itself, the

young lecturer would pay for his act of *hubris*. Alas for him, that opportunity was not long in coming.

Circumstances (or, if you will, Fate) conspired against the unfortunate lecturer in one small but highly significant detail: he was suffering from a head-cold. The inevitable happened; he had to pause and blow his nose, spontaneously and unthinkingly producing his handkerchief to do so. Then chaos broke forth: peals of hugely exaggerated laughter rolled down through the lecture-theatre from the back rows. When the other students realised what was happening, they either joined in with false laughter or else, more probably, began to laugh, genuinely, at the way in which the lecturer had had the tables turned on him by the alert reaction of the hard men. In vain did the young lecturer try to raise his voice above the tumult; in vain would he have tried to explain that the handkerchief was not a signal for laughter. He was hooted from the lecture-theatre, and possibly became, as a result of that collective Northern Irish resentment, a sadder and a wiser man. What now strikes me as significant is that the 'Loyalists', no less than the Nationalists, were not prepared to accept any affectation of English superiority.

*

My discovery of new horizons through the experience of reading began early at Queen's, and I have reason to be grateful that in my very first week there (when I had just turned seventeen) I found my way to the bookshop and bought two paperbacks which were to influence me more profoundly than any books before or since. Both books were purchased out of curiosity, neither being recommended reading. One of these was Plato's *Symposium*, which converted me straight away and perhaps irreversibly to its dualistic ontology, whereby there are two levels of being, the immediate world of appearance and the 'higher' world of ideal forms. I received this insight, in truth, as an extension of Catholic teaching on the distinction between the different categories of the physical and the spiritual; if you had already been taught that the bread of the Eucharist was simply the material embodiment of the otherwise hidden or invisible body of Christ, then it was a natural step to accept the notion that the immediate physical world could in general act as a medium for some higher and invisible reality. What I found in Plato was an additional aesthetic dimension, having to do with the revelation of beauty, which had not been emphasised in Catholic tradition. This Platonism, eagerly accepted, prepared me for a deep imaginative attraction to certain aspects of Romantic poetry (Shelley is the most obvious example), such as the emphasis on the symbol (which 'transparently' reveals an order of reality beyond its own concrete immediacy) and the yearning for an ideal order which might fully satisfy the desire for beauty. But this Platonism carried over also into my reading of Gerard Manley Hopkins, whose attempts to depict the 'inscape' (or essential properties) of the object described were likewise grounded in a desire to see through the object to its ideal form.

As usual, biased as I always have been towards the immediate and the concrete, I evolved in my own mind the requisite image that could make sense of this abstract thinking, and bring it into clear focus. The image is that of a tree seen in bright autumn sunlight: we know it to be a real, solid tree, yet in the brightness of the sun, its leaves seemingly turning to vivid flame, it creates the illusion of insubstantiality, so that we see it no longer as a solid object but as a glowing form, an ideal presence. Thus I 'Platonised' one of the common appearances of nature. Later, when I first went to Venice, I applied the same perspective to the even more solid and substantial Palace of the Doges there. Massive and stone-built it certainly was, and, like Dr Johnson refuting Berkeley's idealistic philosophy, you could if you chose kick it until you rebounded off it, in order to prove the reality of its substance; but when you saw it in the powerful Adriatic sunlight, its solidity seemed to melt into luminosity, and you were looking not at stony substance but at the pure architectural form – Goethe's 'frozen music' – that we are supposed to see in great monuments but often fail to see.

The other paperback I bought in that first week was utterly different in its import, but equally profound in its lasting influence. This was the *Maxims* of the seventeenth-century French writer, La Rochefoucauld; and if I took my sense of the nature of being from Plato, then from La Rochefoucauld I derived the whole basis of my ethical sense. What the

French writer sets out to inculcate, with sustained wit and acumen (and a dash of healthy cynicism), is that the basis of all human action is egoism or self-love (*amour propre*). There are many obvious instances of selfish human behaviour; but La Rochefoucauld's ambition is to go further and expose the egoism latent in what are apparently neutral or even unselfish acts. So one pithy summary informs us that our apparent humility may simply be a subtler form of pride: 'To refuse to accept praise is to want to be praised twice over'. Or our seeming devotion to a high standard may arise not from a regard for virtue but from a selfish sense of our own vulnerability: 'In most men love of justice is only fear of suffering injustice'.

There are readers who find La Rochefoucauld too pessimistic or one-sided; but not only did he seem to me to be a realist who removed the veils of hypocrisy in order to reveal the truth, but in addition did so as part of a psychological dissection of the human character which owed much to the culture which produced him (that is, the France of Louis XIV, which encouraged such astute analysis of men and manners). He was, in a sense, a novelist *manqué*, who was undertaking a depiction of human beings as they actually were. As such, he served me well in my later readings of fiction, in particular in my encounter with George Eliot's *Middlemarch*, which so repeatedly exposes the egoism which dictates our actions and makes us blind to the needs and the reality of others.

Egoism has always since remained for me the core of the ethical problem; in its many forms (desire for power, antipathy to others, harsh judgment or denunciation arising from self-righteousness, or, worst of all, envy in its manifold and often unacknowledged guises) it is ego which comes between one human being and another, repeatedly putting at risk the possibility of genuine human community. Egoism is in George Herbert's phrase the 'cunning bosom-sin' which is too closely implicated in the very core of our being, and can perhaps never be fully extirpated. And just as Platonism could be seen as an extension of certain aspects of Catholic teaching, so La Rochefoucauld's exposure of egoism seemed to me entirely commensurate with Christianity's emphasis on pride as the sin of sins.

Egoism was in fact pride under a different name. And following on from that, it seemed obvious that the whole meaning of the teachings of Christ could be centred on his insistence on charity and selflessness, which are the exact antithesis of self-love. On further reflection, it seemed that self-love derived from a deeply ingrained instinct for self-preservation; for we are often selfish from a sense of our own vulnerability, or out of fear of being caught out or exposed. Before the Fall, that instinct for self-preservation had no role to play, and it came into being only as a result of our exile from Eden and our exposure to an uncertain existence in a world of contingency.

Thus it was that as an adolescent theologian I puzzled it all out and created my master-narrative: once exiled from Eden, we fell into self-regard in our struggle for survival, and in Christ we had the second Adam who attempted to restore us to Eden by trying to remove our selfish fears and promote an ethical code of selfless behaviour. I admired the symmetry of my own mythical construct; and was perhaps, indeed, beguiled into a proud self-congratulation at the ingenious completeness of it all. I shake my head now over the presumption of that much younger man; but, nevertheless, I have never lost the feeling that ego is the great enemy of human welfare, and that the Christian ethic is one possible cure. The most insidious and destructive form of ego is surely envy; and if some of us find such parables as that of the Labourers in the Vineyard especially 'difficult' or 'challenging', then that may be because they specifically target our habit of comparing ourselves with others in a spirit of envious resentment (surely, the clamorous ego is ever ready to claim, *I* deserve better?) We Irish in particular should perhaps bear in mind that when, on one occasion, Joyce was allocating the Seven Deadly Sins to the various nations of Europe, the sin he reserved for his own native land was just that unlovely one of Envy.

*

In due course, having taken Latin, French and English in my first year, I opted for a 'pure' English degree, which meant that I spent the next three years concentrating almost exclusively on English literature, from medieval times up to modern. Given the very limited exposure to English poetry, drama and fiction we had had at school, much of the syllabus was entirely new; and even where we might have studied a major author previously (Milton, say), we would have dealt only with such minor works as the ode 'On the Morning of Christ's Nativity'. Now, however, we were plunged into *Paradise Lost* in its full extent (a real challenge, given Dr Johnson's honest comment: 'None ever wished it longer than it is').

Paradise Lost, however, posed a challenge of a different kind for a reader such as myself. When at school we had read Milton's 'Nativity' ode, it had seemed a straightforward Christian celebration of the birth of Christ, and no doctrinal questions or differences arose. We were vaguely aware that Milton was a Protestant, but we could take this poem, on an event central to all Christians of whatever shade, in broadly ecumenical terms. But when we came to *Paradise Lost*, we had to reckon not only with Milton's unorthodox views on the Trinity, but, more urgently, with a Puritan Protestantism which was associated with the hated Cromwell, and the additional fact that the poem contained some quite explicit anti-Catholic propaganda.

To take the most obvious example, there is the sequence in Book Ten of Milton's epic where, after Satan's successful seduction of Adam and Eve to disobedience, thereby bringing about the Fall, Sin and Death decide to build a bridge across Chaos and meet him on his return. Milton introduces a Latinate pun: as bridge-builders, Sin and Death proceed by 'wondrous art/ Pontifical', where the last word literally means 'bridge-making'. But intentionally the word also implies a sardonic judgment on the Pope, known familiarly to Catholics as the Pontiff (from the Latin title Pontifex Maximus, whence the adjective 'pontifical' derives). This, then, is Milton's satiric dismissal of Roman Catholicism and its false and grandiose claims; and if for some extreme Protestant sects in Northern Ireland the Pope was (and is) the Antichrist and Whore of Babylon, then in Milton's poem he is similarly evaluated as synonymous with Sin and Death.

I am happy to report that I took all this in my stride. In fact, I quite enjoyed the ingenuity in the punning use of the word 'pontifical'. And while I regretted the fact that Milton had found it necessary to satirise Catholicism in this way, I allowed for the historical circumstances (the poem was written in the latter part of a century which had seen protracted religious war in Europe), and perhaps even respected a poet (and a century) that paid religion the compliment of taking it seriously. In any case, such incidental anti-Catholicism could not spoil for me the imaginative impact of the poem, and I happily involved myself in those critical arguments about the true hero of the epic: not Satan (as we might at first be beguiled into thinking) but hard-pressed humanity. Moreover, Milton had deliberately aligned himself with a pan-European tradition in the epic, reaching back as far as Homer and Virgil. He had, transcending his insular origins, gone to Italy in the cultural tradition of the Grand Tour; and his impressive learning, as displayed in *Paradise Lost*, was a reminder that he was a European humanist as well as an English Puritan.

What *Paradise Lost* posed was a challenge to one's discrimination: you had to learn to sift the valuable wheat from the offensive chaff, and thereafter acknowledge the unqualified worth of great poetry. The exercise was, nonetheless, of a negative kind. I was not placed in a position where I said, 'This is good in the very fact of its Protestantism'; but rather, 'In spite of its Protestantism, this is still pretty good'.

Far more positive, though, was my response to the seventeenth-century Anglican poet George Herbert, who came, in a number of ways, as a revelation. The fact that he was Anglican rather than Puritan might in any case have prepared me for a more sympathetic response, given (as I was later to learn from reading Newman) the proximity of certain aspects of Anglicanism ('Anglo-Catholicism') to Roman Catholicism. But it was indeed at a later date that I learned of that proximity; and it pains me somewhat to recall that when I first came across the poetry of Herbert at the age of eighteen, in my second year at Queen's, I was more or less oblivious to the differences in belief and emphasis across the Protestant spectrum. True, I knew that some were Presbyterian, others Church of Ireland, others still Methodist; but in keeping with my inherited 'Them and Us' mentality, I had little time for a subtler taxonomy of that kind. We were taigs, they were (all of them) Prods, and that was it. So I read Herbert not primarily as an Anglican poet, but, to begin with at least, as a poet indiscriminately associated with the 'other side'.

Partly because of a deliberate espousal of simplicity in style, Herbert's poetry is rather more accessible than Milton's (or, for that matter, the poetry of his near contemporary, John Donne). But what surprised me at first was the familiarity of the terminology and the imagery. I mean, of course, not just the central images of Christianity (such as the Crucifixion and the Resurrection), but the liturgical imagery of the Eucharist, or the references to the season of Lent and to Good Friday, or the fact that one of the poems was an 'Anagram of the Virgin Mary' (for had we not been taught that, unlike us, the Protestants did not venerate the Virgin Mother of God?). Above all, I felt obliged to acknowledge that what Herbert conveyed in his poetry was not just a doctrinal sense of Christianity, but the spiritual experience of being a Christian. Most obviously, this is the case in what is perhaps the greatest of all his short lyrics, 'Love' ('Love bade me welcome'), a poem about the Eucharist but, even more centrally and powerfully, an affirmation of God's unconditional forgiveness of sinful and imperfect man. But in other works (such as 'The Flower', which begins: 'How fresh, O Lord, how sweet and clean/Are thy returns!') Herbert seemed successfully to have conveyed the vivifying experience of grace in terms immediately recognisable to any Catholic.

Why, it may be asked, should I have been so surprised at this discovery? The answer is one that makes me blush. So incessantly had it been dinned into us in our education that the Catholic Church was the 'one true church' that all Protestant religions were regarded as sadly deficient in anything approaching true spirituality. If, for instance, they could not accept the doctrine of transubstantiation, whereby the bread and wine of Holy Communion become, really and truly, the Body and Blood of Christ, what could they know of the intensely spiritual experience of receiving that sacrament, which for the Catholic possesses such absolute meaning? Indeed (I blush again) I recall how at primary school, when I was nine or ten, one of the Christian Brothers pointedly mocked the whole notion of the Eucharist as administered in the Church of Ireland,

and although I can still remember the exact words he used, I cannot bring myself to repeat them here, preferring at this point to spare the reader.

In his superbly acerbic short story 'Grace', Joyce hilariously exposes the limitations of Irish bourgeois Catholicism. In the course of one of the earnest conversations between the Catholic 'gentlemen' in the story, distinctions are drawn between themselves and their Protestant neighbours. Mr Cunningham 'quietly and effectively' summarises the consensus among the group as to Catholic superiority. 'But of course,' he remarks (of course!), 'our religion is *the* religion, the old, original faith.' Such triumphalism, however quietly expressed, is the basis of the intolerant dismissal and devaluation of any alternative version of Christianity, and it was to that tradition that I was frequently exposed in the early and formative years of my education. What it meant was that while I could readily accept that there were 'good' or morally admirable Protestants (and in fact there is a widespread Irish Catholic tendency, which may arise from some obscure law of compensation, to extol the honesty and probity of Protestants), they were nonetheless excluded from the spiritual centre. Ethics was one thing, but genuine spirituality another. And it is against this background, with its inculcation of narrow views, that my surprise on coming across the poetry of George Herbert may be explained (though never quite excused).

Clearly, then, there *was* such a thing as an identifiably Protestant spirituality, less rapturous and more restrained than its Catholic equivalent, but perhaps (especially if you were exposed to the excesses of Herbert's Catholic near-contemporary Richard Crashaw, and the extravagances of the art of the Counter-Reformation) all the more admirable for that restraint. Herbert's poetry was low-key and authentic both in its struggles and perplexities and in its moments of assurance and confident belief. I am inclined to believe, too, that it was this early encounter with Herbert at university which prepared me for a more sympathetic engagement with later poetry which might otherwise not have been so accessible.

Thus it was easier for me to accept the idea of the possible saintliness of the seventeenth-century Anglican Nicholas Ferrar, so central to T. S. Eliot's 'Little Gidding' (one of his *Four Quartets*); or, indeed, taking

Herbert and Ferrar together, to understand why it was that the seventeenth century as a whole can be regarded as a high-water mark in the Anglican tradition. Moreover, it may also be the case that I acquired some gradual understanding of the general Protestant distrust of image or icon, and the preference for a more direct access to the invisible. Herbert's verse is liturgically rich, but in his preference for simplicity of expression and his frequently expressed suspicion of poetic ornament he may be conveying a yearning for an unmediated knowledge of the divine; and his verse is, one might say, as uncluttered as a Protestant church. In terms of poetic simplicity, one of his successors is Wordsworth; and I do not think that I could have come to appreciate Wordsworth as much as I did had I not first learned to appreciate a Protestant tradition of the *unimaged* divinity. For one of the recurrent experiences in Wordsworth is the moment when 'the light of sense goes out', and the poet, departing completely from any reliance on the immediacy of image, surrenders to the 'invisible'. Even if the experience is non-Christian (as for the early Wordsworth it certainly was), it remains a culmination of a spiritual and, perhaps, 'post-Protestant' kind.

*

If, however, one was challenged in one's reading or study to respond to difference and learn to see things from the perspective of the other, it remained the case that 'on the ground' the old familiar sectarian divide was still very much in evidence. Catholics and Protestants mingled, of necessity, in the classrooms and lecture theatres, and to some extent socially; but each side continued to define itself in its own chosen enclaves. Protestants had their Bible Union, Catholics their Chaplaincy; Nationalists were members of the Gaelic Football Club, the other side played some such game as hockey (never, ever played at Nationalist schools, and often dismissed as a 'cissy' version of hurling). Even if all the students did not subscribe to these structures, they nevertheless remained normative.

Not all Protestants were members of the Bible Union (some would have found it too fervent or fundamentalist), but nearly every Catholic visited on a regular basis the Catholic Chaplaincy. For the Chaplaincy was not just a spiritual resource, but a social centre. I suspect that a number of Catholics met their future marriage partners in that context, whether attending the nightly recital of the Rosary or else browsing the reading material available there. (The alternative venue might be one of a number of dancehalls in the city of Belfast, in particular Fruithill on a Sunday night, a place where you were guaranteed to meet only co-religionists.) A Chaplaincy is, to some extent, what the Chaplain makes of it; and in my time at Queen's the Catholic Chaplain was, in terms of doctrinal orthodoxy, rather further to the right than John Paul II. As I recall it, we had numerous orations from him on abortion, the gist of which was that not only did the foetus have an equal right to life with the mother, but, in circumstances where the life of the mother could be saved only by terminating the pregnancy, then that was strictly forbidden and the mother would forfeit her life. This was not, of course, simply a matter of theological debate of merely academic interest; the Chaplain would have known that among his listeners were a number of Catholic medical students, and the determination was to ensure that when they began their practice (some as specialists of various kinds) they would follow orthodox (or, in the Chaplain's case, ultra-orthodox) Catholic teaching.

The serious tone of Chaplaincy proceedings in general was memorably indicated in one brief sentence in the Chaplaincy handbook, which was handed out to impressionable freshers. The sentence read (and I can still recall it almost word for word): 'You are welcome to relax and spend as much time as you please in the Chaplaincy during opening hours; but do remember that time wasted around the Chaplaincy is the same as time wasted anywhere else; and' (the punchline) 'time is given to us to prepare for eternity'. How is it, one repeatedly wonders, that Christianity is so frequently seen to be compatible with a total humourlessness? One recalls, gratefully, the suggestion by G. K. Chesterton that there was only one thing that Christ hid from us when He was on earth: a divine sense of humour. We might not have been able to cope with humour on that scale.

In my second year at Queen's I was myself guilty of an unduly orthodox gravity in my dealings with the Chaplain (call him Father Michael). I had been asked to write an essay on the great seventeenth-century English prose stylist, Sir Thomas Browne, with specific reference to *Religio Medici*. Somehow or other, acting with a misplaced zeal, I discovered that the works of Browne (including *Religio Medici*) had been placed on the Catholic Index of Prohibited Books. As a dutiful son of the Church, therefore, I wrote a letter to Fr Michael explaining the situation and asking him if it was all right for me to go ahead and read the book by Browne so that I could fulfil the essay requirement. Back came a prompt reply. I suppose that I had expected that the whole matter would be treated as a formality, and that my asking for permission to read the forbidden text was merely a requisite gesture; but not, it turned out, when Fr Michael was alerted to the least whiff of heterodoxy.

'Dear Brian,' the letter ran, 'thank you for making me aware of your moral predicament. You may, of course, read the book in question in order to satisfy your tutorial requirements. But please read only those parts of the book that are relevant to your essay; and on no account allow the book into the hands of another.' When, later, I got hold of the book I was quite unable to convince myself that what I was carrying around with me was some kind of moral timebomb or devastating moral virus. I was later to discover that Browne had fallen foul of the Vatican authorities because he was regarded by them as tainted by fideism. Fideism may be defined as an excessive dependence on faith (*fides*) or revelation, at the expense of reason or the intellect; and, arcane and remote from common experience as the denunciation of fideism may seem, there is in fact an understandable logic in the Church's suspicion of this tendency to play down the role and importance of reason as a means of access to the truth.

The Catholic Church's argument is that the natural and inevitable outcome of such a distrust of reason as is found in fideism is scepticism: if reason cannot guide us to the truth, then one argument becomes as valid as another. The Church further holds that a fideistic attitude encourages agnosticism, which in itself, in any case, is an extension of a radical scepticism. Unlike the debates over duelling which earned Alexandre Dumas (Dumas *père*) his place on the Index, and have, by now (and for some considerable time), been consigned to the pages of history, the ideas of fideism might be seen, from the Church's perspective, to pose a continuing threat. But while one might concede so much to the ecclesiastical point of view, there remain two aspects of this experience which later struck me as particularly ludicrous.

The first was that on any Sunday of the year I could freely purchase *The Observer* or *The Sunday Times* and find in its book-pages and elsewhere a vigorous agnosticism which was much more challenging to religious belief than anything in the pages of Thomas Browne. If the fear was that I in my innocence might have become a fideist, and (who knows?) might have spread the destructive virus of scepticism or agnosticism among my peers, corrupting them all in ways unforeseeable, then it should have been obvious that the British Sunday papers had already done the utmost damage that could have been done, both to me and to them. The second thing is sad as well as ludicrous. Of all the English Protestants in the seventeenth century (a time when contentiousness in religious matters was the norm), it would be difficult to find one more tolerant and ecumenical than Thomas Browne; tendencies that were promoted by his early travels on the Continent and his sojourns in Montpellier and Padua. Yet this was one of the writers whom the Catholic Church had chosen to proscribe!

Looking back, I marvel not only at the intransigence of Fr Michael, but at my own uncritical orthodoxy. I am now, unlike my youthful self, clearer as to where I stand on matters of this kind; and feel that if the Catholic Church comes into conflict with the principles of a liberal education, so much the worse for the Catholic Church. It is fortunate, then, that the Church can count among its luminaries John Henry Newman, who, sustained in *The Idea of a University* by his own 'great and firm belief in the sovereignty of Truth', repeatedly urges on us a respect for that Truth, so that we should be ready to accept it 'without fear, without prejudice, without compromise'. Moreover, there can in his view be 'no intellectual triumph of any truth of religion' unless it has been 'preceded by a full statement of what can be said against it'. It is only out of such liberal debate that the possibility of truth might begin to emerge.

*

In my final year as an undergraduate at Queen's, in the run-up to my BA examination, I moved out of a flat I shared with a number of other students, some of whom had already done their finals and felt that they were no longer under pressure to lead a sober and industrious life. Life in the flat had been fun while it lasted, but there were signs for me (if I was wise enough to interpret them) that I was, among other things, drinking more alcohol than was good for me. I remember in particular one occasion when, following an evening in the Club Bar or some other hostelry, I was being sick into a washhand basin in the toilet, and was put on the spot by one of my flatmates, an unfortunate and rather immature man called Ed, who was going through a late adolescent quarrel with God and religion. I still had at that time a reputation as a practising Catholic (I was to lapse for a brief while only some years later), so Ed saw his chance to 'put me to the test'.

His insistent voice is at my ear, while I retch repeatedly (though with awful, lingering gaps between), and feel that oblivion would be a merciful release.

'There you are, you see now? That's what your God does for you – lets you suffer in this way. Look at the state of you!'

Heroically, as I find a brief space between the heaves, and struggle to make my voice function, I summon up my highest moral sense.

'My own fault,' I reply with faultless logic, even in my appalling state. 'Drank too much.'

Ed was a troubled soul, and doubtless felt not that my reply represented a victory for the angels over his diabolical attempt at subversion, but that it was, rather, a revelation of just what a tight-arsed little shit I was. Poor Ed, alas, was one of those who, however troubled and pained they may be, fail to achieve anything approaching tragic grandeur, and remain on the level of the ludicrous. One particularly wild night, after much drink had been taken, we were up in the top storey, and about to indulge in one of our party-pieces, known as 'the Sinking of the *Titanic*'. This was the brain-child of the inventive 'J.J.', an engineer who had more comic imagination than anyone I have ever known. The routine consisted of staggering in a ragged knot or knots (depending on our numbers) from one side of the room to the other, kicking over the furniture as we went (all to do with the fatally sloping deck), and, the crowning touch, singing 'Nearer My God to Thee'.

It was on this night that Ed decided he would allow us to hear some of his poetic outpourings – a decision all the more badly timed given that one of our visitors that night (though not a member of the group) was the youthful Seamus Heaney, who even at that early stage (before the publication of his first collection) was known to have an unusual gift for poetry. To an audience made all the more sceptical and unheeding by drink, Ed insisted on voicing his poetic clichés.

'Death is the one reality', he told us in something approaching regular metrical form; a suggestion greeted by the whole group with raucous and sustained laughter. Ed, however, was not inclined to release himself from the close embrace of his existential angst; and promptly announced that he was going to end it all by throwing himself off the gable roof. As he struggled to open the window into the night air, willing hands assisted him, with cries of 'Good man, Ed!' and 'Good luck now!' So out he went, onto a fairly broad window ledge, and, as we continued our chat inside, someone decided to close and lock the window behind him. As we subsequently went through our *Titanic* routine, we could hear at first tentative and then increasingly louder and more desperate knocks on the window-pane, as Ed decided that this was not, after all, the night for him to face the 'one reality'. Eventually he was ignominiously readmitted, and had to bear his ignominy as best he could. Queen's could be a tough school in the early sixties, and you had to be prepared to take the rough with the smooth. I can recall other instances of casual victimisation, and at this stage am not proud of my own participation in those (limited as I hope it was).

Clearly, though, I could not hope to apply myself to my studies in English, as the imminent examinations required I should, if I continued in a lifestyle of the kind just described. So I resolved to go back into 'digs', choosing to return to a household where I had stayed the previous academic year. This was a house quietly situated on Botanic Avenue and run by an unmarried Catholic woman who lived there with her widowed mother. It was a choice not just for the quiet life, but for the regular one: breakfast and the evening tea were served at set times, and that meant, in addition, that I did not have to waste time preparing my own meals (lunch was in the student canteen). So I determined to spend my spare time in the library, getting up reasonably early in the morning, and often working late at night, not just in the main library, but in the small library room in the English Department.

It was there that I got to know somewhat better than I previously had Stewart Parker (who was later to die tragically young from the cancer that had afflicted him early in his life, and cost him the lower part of one of his legs). Stewart would also be reading in that small departmental room, and at times, when I raised weary eyes from D. H. Lawrence's *The Rainbow* or whatever it might be, Stewart was always affably available for a chat. The word 'affable' means, literally, someone you can talk to; and that, I think, was one of Stewart's great charms. However lively he could be in conversation, he had no noticeable self-assertion, so that you always felt that here was someone who (usually with a smile on his face) was ready to listen to you.

I am still grateful for the company he provided at a time when I felt under acute pressure to deliver a good degree. As those who are familiar with his work will know, Stewart had a great love of music; and we discovered that we had in common a growing interest in forties' swing, including Glenn Miller. One abiding memory I have of Stewart is his rendition one night, with all the appropriate imitation of the orchestral instruments, of 'Tuxedo Junction', in which, I think, I eventually joined. He dearly loved the obvious syncopation, and, as his walking-stick leaned on the chair beside him, his one good leg moved up and down to the time of the music.

I should take this opportunity to correct any false impression which may have been given with regard to relations between Protestant and Catholic at university level. There was indeed social interaction between us. Stewart was, as I knew (and alas we in the North always made it our business to know), a Protestant; but that simply did not feature as a factor in our acquaintance. Moreover, in the digs I went to on Botanic Avenue the majority of the residents were Protestant, and we coexisted on the most cordial terms. Two or three of these were studying medicine, and we swapped jokes of the kind you might expect from medical students. One of them was a gentle giant who played rugby, and I was intrigued, in watching out for him subsequently, to see if he would make it to the inter-provincial level and play for Ulster.

We even had among us a research student in chemistry who was a member of the notorious Northern Irish auxiliary police force (now disbanded), the B-Specials. I do not remember having had any trouble with that, though on the whole we tended to move (by tacit agreement) in different social circles. Yet if Trevor (such was his name) invited me to join him for a drink, I had no hesitation in doing so. He was a mature student by the time I got to know him, and had a good sense of humour. Only on rare occasions did he cause me some passing unease (and then it resolved itself quickly into an anecdote to be relayed to fellow Nationalists).

'You know who you remind me of, boy?' ('Boy' is a common form of address in the North of Ireland.)

I looked back across the table at him through my glasses, which I had been wearing for some years; at that time, too, I was clean-shaven, so the comparison Trevor came up with is explicable.

'Who?'

'De Valera. No, really, you have a definite look of him about you.'

I did not allow my imagination to dwell too long on the question as to how 'Dev' would have been perceived by a Northern Protestant who was sufficiently devoted to his province to serve in the B-Specials. It was, at best, a dubious compliment, though offered in all sincerity and without any hint of threat. That, however, was in the early sixties; and a similar exchange at a later date would have carried a much more sinister import.

*

Even in the early sixties, however, Belfast could easily display its more violent side, and at or following the Saturday night 'hops' at Queen's, there were frequent clashes of a vicious nature between city youths and students. But my own most vivid memory of violence occurred off campus, and, innocent enough as it finally proved to be, disturbed me much more than the occasion seemed to warrant. It was the year after I had graduated, and I had moved accordingly from the secure haven on Botanic Avenue into a less structured and more liberated existence in a house shared with a number of other lads on the Lisburn Road.

There were about seven of us altogether, all but one, as I recall, graduates or undergraduates. The one non-university representative was in a junior 'white-collar' job; and whatever his difference from us in university terms, he had at least the recommendation that, like two or three of us, he too was from Newry. We were, then, a fairly homogeneous group; that is, up until one of our number (a man pursuing a university degree as a mature student in his early twenties) suggested that we fill a vacant bed with a mate he had come to know, a man I shall call Bobby. It is easy to be wise after the event, but we should have proceeded with greater caution. Whereas all of us in the lodgings had known each other for some time, the newcomer was a stranger to everybody except the man who introduced him into the group. Inviting a stranger like Bobby into our tight, closely knit group was, at best, a major gamble.

There were two further complications. Bobby, from County Antrim, was a Protestant (we were all Catholics); and Bobby was as far removed from a university education as it is possible to be, having been apprenticed as a carpenter from an early age. By the time he joined us, he was about twenty-two, a strapping figure whose biceps bore witness to the vigour of his manual labour (whereas we, by comparison, were a pretty weedy lot). Bobby, in other words, was significantly different to the rest of us, on at least two major counts; but we all felt young and tolerant and adaptable, and at first all went well. Until, that is, the Night of the Big Booze-Up.

A group of five, including Bobby, went drinking. It seems (for I was not there to witness the proceedings) that not only did one drink lead to another, but one kind of drink led to another. To crown it all, the gang bought a 'takeaway' in the form of flagons of the poisonously potent Merrydown cider, cheap and staple fare for the impoverished student. By the time they arrived back in the lodgings (where I and two others were spending a sober night) they were in a chaotic state; and they still had some cider to drink. They were all on a downward and degenerative spiral to utter irrationality; friction was in the air, and quarrels on the flimsiest of pretexts seemed imminent. Some of us who were sober tried to keep potential combatants apart from each other; but the situation was increasingly getting out of control. And it was Bobby who emerged as easily the most dangerous, if only because of his physical strength.

Apart from that consideration, Bobby had decided to take it upon himself to defend his self-worth by challenging all comers. Just because he was not a clever dick university student, that didn't mean he was not as good as everybody else. So he went around the house, putting it up to anyone who crossed his path, that he was as good as they were any day. My own turn came when he cornered me on my own in the kitchen; it remains for me a frightening experience.

'You think you're better than me, don't you? Think you're better than me?'

'Not at all, Bobby,' is my measured reply. I smile in what I hope is a reassuring way, noting as I do so that Bobby is clenching and unclenching his fists, and bringing up the veins on his exposed upper arms.

Now he is reaching his hand out and stroking my cheek softly but with a menacing caress. All he can do now in his speech is repeat the same question over and over.

'You think you're better than me, eh?' (the menacing stroke on the cheek is more definite and pronounced). I decide that at all costs I must stay calm and reasonable. The kitchen is empty apart from the two of us; and this guy is big and strong, and may not (as the saying is) know his own strength. I try to reach some court of appeal in his eyes, man to man. And then it was that I experienced the most frightening thing of all. For when I look into Bobby's eyes as he stands in a truculent posture a few feet away from me, I see pure void, absolutely nothing. There is not the vaguest, slightest point of human rationality in those eyes. The man who stands before me is as irrational as an automaton, and strong enough to kill with his bare hands if that is the way his inclination leads him. I am really frightened now, but continue to deny myself any sudden movement.

Luckily, a distraction: the friend of Bobby who introduced him to the lodgings has entered the kitchen, and he is one of the sober ones. He goes out with Bobby into the front room. Later I learn that, as his friend is trying to talk him out of his aggression, Bobby smashes the backs off a couple of chairs with his fists and then collapses in hysterical weeping. The crisis is over, and we all go to bed. Next day, not surprisingly, Bobby has absolutely no recollection of what happened the night before. All the time he was at his most aggressive, he had been as unconscious as an automaton, and could have done anything without realising the nature of his actions. In retrospect, the escapade seems to me more frightening than ever.

What kind of terrifying nothingness was it that I clearly saw in Bobby's drink-crazed eyes? Pure irrationality, perhaps; but I must resist the temptation to see in those eyes a dire prophecy of events that were to afflict that society on a larger scale. So it might be extravagant to claim that what I saw in those mad eyes was a foretaste of the destructive sequence of sectarian hatred and terrorist mayhem that was to engulf Northern Ireland in the seventies and eighties. Moreover, the episode may reveal as much about me as it does about Bobby or Northern Irish society. Did I overreact at the time (do I do so even now)? For in the immediate aftermath, when I tried to express how I had felt, the other members of the group teased me unmercifully about it ('Look out, boy! Here comes Bobby!')

I appear to have both a considerable fear of and fascination with the irrational, and perhaps this induces me even now to make too much of the Bobby episode. I am appalled by Schopenhauer's idea that the world and we who are in it are driven by an irrational force (most evident in the sexual act) called the Will; yet at the same time my imagination repeatedly comes back to such a notion. Reluctant as my acknowledgment may be, I do nonetheless pay heed to Lacan's suggestion (as mediated by Slavoj Žižek) that we are inhabited by an amoral, cruel and meaningless force which he calls 'the Real'. Was this not the part of my nature that led me as a child to smash the crabs to pieces on the seashore at Warrenpoint? Is this, too, not the part of our nature that Shakespeare tried to describe in his famous sonnet on lust (number 129), as 'Savage, extreme, rude, cruel, not to trust'?

Yet on the other side I am committed to the claims of reason, provided they do not become overweening. I acknowledge the moral force of the warning against our potential irrationality and barbarism in Conrad's *Heart of Darkness*, when Marlow observes that the 'human mind is capable of anything – because everything is in it, all the past as well as all the future'. (In the self-destructive fate of Kurtz, the point is graphically illustrated.) Again, I applaud Freud when he announces it as part of the civilising programme of psychoanalysis that 'where id was, there ego shall be'. So, in some senses, I remain a child of the Enlightenment.

Nonetheless, I am uneasy with those rationalist tendencies which would abolish all sense of mystery (hence one source of my interest in Romanticism), or sceptically dismiss religious experience out of hand. One reason why the *Pensées* is to me so attractive is that Pascal consistently attempts to prescribe limits to reason ('There is nothing so consistent with reason as the denial of reason'). And perhaps it is Pascal, too, who strikes the correct balance when in the *Pensées* he warns against not one but two excesses: 'Excluding reason, admitting only reason'.

I suspect that one of the major motives for my interest in literature is that literature is in its own way a response to Pascal's admonition, in that it finds itself at home on the problematic interface between the rational and the irrational. While committed to a programme of inclusion from which nothing should be omitted, not even the darkest and most troubling aspects of human experience, and ready at all times to hearken to the voice of unreason, literature holds itself equally obliged to honour the severe and civilised discipline of clear articulation. The tension between these contrary claims is never easily resolved, and the process may involve what Arnold called 'imaginative reason', rather than pure rationalism; but it is a positive form of reason nonetheless. And this, in literature, is the Apollo that must repeatedly engage with Dionysus.

CHAPTER TEN

The Circle Broken

In the late spring of 1960, my mother became ill. It was some six months before my nineteenth birthday, and I still do not know if the other members of the family realised at the time how serious her condition was, or might become. What I do know is that I myself had little or no inkling of the gravity of her plight; in large measure because my brothers and sisters conspired (and I think that that is the correct term) to keep from me the details of her condition. I have no doubt that they acted in that way to 'save me from the worst'; but it was to prove the most misguided type of kindness, in that, when the end eventually did come, I was even less prepared for it than I might have been.

But it may also be the case that I conspired against myself; that I refused to admit to the centre of my consciousness the fact that she was indeed gravely ill, because the recognition of that possibility would have been intolerable. She had been diagnosed as having cancer of the breast, and underwent a mastectomy. I cannot recall the extent to which these details registered with me; certainly, it seems to have been the case that the implications of these facts hardly registered at all. I had a dim sense that all was not well, and I was recurrently troubled to think of her lying up in her bedroom all day; but she herself tried as hard as she could to be cheerful and positive, although, towards the end, as her suffering became more acute, she began to reveal her anguish.

At first all was well, and the darker implications of her illness were covered up in a flurry of family activity. The summer following her operation, our cousins from Boston came over on a visit to Ireland, and a touring party was organised to convey them round the island. Other Irish cousins, as well as our branch of the 'clan', pitched in, and the touring party (including my mother and, more remarkably, my father, who was rarely known to take a holiday) travelled west and south, ending their excursion on a high note by 'doing' the Ring of Kerry. They came back to Newry in due course; there were a number of photo sessions; then the American cousins were gone, and the dust settled. It was shortly after that that my mother's health began to deteriorate; and I suppose that it was only at a much later date that I recognised that the trip round the country with the Americans had been either a last attempt to bring her back to a normal state of health, as part of a convalescence, or else a farewell present for her, a final holiday.

For most of the last nine months of her life she was confined to bed. Am I right now in thinking that when I went up to see her I sometimes experienced a certain awkwardness, as if she did not want me to know how poorly she was, and felt obliged to act in a way that would keep up her spirits and mine? Next door to the bedroom was our drawing-room, which contained a splendid radiogram, with a handsome walnut exterior. It was at this period that I was beginning to discover the delights of music other than that of the most popular kind: not, to begin with, classical music, but Richard Rodgers and George Gershwin. We had a '78' of Rodgers' 'Slaughter on Tenth Avenue', and for a few months this became for me the most intense musical experience I could experience, especially in the soaring climax. After that, I graduated to Gershwin's 'Rhapsody in Blue', and, eventually, with Tchaikovsky and Rachmaninov, moved on to classical music proper.

So I would put on one of these favourite pieces, ask my mother if she would like to listen to it, turning up the volume so that she could hear the music. I think now that she, in her sickbed, was still concerned to humour me; for the truth was that her tastes in music were for pieces quieter or more melodic – such as John McCormack singing 'Bless This House', Liszt's *Liebestraum*, Elgar's *Chanson de Matin*, Puccini's 'One Fine Day' or the 'Humming Chorus' from *Madam Butterfly*, or (a great favourite) Debussy's 'Clair de Lune'. But it was one way for us to communicate, even if in my immaturity I was far too self-centred, and not sufficiently alert to either her condition or her needs. She would acquiesce in my choice of music, though occasionally hinting that she also liked the quieter pieces I have mentioned.

As is usually the case in such circumstances, a routine established itself. By now my mother's sister was living with us, an ageing spinster whom we knew as Aunt Bella (Isabella). She had worked for years in Boots the chemists in Manchester, and possessed what seemed to us, in its unfamiliar Englishness, a peculiar accent. She took over the running of the house, including the kitchen; and I was particularly grateful that she was such a good cook, because it meant that the kind of meals my mother had made continued to be served up in the usual way. She was also able to make the apple tarts and sponge cakes that my mother had provided; and it is a startling revelation of my selfish reluctance to face reality at that time that it was on those limited terms that I could reconcile myself, in part at least, to my mother's absence from the running of the household.

But the atmosphere in the house was changing. It was becoming clear to my father, and to my sisters and brothers, if not to me, that the illness was a grave one. All I was conscious of was a growing unease, a sense of something happening which did not declare itself openly. I would enter the kitchen perhaps, and catch my sisters in the midst of an earnest conversation carried on in low voices; and the conversation would change. On Saturday nights, I would go out with some of the lads for a few lagers in the local hotel bar, and return in time to see the controversial but highly entertaining *That Was the Week that Was* on television. The euphoria generated by the drink and conversation in the bar would persist up to a point, but there would inevitably arise in my mind the thought of my mother lying ill upstairs, and I was possessed by a strange confusion of feeling (to which the effect of the alcohol consumed earlier contributed). Sometimes the feeling would assume the form of vague irritation, as if I resented any reminder that life might be a major problem. 'Leave me alone,' part of my mind was saying, 'let me immerse myself in these trivia. Let me entertain myself. Don't annoy me!'

The Christmas before my mother died was a particularly fraught time for all of us. You can establish a mind-numbing routine for most of the yearly round, but on occasions which have such a powerful association with family solidarity, such as Christmas, the feelings below the surface begin to assert their claims. It was unthinkable that on Christmas Day itself our mother was to be laid up in this invalid fashion: nothing would be the same. The festivities would be a mockery of what they once had been. It was during this Christmas period that I saw for the first time, one Saturday night, Frank Capra's *It's a Wonderful Life* (on television), fell in love with Donna Reed, learned off some at least of the words of the song 'Buffalo Billy, won't you come out tonight?', and yielded to the masterful exploitation of sentiment in Capra's masterpiece. I was profoundly moved by it all, as many have been before and since; but I cannot help wondering if in my case the film provided a safety-valve for pent-up emotions that I was not even aware of having. So it is that the film retains forever for me not just the association with Christmas that it has for all who see it, but its relationship to that special Christmas, the last my mother was to spend on this earth.

Yet the Capra movie was the occasion also of a particularly memorable form of that irritation I have mentioned. As I recall it, there came a request that I, along with the other members of the family, should convene in my mother's bedroom to say the family rosary, and the request came before the film was over. My irritation arose from having to leave a film halfway through, but there may have been deeper motives at work. I was more than ever reluctant to abandon that world of fantasy, where my emotions had free range, and return to a reality where my feelings were at best confused, at worst intolerable. But submit I did (with shamefully bad grace), and after the rosary I went back to the TV to catch the end of the film.

My brother Art was by this stage in his final year as an undergraduate at Queen's, and would face his final examination in history in the summer. He was expected to do well, but as my mother's health deteriorated, the pressure on him became considerable. He was fortunate at the time to have a steady girlfriend, and I imagine that she gave him emotional support of an invaluable kind. For it was increasingly clear, even to me, who would rather not have admitted it, that my mother's health was in a state of slow decline. Yet I could not bring myself to allow any hint or whisper within my mind of the terrible word 'death'. One afternoon I had what was one of my most painful experiences with her, and, indeed, one of the most painful in my life. Even now I find it difficult to put into words.

Bedridden as she was, she had to rely on a bedpan to relieve herself; and this was usually provided for her by someone other than myself. But one day when I was the only one available, she called for my help. I duly handed her the bedpan, then realised with horror that she was pulling up her nightgown, revealing her pudenda, and that it was my task to help her to place the bedpan beneath her. I froze; at that stage I was uninitiated sexually, and this was the first time in my maturity that I had seen the female genitalia. I tried awkwardly to manoeuvre the bedpan into place, and she, too, struggled to help herself. But the awful thing was that she was in considerable discomfort, and her groans and gasps of pain served only to disorientate me further. Had I been only adult enough to seize the initiative, act firmly but gently, raise her bodily, and take command of the situation, as a nurse or doctor would do with a patient! But my false delicacy simply contributed the more to her suffering, so that for me the abiding memory of that moment is the anguish in her eyes, the desperate recognition of her own painful state.

My mother was, as I have made clear, deeply religious; but equally she possessed a great love of life. As she came to the end, it was the latter which seemed to predominate. I have no sense that she was resigned to her own death; as, indeed, how could she be, when she had but recently reached the age of sixty? No doubt she must have gone over repeatedly in her anxious mind the consequences for the family, so long nurtured by her, whom she must now leave behind. My two sisters were married, and both had provided her with her first grandchildren. But my two brothers and myself were young and unsettled, and she must have worried about our eventual fate.

In early June 1961, I made the first of two visits to Lough Derg ('St Patrick's Purgatory'), situated on an island in that lake in Donegal, a place for penitential prayer that goes back to medieval times. A sojourn there involves fasting for three days, and missing sleep on the first of two nights, when you are required to spend all night praying in the large basilica. It has featured frequently in Irish literature in the past two centuries, most recently in Seamus Heaney's splendid sequence 'Station Island'. The tradition among Catholics in Queen's was that you went there to pray for a good result in your final exams, a curious version of *quid pro quo* (I shall offer up penitential suffering in order to gain academic success). My finals were not until the following year, but I agreed to accompany a pal of mine who had just done his final exams; and quite an experience it turned out to be.

Record gales for that time of year assaulted the west and northwest coast of Ireland, and part of the vigil night was spent among the external colonnades of the basilica, huddled in blankets or overcoats or anything else that would serve to keep out the cold. One young woman from Cavan with whom I found myself in close proximity, acting in a manner more secular than the spiritual context seemed to require, offered to play footsie with me under a blanket; but, while I was flattered by the attention, I quickly realised that Eros and an empty stomach do not make good companions. Later, while we were inside the basilica, I was to experience an even more blatantly secular moment. At one point, looking around for my companion, Pete, I spotted him soundly asleep (against all the rules), on one of the church seats.

'Pete, Pete!' I shook him by the shoulder. 'Wake up! You're missing all the grace!'

Pete's priority was obviously not best served by my intrusion, and, almost before he was awake, he gave fiercely instinctive vent to the feelings of natural, post-Adamic man.

'What the fuck's the matter with you?'

In spite of the pain of the penitential fast and vigil, one can recommend Lough Derg to those who have not been there, not because one has any wish to see others suffer (on the basis of 'if I went through it, then so can they'), but because it offers an experience of a unique kind. There is no place on earth, I suspect, like Lough Derg, and its increasingly anachronistic quality confers on it an odd kind of singular appeal. At the particular time I first went there, it provided a welcome escape from the tragic circumstances of home; given that, in a state of physical discomfort, we are less likely to be aware of distress of a psychological nature. Lear in Shakespeare's play discovers that

> the tempest in my mind
> Doth from my senses take all feeling else
> Save what beats there.

The reverse, however, is also true: pain or discomfort in the physical senses can take away all feeling of the tempest in the mind.

But when I arrived home, I had to acknowledge the problem that persistently awaited there, now becoming more acute than ever. I was first of all taken back by coach to Belfast from Lough Derg, and had time to kill there before travelling on to Newry. This was the last of the requisite three days of fasting, and the convention was that you stayed up until after midnight of the third day and then broke your fast with a vengeance. My favourite dessert at that time was strawberries (with cream); so I purchased a punnet of these for myself in Belfast, and fantasised about them on my way back to Newry. What I soon realised, however, was that the home environment offered no haven for such unthinking pleasures. After midnight, in a subdued ritual, I duly ate the strawberries and cream, but they were, if not quite tasteless, then lacking in their usual exotic piquancy. Like Bergman's wild strawberries, they were fading into a simpler and richer past. Some days later my mother was dead.

A midsummer evening, 20 June 1961. The evening meal is suspended. The doctor is with my mother, who lies in a semi-conscious state upstairs. All day, and for the past number of days, heavily sedated by painkillers, she has drifted in and out of consciousness. On a summons from the doctor, I follow my sisters and brothers up the steep staircase to the landing, then on up a further flight of stairs to my parents' room. My father is already there, but slumped in the old green wicker chair. He looks wretched. In the gathering stillness I have time to notice also the grave demeanour of the young doctor; he is the assistant to our usual family doctor, and has prepared himself to do what must be done. Standing close to my mother's unconscious form, he contributes to an ominous tableau. Yet, astonishingly, I have failed still to take in what is happening. So that what the doctor is shortly to say falls upon me like a sudden affliction, tears me to pieces, plunges me into a chaos of feeling in which part of me seems to drown forever.

He is holding a syringe in his right hand: morphine.

'I am going to give her this now.'

His voice is low and compassionate, but firm, steady, professional. What he says next is simple and appalling.

'She won't come out of this.'

He is injecting the morphine. I am shattered. I am no longer conscious of anyone else in the room, or of my surroundings. A great bitter hammer-blow is at the back of my throat, physically painful if I had the leisure to attend to mere physical pain. She has gone forever, my mother. She will never be again. I am blinded less by tears than by a consuming grief that has no physical shape, cannot assume any such shape, or find any adequate voice. Her death comes as an absolute, with absolute force. The others in the family had tried to conceal the truth from me, and all too willingly I had connived at the concealment. Now, without preparation, with no sense of anticipation or gradual approach, the unspeakable is upon me, and I am helpless in its merciless ravage.

How long the experience lasted I cannot say. It was something outside of time, or at least something not measurable in time as we normally understand that. But the spasm passes, leaving behind only its traumatic residue; the experience comes, as all experiences must do, to an end. I am released back into time, into a world that is now absolutely altered from the world I had inhabited but a few moments before. My mother is still breathing, she is not yet dead; but she will never wake again.

Mechanically, I join the other members of the family as we kneel around the bed and someone, one of my sisters, starts up the family rosary. Is the young doctor gone? I hardly notice. At some stage he removes his presence, but I cannot remember when. One of our female cousins from Lislea, a nurse, has been present for some days, and he can leave things to her professional care. We pray on, trying to deliver the responses with some clarity, trying not to fail the occasion. My mother's breathing is growing more stertorous; then it is gentle, then gentler still.

At last she breathes her last. Someone stands up to check her condition. She is gone.

I look at the Westclox alarm clock that stands on the dressing table along with her Yardley eau de cologne, her Pond's Cream, her hairbrush. The clock that roused her over many years to her daily duties, beginning with attendance at mass and reception of communion. The clock that will never wake her again.

It is twenty minutes past six. The midsummer sun shines uselessly beyond the bedroom window. I am some months short of my twentieth birthday, and am to sit my final exams at Queen's in less than a year.

My griefstricken father somehow roused himself to make the funeral arrangements, and place the notices in the newspapers. But his self-possession could not last. By the time of the funeral, only days later, he had abandoned himself to a futile attempt to anaesthetise his pain by consuming neat whiskey. Looking at him then, ignominious in his drunkenness, I felt a pure hatred, justifying it to myself by accusing him of a lack of dignity in the presence of death. How could I recognise, ravaged as I then was by emotions with no adequate name, that what I was doing was targeting him as an available scapegoat? That I was directing towards his bowed and greying head an anger whose proper mark would have been those invisible agencies that had robbed me of my mother. But those were out of reach; and, as others have done before and since, I expended my silent rage on the most available victim. May God (and my father) forgive me that I should have been so blind at that moment to his own inner anguish.

*

On only one other occasion would I experience a greater pain; and that would be at the time of the cot-death of my infant son in 1977. I am still surprised at the vehemence of my grief at my mother's death, given that I had, as I had so rationally thought, distanced myself from her in my own nascent sexuality. Tidal and intensely terrible for every second of the brief spasmodic period it lasted, my grief plunged me far down into realms where I had never been. But deep and strong and obscure are the bonds between child and parent, and I am not the first (nor shall I be the last) to feel that powerful tug of nature in the moment of the last parting.

It was, in truth, an experience in the face of which all attempts at description confess their impotence. It opened up within me a space quite inaccessible to words or to what the French have taught us to call 'discourse'. So it is that I have always looked kindly on the similar yet significantly different terms, 'ineffable' and 'unspeakable'. And it is precisely because our language is normally so inadequate that we need the full range of creative exploitation that the poet, dramatist or novelist tries to bring to bear on our inadequate linguistic tools. Sometimes all he or she can finally do is bring us to the very edge of language (as Shakespeare does, for instance, in the last great speech of Lear), and leave us attentive to the ensuing silence.

I was devastated by my mother's death, but I survived. I had to accept the strange sight of her body laid out in the brown robes of the Franciscans (for she had been a member of the Third Order of St Francis, an order for the laity). At first I resented the change wrought in her appearance by the unfamiliar garb; I may even have felt rebellious, and regarded it as another exmple of the way in which 'they' were taking a beloved and familiar figure away from me and replacing her with something too different to be her. But deep down I knew that the real change was death itself; and when I entered the room on my own, as I sometimes did over the next two days, to look at her stiff body, I came to accept that she was no longer there, and that her body remained only as a sad parody of what she had once, so energetically and enthusiastically, been in life. I tiptoed out of the room across the cold linoleum, polished to a flawless sheen. It was no longer her bedroom, no longer either the bedroom in which, as a child, I had sought refuge from my nightmares. It was a mausoleum, a monument to vacancy, a void.

I survived, too, the funeral, hating as I did so, like a less exalted Prince of Denmark, the exposure of my mourning to the public eye. We were a well known family in the town, and both the visitors to the house and the numbers who attended the funeral were considerable. I discovered, in addition, how stubborn the life-urge was within me; a testament, I would now say, to the strength with which my mother had cherished me through the years. One incident in particular stands out, from the day after her death. Sullen and unsmiling, I sat down to lunch, which consisted that day of my favourite dish of brown stew, served up by my Aunt Bella, and made just the way my mother used to make it. I glanced with contempt at the meal set before me; and wondered how I, in my great grief, could be expected to have any relish for those trivial pleasures of a more innocent past! But my hunger was not to be denied, and the chunks of succulent steak were as welcome as they had ever been. Since that moment, and on more than one occasion, I have had reason to be grateful for those animal spirits that sustain me, and put to flight that stubborn pessimist in his 'inky cloak' who would be content with mere spectation and sour commentary.

*

I suspect that I acquired around the time of my mother's death the habit of surviving largely by strength of will, a habit which proved essential when, following her funeral, I found myself saddled with the business of answering the many written expressions of sympathy which flooded in and required acknowledgment. The other members of the family seemed to melt away; and it may in any case have been a sure instinct on my part that led me to busy myself in this way, filling up what would otherwise have been painful hours of vacancy with self-imposed activity. For in truth I overdid it, writing numerous letters where, perhaps, the simple acknowledgment card would have sufficed. But it was an activity of the kind noted by Vladimir in Beckett's *Waiting for Godot*: it 'passed the time'.

I resumed my studies at Queen's the following autumn, and steeled myself eventually to face my finals. I was expected to do well, and this was an additional burden. Anything less than the best would have been regarded not just by me but by others as the equivalent of failure; so that it was an 'all or nothing' situation. I found myself relying on my strength of will to see me through, which produced a state of mind not really conducive to the subtlest engagement with literature. The best way to read literary works is perhaps in a paradoxical state of relaxed alertness, with the kind of balance between the mental faculties advocated in a famous passage in Coleridge's *Biographia Literaria,* where he recognises the relevance of 'the will and understanding' in the functioning of imagination, but allocates to them a subordinate role. The imagination is to some extent under the 'controul' of the will, but, in the phrase Coleridge quotes from Virgil's *Georgics, laxis effertur habenis* ('is borne onward with loose reins'). In my last year at Queen's, I was sometimes clenching those reins so grimly that my imagination had to struggle for a more comfortable freedom: had, in a sense, to fight for breath.

I needed, though, that strength to see me through. As I have already suggested, Queen's in the 1960s was a tough school; and, in my own case, I can best illustrate that by one brief anecdote. Not long after the start of the first term, following my mother's death, I was on my way out from the student canteen after lunch, when I passed a bunch of 'cronies' whose central figure was one who had just successfully completed his degree in English. Always introspective by nature, and at this time more so than ever, I was shocked by an obscene phrase hurled at me with a casual brutality by a member of the group noted for his sexual conquests, the implication being that I was not man enough to have any success in that sphere.

My ears burned as I retreated before their collective sniggers. The imputed ignominy was as nothing compared to the revelation that someone who had been as recently bereaved as I had been could be treated so callously. I retreated, though, with a firm step, as deep within me the resolution hardened to see the challenge of my final year through to the end. I was too sensitive for my own good, but I was also strong-willed; even if that strength of will was, for someone in my situation, a dubious blessing.

I had read enough of D. H. Lawrence (possibly at that time my favourite author, and certainly my favourite novelist) to be aware of his repeated warnings against allowing the conscious will a destructive dominance. It is, for instance, the ruthless will of Gudrun and of Gerald (so memorably played by Glenda Jackson and Oliver Reed in Ken Russell's film version of Lawrence's novel) that proves so destructive in *Women in Love.* Among the other texts by Lawrence I studied for my finals was *Sons and Lovers*, which, as I reread it, acquired a new depth of meaning and relevance, especially in its closing pages, which deal so vividly with the death of Paul Morel's mother.

The sequence is based on Lawrence's own experience of the death of his mother from cancer; and I both identified with Paul Morel and at the same time distinguished my experience from his. I had no sense that my own attachment to my mother had been in any way Oedipal (as Lawrence's, and Paul Morel's, evidently was). My own relationship with her was, rather, similar to that between Seamus Heaney and his mother, as so perfectly memorialised in one of his most moving poetic sequences, 'Clearances', in *The Haw Lantern*. It is in the course of that poetic tribute to his mother that the poet, looking back to a much younger self, recalls 'our *Sons and Lovers* phase'. I, too, had been through that phase; but now, with the emergence of the challenges ahead, I had to leave it behind. The parting had come far too early (and, to this day, I am aware of the difficulty of acquiring an objective estimate of that remarkable woman, given that I had not sufficient time to 'grow away' from her); but, like Paul Morel at the end of Lawrence's novel, I could not follow her to 'the darkness'. I took my cue, rather, from Robert Frost's succinct statement of necessity at the end of 'Out, Out – ':

> And they, since they
> Were not the one dead, turned to their affairs.

*

Partly because I had never worked for a substantial period in our bar, I had had few opportunities to get very close to my father; and few indeed are the childhood memories of time spent in his company when I was the sole object of his attention, or of exceptional personal acts of kindness on his part. I have one vague memory of walking out the Armagh Road from Newry one autumn day (perhaps I was seven or eight), when he pointed upwards to the dark englobements in the trees (now visible, since the leaves had been stripped away), and told me that those were nests – now abandoned – the crows had earlier made. As I am usually oblivious to the natural environment (and could never have been a naturalist), the incident is all the more deeply implanted in my memory, as one of the rare occasions when I *was* made aware of the natural world.

More vivid still is an episode from one of the months in Warrenpoint, when I might have been about eight or nine. I was feverish with a 'flu bug, and tossed and turned in my bed. My mother tried repeatedly, but in vain, to persuade me to take Aungier's Emulsion. The very thought of that creamy-white liquid sliding coldly down my throat was too much to bear, and I could in no way face the reality of it, no matter how often my mother placed the spoonful under my nose. The evening wore on; through the bedroom window I could see, as usual, across the darkening sea, the comfortingly rhythmic lighthouse beams. My mind idled on those till I drifted off into a fitful sleep, only to wake up later still in my uneasy condition.

It grew very late, and all was dark outside. My father would soon be home. Then there were voices below and a sense of activity, something stirring. Now my father is there in the room, at the foot of my bed.

So I wasn't feeling well?

No, Daddy.

Would I not take the Emulsion?

Oh no, no, couldn't!

'Look,' my father said, producing a shining silver half-crown from his trouser-pocket, 'I'll give you this if you can be a brave man and take the medicine. Come on now.'

My father knew me well. Half a crown! I could do nearly anything for that kind of wealth. So I dragged myself up in bed until I was sitting straight, braced myself as my mother poured the awful stuff onto the spoon, and as fast as I could opened my mouth and swallowed it.

'Good man!' said my father. 'I'll leave this here for you beside the bed.'

More soothing noises from my mother. Then they are both gone, leaving behind my silver trophy, the prized half-crown. It is more than money; it is the token of my father's loving care.

But an occasion such as that one sticks in the mind precisely because it was so unusual. My earliest memories of my father include his impatience when I ventured, at the age of seven or eight, into his busy bar, where, it is abundantly clear, I am a nuisance, getting in the way of those who scurry back and forth serving drinks to the customers, often carrying them on precariously balanced trays to the partitioned 'snugs'. I am told in no uncertain terms to 'get out of here!' My father can barely find a moment to express his annoyance; but there is no doubt that my presence is not only unnecessary but unwanted. I grow up envying my brothers, who are not only welcome to help my father, but feel at home behind the counter. I am not a part of it, and begin to play my fated role (so it seems) of outsider.

But following my mother's death I was increasingly called upon to participate in the running of the family business. Possibly this would have been the natural development in any case, as I grew older and more mature; my brothers, moreover (especially Art), owing to changing circumstances, were not always as available as they had been. So it was that I underwent a rather belated rite of passage, as, for the first time, I worked long stretches in the bar, especially in the summer following my final examination at Queen's. What I am most grateful for is that I had that last opportunity to get closer to my father in his latter days (he survived my mother by two and a half years). I worked hard and served him well, and took pride in doing so; but it was I who was the winner in the transaction. There finally fell upon my shoulders, however belatedly, the mantle of paternal acceptance. Truly I was his son, and he, as truly, my father.

I was carried through the long demanding work-day (from 10 o'clock in the morning to 10.30 or later at night) not just by the sense of liberation which followed from the successful completion of my undergraduate degree, but also (doubtless) by the thought that now at last I could prove my worth and take my place behind the bar counter. I was sustained by a remarkable flow of energy, and relished the demanding labour as a release from all mental exertion. True, I still had to keep my wits about me, remembering the different prices of the drinks and engaging in some tortuous mental arithmetic (a bottle of stout and five Woodbine, one and tuppence plus tenpence ha'penny, equals two shillings and a ha'penny, change from half a crown fivepence ha'penny, next please!) All transactions were carried out at speed, especially when the clients poured in just before the televised horse-racing, and stood three or four deep around the counter, calling, waving, giving in their orders: 'Bottle of stout, Jimmy!' 'Hey, Jimmy, a Bass, for Christ's sake!' I quickly got used to thinking of myself as 'Jimmy' (a generic title, it seemed, for any male whose name you were not familiar with).

The busy times were best not just because they kept you active, but because you could taste the sweet satisfaction known to the capitalist as 'profit'. The cash register steadily accumulated throughout the day its freight of ten-shilling notes and pound notes, and there in that delightfully tactile form was the immediately visible reward of your labour. I rapidly learned that the accumulation of capital has more to do with psychological than with financial satisfaction. In a similar way I came to appreciate not just the quality of the Guinness which at that time we bottled ourselves (it was clear from customer reaction that such stout was far superior to the factory-produced version), but the sense of fulfilment attendant upon the lengthy process by which that quality was achieved.

The process itself was (like some of Robinson Crusoe's productive ventures on his desert island) interesting in its own right. First, the bottles were washed in a huge wooden tub, some three or four feet in diameter and a similar extent in depth. The old labels floated free from the bottles in the warm water, and each bottle in turn was then plunged onto a rapidly spinning automated wire brush for an internal rinse. After that, the bottles were serially stacked (upside down, for purposes of drainage) in special wooden containers. Next, the bottles, once dry, would be stacked in shallow cases, each of which held two dozen. And then came the bottling proper, which required some dexterity.

The first skilful undertaking was the hammering of the spigot into the barrel of Guinness (placed on its side, just above the trough which would in due course feed the bottles). My father always wrapped this tight with newspaper, in order to seal in any potential leakage; then the spigot was hammered with the wooden mallet as quickly and firmly as possible into the barrel-bung, though rarely quickly enough to prevent an initial burst of frothy stout which skited out and spattered the wielder of the mallet. Once the spigot was firmly in place, it only remained to turn it on and allow the Guinness to flow into the trough, from which descended four feeder-pipes (with holes placed along their length, just like flutes). Below the pipes was a shelf or ledge on which the empty bottles were placed to receive their fill of black liquid; and here again you required sustained skill and attention.

For you had to keep changing the bottles as they filled up, sliding them off the pipes, making sure that they were neither too full nor underfilled. Above all, you were obliged to move your eyes from one bottle to the other to make sure they did not overflow, deftly removing the full bottle and replacing it with the next empty one and keeping the whole process going. Each bottle, once filled, was stacked in the case again, and would be ready for corking soon afterwards; and this was by far my favourite part of the whole process.

We had a special corking-machine operated by a foot-lever. The corks were soaked in warm water to soften them up and make them yield to the pressure of insertion; then you would take a handful of corks at a time, drop one into the small space below the plunging rod which would drive the cork in, and with your other hand place a filled bottle accurately beneath the plunger on a round stand. The corking itself occurred when you depressed the lever rapidly with your foot, at which point the plunger descended with force and rammed the cork home. The great joy in the exercise consisted of an increasingly confident momentum and coordination, so that you could surrender to the mindless rhythm of it all, making optimum use of the time and the mechanism at your disposal.

Thereafter my father's expertise was needed for the carefully supervised storage (for the stout could be served to the customer only when it was in perfect order). The bottling-store was lined with storage shelves, and the stout was placed on these for a number of days, the number in part depending on the weather and the time of year (it 'came good' more quickly in the warm summer than in the winter). This productive process was a pleasure in itself, but there was, in addition, the satisfaction of knowing that you had created a product of unusual quality. This became abundantly evident when the stout had to be repeatedly poured with maximum care and attention for the fastidious 'regular', the connoisseur of bottled Guinness. It was only subsequent to all of that creative activity that you could begin to savour the satisfaction of a purely 'capitalist' kind, that raw material plus labour equals profit. It would be rash to give the profit motive automatic priority.

But hard work could be in any case its own reward. 'The labour we delight in physics pain', as Macbeth (in one of his more sententious moods) observes; and Freud famously declared that the two sources of human happiness are love and work (*Arbeit*). If business was slack, then I happily made work for myself. One day when I knew that there would be few if any customers (it may have been a Monday morning), I devoted hours to a thorough cleaning of the gents' toilet, scouring the urinals that had not, it seemed, been cleaned for years. I obtained an inordinate satisfaction from the accomplishment of this task, perhaps because it was my own version of the Herculean sweeping of the Augean stables. But I was just happy to be active and 'doing'; and not only doing, but seeing (which one hardly ever sees in academic life, either as an undergraduate or thereafter) the immediate results of the doing.

The worst times in the bar were the long monotonous stretches when either there were no customers at all, or (worse still) when there was one boring customer who insisted that you maintain a conversation. It was only as a result of these purgatorial moments that I learnt the full range of meanings in the word 'bore'. My father, though, had always said (as those in business do) that the greatest education comes from dealing with the public; and the bores, along with the other examples of humanity who frequented the bar, were a part of that education. Sometimes the two kinds of education (the academic and the practical) came into minor conflict, as I attempted to keep up my reading during those hours when business was slack.

The sweet scenes of autumn were for a while put by – unless some tender sonnet, fraught with the apt analogy of the declining year, with declining happiness, and the images of youth and hope, and spring, all gone together, blessed her memory.

Propped on a stool behind the bar counter, I am beatifically immersed in Jane Austen's *Persuasion* (one of the many canonical novels which I had failed to get to grips with as an undergraduate). A little earlier, I had read George Eliot's *The Mill on the Floss*, and had been dismayed to discover how completely I identified with the heroine, Maggie Tulliver. Was I undergoing, in my late adolescence, some kind of fatal gender-confusion? But these were passing thoughts only (and I have since come to understand my identification with Maggie as something which transcends gender, having more to do with my image of myself within my own family structure). That experience did not, in any case, deter me from identifying (though less passionately) with the heroine of *Persuasion*, Anne Elliott, whose inner life and intense feelings evoke my immediate sympathy.

She roused herself to say, as they struck by order into another path, 'Is not this one of the ways to Winthrop?'

'Jimmy!'

But nobody heard

'Jimmy!'

or, at least, nobody answered

'Jimmy! Are you deaf or what? A bottle of stout! If it's not too much trouble, like!'

'Right, right!' I lay the paperback carefully to one side, intent on not losing my place. Inwardly I curse him for intruding so insensitively on my own inner world. I serve up the Guinness with as much good grace as I can muster. Back to the book.

nobody answered her.

Winthrop, however, or its environs

'Do a lot of reading, then, Jimmy?'

Christ almighty, he is determined to have a conversation. I raise my eyes from the paperback.

'Yeah, a bit.'

'Do a lot of that myself. Though you mightn't think it to look at me. Ever read any of Marx?'

This is getting out of hand.

'A bit, but I'm no expert.' Which was true, because my knowledge of Marx was second-hand.

'You're a student, right?'

I confess as much.

'And someone like you would have a lot of what's-the-word *leisure*. Right?'

Again, I can't deny it.

'Know what Marx would call you? Marx would call you' (he enjoys the pleasure of articulating the definitive phrase) 'a *non-productive agent.*' The index finger is tapping the counter with quiet emphasis. 'A non-productive agent.'

I cannot escape now. I have to defend my honour. The Marxist auto-didact leaves some thirty minutes later, and even I ('smart' college-boy though I am) have to admit that, at best, honours are even, though I have a sneaking suspicion that he has won the debate. I return to my book, hoping that its urbane prose will soothe my ruffled sensibility.

and after another half mile of gradual ascent through large enclosures, where the ploughs at work, and the fresh-made path spoke the farmer, counteracting the sweets of poetical despondence, and meaning to have spring again, they gained the summit of the most considerable hill ...

Those farmers, it now seems to me, are genuinely productive agents; and dreamy Anne, with her self-indulgent melancholy, is out of touch. Perhaps she should get herself a job, and leave herself less time for intro-spection. A spell, maybe, as a barmaid in a market town.

*

I inevitably came to know by close observation the extraordinary changes in character that drink can bring about. Some became aggres-sive, others turned maudlin, others still grew foolish in a way that could hardly have been foreseen. From behind the bar counter, you have the privilege of detached spectation; sober and responsible as you have to be, you are not directly involved in the 'goings-on' of those rendered less inhibited, more spontaneous in their behaviour by the consumption of drink. Increasingly, I now begin in retrospect to think of the bar counter as a richly symbolic divide. Behind the counter was the realm of order, stability, and authority, perhaps, too, the realm of bourgeois security; on the far side was the world of fluidity and contingency, and, on occasion, of a dangerous irrationality, a world which tried to realise a bohemian ideal of freedom and irresponsibility.

The final authority rests with the barman, and he is often called upon to exercise it in a spirit of firm and clear-sighted diplomacy. I witnessed my father in action one tricky night after closing-time, when rationality began to fray at the edges and it required a cool head to defuse a potentially explosive situation. It all began innocently enough. The bar doors had been closed for the night, and a group of three had remained behind for a last round. One of the group was a large, heavily built man in his late thirties, the son of a regular customer who was well known to my father; he had been in his time a contender for an Irish heavyweight boxing title, but had failed to make the grade. Also present was a truck-driver, equally well built and physically capable. The third late drinker was a Scot who had been resident in the town for years, and was, inevitably, known as 'Mac'. Mac sober was a gentleman, a well dressed businessman who spoke with authority on the affairs of the day; but Mac drunk (after a day spent throwing back gin and tonics) was a very different personality – tetchy, foul-mouthed and aggressive. And, in some ways worst of all, mischievous.

It was Mac who played the part of *agent provocateur*. Absurdly (given that in his present company he was a lightweight), he wanted a demonstration of wrestling procedures; so he allowed himself to be picked up in a wrestling-hold and than thrown to the ground by the ex-boxer. His next ploy was to egg on the other two, the ex-boxer and the truck-driver, so that they embarked on their own wrestling match. I grew increasingly uneasy as the huge forms grappled with one another and each in turn was thrown through the air, to fall with a shocking thump on the floor. I looked apprehensively towards my father. He was taking it all in with a wary eye.

Meanwhile the wrestlers threw bulk against bulk like amorphous mastodons, becoming increasingly unreasonable in their struggle. For drink had been taken on all sides, and as the wrestling match grew more earnest, and each man strove to best the other, an element of uncontrolled aggression entered into the 'game'. Mac all the while played the role of 'loose cannon', liable to say any number of provocative things that would raise the temperature. My father, though, was keeping a steady eye on it all, and biding his time for an intervention that would bring an increasingly uncontrollable situation to an end.

What he did was simple, but it was carried through with exemplary judgment and diplomacy. He persuaded all concerned that it was well past official closing-time, and that he could give them all one more 'on the house', but only on the understanding that they would quickly consume that last drink and get off home. His well timed intervention broke the rhythm of proceedings that were beginning to generate their own dangerous momentum, and something like rational decorum was restored. I was glad to have my father's authority to rely on at that juncture, for there is no doubt that the developing situation would have run well away from any control I could have tried to apply had I been there on my own. He was the one source of stability in a rapidly disintegrating situation. I felt a huge relief when the men had left the bar, and, along with my father, surveyed with pleasure its vacant space, as I washed up the last of the dirty glasses behind the counter.

I can live on both sides of the counter, and have done so, both in reality and vicariously; I acknowledge, above all in literature, the divisions between reason and unreason, the wild and the civilised, nature and culture. But I am finally conservative in my insistence on the necessity of such divisions. If we are wrong to privilege 'male' over 'female', then it still may be essential to the survival of civilisation to prioritise reason over unreason. I feel in myself the persistent need for some sure point of orientation; and for that reason (speaking metaphorically) I would hate to see the bar counter removed.

*

In his last days my father forswore all alcohol, remaining sober and stoic; and I made the most of the increasing opportunities I now had to get closer to him. His health, though (always a problem throughout most of the years I had known him) steadily declined. Besides the numerous operations for duodenal ulcers he had had in the course of his life, he suffered, in addition, from a severe stiffness in his joints as he grew older, and found it increasingly difficult to walk. The last indignity was incontinence, and I remember in particular one occasion when I was to minister to him in that condition. An attack of diarrhoea had left him sadly compromised; life's last scatological joke, of which he, who had in his time told many such jokes, was now the victim.

Because of his stiffness and immobility, he was unable to do very much for himself; so, as he leant forward, heaving repeated sighs, and clutching at the wash-hand basin in our main bathroom, I wiped clean his withered buttocks. Throughout the whole messy business he kept apologising for the trouble he was putting me to, even as I repeatedly tried to assure him that it was no problem. I worried, in a passing moment of late adolescent self-doubt, whether my caring behaviour might be construed as too 'feminine', as if, in my submissive ministration, I had momentarily turned into a female nurse; a fear which in turn reactivated the memory of how, reading *The Mill on the Floss* for the first time, I had so passionately and problematically identified with the female protagonist Maggie. Yet I did not and now do not regret my brief ministration to him: far from it.

Was such attention to my father a kind of penitential act to atone for earlier criticism and neglect? So, now, at this remove, I question my own motives. But, at the time, I rejoiced without self-questioning in the opportunity to help him. I was glad to be of service, in however minor a way. No, it was no trouble – no trouble at all.

*

My brother Art had been appointed to a teaching position in the History Department at University College Dublin, and in the autumn of 1963 I saw him off to Dublin at the train station in Newry, in what was, on his side certainly, an emotional parting. I was still, I fear, living according to the dictates of the will, and was steeling myself for my own imminent challenge. I was shortly to go to Oxford to pursue research, and regarded it as a major step into the unknown. In our different ways each of us recognised that this was a significant parting of the ways; his boarding of the train for Dublin gave symbolic expression to our deeper awareness that the family unit was indeed gone, and that we would both, from now on, have to fend for ourselves.

Not long afterwards, I travelled to England, and took up residence in Balliol College. I hoped that my father, though he never made any fuss about it, might derive a degree of wry satisfaction from seeing his youngest child enter one of the bastions of British culture; and I imagined him musing in the bar, as he sat on the couch there, on the strange ways of the world, whereby he who had left school at fourteen, and done his own small bit for Irish independence, could now speak of his son at Balliol. But I was to spend a very uneasy first term at Oxford, partly because the way of life was so utterly strange to me and I experienced a degree of culture-shock; partly because I discovered shortly after my arrival that my chosen thesis-topic had already been poached by an American doctoral student in Texas; but mostly because I sensed that my father (who had never fully recovered from my mother's death) was slowly dying back home in Ireland, and I feared that he might die while I was absent.

Throughout that first term, as I passed in and out through the gates of Balliol, I would look towards the pigeon-holes into which the mail for the students was alphabetically sorted, dreading to see, pinned above the pigeon-hole marked 'C', a telegram informing me that my father had died, and that I should come home at once. When no such telegram materialised, I still looked through my mail with apprehension, anxious lest a similar message had been relayed by post. But I got through Michaelmas Term without any summons, and, shortly after my return to Newry, my father was hospitalised. He died in the course of my first vacation from Oxford, on a dull day in January.

During that vacation, I was able to visit him in hospital two days before the end. He was unable to speak, but his eyes were open, and he recognised everyone who came to see him. What I especially remember was a curious and compulsive movement of his left hand, which he passed repeatedly in front of his eyes, as if he were trying to brush away some cobweb visible only to himself. The eyes remained shrewd and bright. I should have hugged him and said farewell, but my habit of self-restraint (now increasingly ingrained in me) held me back. Two days later he was dead, having passed away in the stillness of his private ward.

I returned to Oxford. I would, at all costs, finish my thesis as quickly as I could and try to move on to a fuller life elsewhere (for Oxford was a severe trial in its unnatural constraints). A steady routine of work during the week and 'piss-ups' on Friday and Saturday nights became the norm. It saw me through to the successful completion of my research; but I suspect that for much of the time in Oxford I cut a sorry figure. I had failed to indulge properly in the therapeutic process of grieving, not only for my father but for my mother too; surviving by strength of will, I had suppressed a natural grief, and (like neurotic Hamlet, or his later avatar, Stephen Dedalus in *Ulysses*) failed to come to terms with death. Poor youth, I think, as I look back on that melancholy figure at Oxford across a great swathe of time: solitary, orphaned, rootless, tempted by an ultimate kind of bitterness, yet saved from that by his own sporadic sense of humour and by the humour and fellowship of others.

I long to reach across the dividing years and put my arm around his shoulder, console and sustain him, tell him that the future, if not as bright as he might wish, is at least more tolerable than he may realise; but too well do I know how quickly, how impatiently, he would shrug off that sentimental gesture.

Epilogue

He must have been deeply asleep, because his mother's voice took time to penetrate his consciousness and he did not at first recognise it nor know where he was. His eyes opened on the gloom of the bedroom; he was covered by the bedclothes, a sheet and one light blanket.

What was it? Was it time to get up and go to meet his father coming back from his trip to America? But that had already happened. Years ago.

'Wake up, there's the boy! We have to meet your father.' His mother's voice again.

So was it his father returning from America, after all? He is still sleepy and confused.

'Where, Mammy? Where are we going?'

His mother laughs.

'To meet your father off the bus, as usual. I'm nearly sorry now I woke you up at all, if you were that sound!'

Off the bus? He looks around. It's Warrenpoint, not Newry – that's it! But he is still not fully awake. He notices that, apart from his missing sandals, he is pretty much fully dressed.

'What time is it?'

'After ten, sleepyhead! Come on, we don't want to disappoint your father. We don't want to be late for him, do we?'

After ten? But it was after ten in the evening, he realised, not the morning. Not the autumn morning he had risen to greet his father, returning across the wild ocean-waste of the Atlantic.

Puzzling, it was all so puzzling... He pulled himself out of bed, and things began to make more sense. It was late in the day and that was why it was dark, and they were going to meet his father off the bus from Newry on this Saturday (yes, it was Saturday) night.

His mother has left the room. He puts on his sandals, struggling a little with the fastening straps. Then he is down the stairs. His mother is already at the front door, her hand on the latch. She goes out; he follows. They cross the road to the far side where the sea sounds.

The night is moonlit and quiet; the waves are throwing themselves gently, almost apologetically, against the concrete walkways below. The boy runs his hand along the rough top of the sea-wall; the smell of the sea embalms the night air; the mountains loom in the darkness across the bay.

There, now! the lighthouse shoots forth its never-wearied beam.

From one of the brightly lit windows across the road from the seafront comes the sound of a gramophone. Through the window, open to the mild and balmy night, the sound carries easily across the still air. A soprano voice, rich, impassioned, controlled. (The music is that of Richard Strauss's Four Last Songs.*)*

The bus arrives and here, descending, is one figure only, his father, smiling. He embraces Mother, ruffles the boy's hair. The Saturday night is complete, now that Daddy is here! The next day is Sunday, and the whole family will sit down for Sunday lunch, his father carving the roast. It will be a good day, with all the family united.

On the way back from the bus stop they pass once again the open window from which pours forth the vibrant soprano voice. (She is singing, now, the third of Strauss's Four Last Songs, *the words by Hermann Hesse:*

Und die Seele unbewacht

Will in freien Flügen schweben

It is about the spirit soaring on wings of freedom, carried, sublimely soaring, on the female voice.

Um in Zauberkreis der Nacht

Tief und tausendfach zu leben.

The free spirit winging its way into the magic circle of the night. And there in the depths beyond drinking deep of thousandfold life.)

The bay is dominated by a Douanier Rousseau moon, bright as a half-

crown new-minted. The sea is tranquil and silver. The scene is like a stage-set. But this is no ordinary night. It is a night of magic composure.

They walk, the parents and the child, back to the holiday home, beside the familiar sea-wall above the calm, expansive sea. The lighthouse pulses like a silent tune. (Zauberkreis der Nacht.) They inhabit, they breathe in, they inhale the magic circle of the night. (Tief und tausendfach.)

The three of them make a happy procession. The waves are scarcely audible. His right hand is gently held by his mother, his left hand firmly grasped by his father's hand.

Index